# COOK'S BIBLE

# COOK'S BIBLE

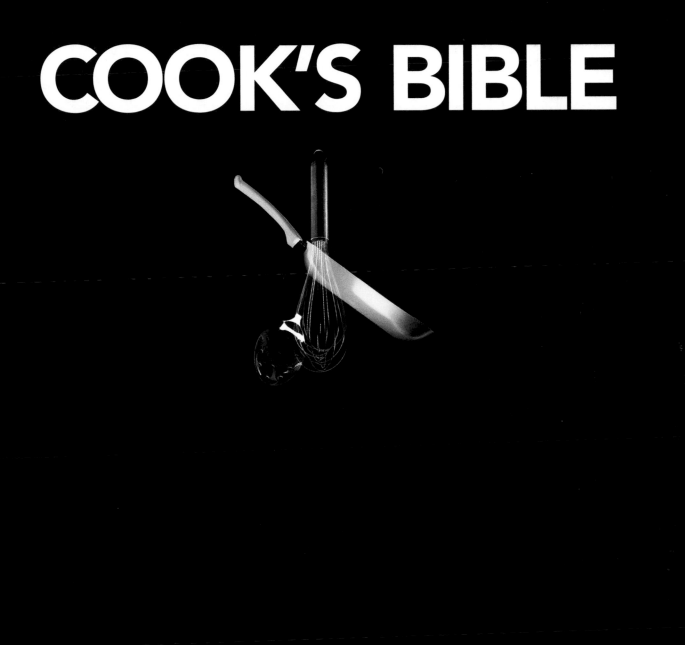

This edition published in 2010
LOVE FOOD is an imprint of Parragon Books Ltd

Parragon
Queen Street House
4 Queen Street
Bath BA1 1HE, UK

ISBN: 978-1-4075-2427-6

Printed in China

Text written by Lorraine Turner
Designed by Talking Design
Photography by Clive Bozzard-Hill
Images on pages 14 and 15 supplied by Günter Beer
Food Styling by Sandra Baddeley and Carol Tennant

## Notes for the reader

This book uses imperial, metric, and US cup measurements. Follow the
same units of measurement throughout; do not mix imperial and metric.
All spoon measurements are level: teaspoons are assumed to be 5 ml,
and tablespoons are assumed to be 15 ml. Unless otherwise stated, milk
is assumed to be whole, eggs and individual vegetables such as potatoes
are medium, and pepper is freshly ground black pepper.

The times given are an approximate guide only. Preparation times differ
according to the techniques used by different people and the cooking
times may also vary from those given as a result of the type of oven used.
Optional ingredients, variations or serving suggestions have not been
included in the calculations.

Recipes using raw or very lightly cooked eggs should be avoided by
infants, the elderly, pregnant women, convalescents, and anyone with
a chronic condition. Pregnant and breastfeeding women are advised
to avoid eating peanuts and peanut products. Sufferers from nut allergies
should be aware that some of the ready-prepared ingredients used in
the recipes in this book may contain nuts. Always check the packaging
before use.

# CONTENTS

PART ONE

# INTRODUCTION

# HEALTHY EATING

THE AMERICAN WRITER MARJORIE RAWLINGS ONCE SAID THAT FOOD IMAGINATIVELY AND LOVINGLY PREPARED, EATEN IN GOOD COMPANY, WARMS THE SOUL WITH SOMETHING MORE THAN MERE CALORIES. WHILE THIS IS TRUE, IT IS ALSO TRUE THAT THE HUMAN BODY NEEDS A REGULAR AND BALANCED INTAKE OF OVER 70 NUTRIENTS—VITAMINS AND MINERALS—IN ORDER TO KEEP IT WORKING PROPERLY AND PROTECT IT FROM DISEASE.

### The five food groups

A healthy and balanced diet needs to contain adequate amounts of five major food groups: protein, carbohydrates, fat, vitamins, and minerals.

### PROTEIN

This food group provides the building blocks for the body. Everyone's protein requirement differs, depending on health, age, and size, but the average minimum requirement is around 1¾ oz/50 g per day. There are two types of protein: complete protein, which is found in foods of animal origin, such as meat, poultry, fish, eggs, milk, and cheese, and incomplete protein, which is found in foods of nonanimal origin, such as nuts, seeds, grains, and beans. Complete proteins provide the proper balance of amino acids necessary to build body tissues; incomplete proteins need to be mixed with small amounts of complete protein in order to provide adequate nutrition.

### CARBOHYDRATES

The main source of the body's energy is carbohydrates. No official daily requirement exists, but a minimum of 1¾ oz/50 g daily is recommended to avoid an acid condition of the blood called "ketosis." This condition occurs when your body has to use fat instead of carbohydrates to provide its energy.

Carbohydrates can be found in starchy and sugary foods. There are two types of carbohydrate: complex carbohydrates, which can be found in bread, pasta, rice, cereals, beans, fruit, and vegetables, and simple carbohydrates, which can be found in desserts, puddings, cakes, chocolate, candies, and sodas.

Complex carbohydrates take longer to be broken down in the body, which means they release energy into the body more slowly and gradually. These are the best carbohydrates to eat. The sugary, simple type of carbohydrate will provide a quick boost of energy, but this surge is quickly used up; such "highs and lows" of energy are not good for maintaining good health and vitality.

## FAT

These days we are encouraged to eat a low-fat diet, but to cut fat out completely would be very unhealthy. What we should be doing is eating the types of fat that are good for us and reducing our intake of the potentially harmful kinds. Saturated fat is potentially harmful in excessive amounts. It can raise our blood cholesterol levels and blood pressure.

A good way to remember which foods are high in saturated fat is to think of the fats that stay solid at room temperature, such as lard and butter. It is these kinds of solid fats that clog our arteries and can lead to heart disease. Healthier kinds of fat are polyunsaturated fats, such as sunflower-seed oil and canola oil, and monounsaturated fats, such as olive oil and peanut oil. We also need a regular intake of essential fatty acids (EFAs). These actually help the body to burn off excess fat. Good sources of EFAs include oily fish, sunflower seeds, pumpkin seeds, and avocados. So it is not true to say that all fat is bad for you. Restrict saturated fat in your diet by all means, but not the other kinds. Remember also that a low-fat diet is unsuitable for children under 5 years of age.

## MINERALS

There are about 18 minerals required for healthy body function, and the six most well-known minerals are: calcium (found in milk, cheese, and beans), iodine (found in seafood, kelp, and onions), iron (found in red meat, egg yolks, oysters, nuts, and beans), magnesium (found in figs, lemons, nuts, seeds, and apples), phosphorus (found in meat, poultry, fish, whole grains, eggs, nuts, and seeds), and zinc (found in steak, wheat germ, brewer's yeast, eggs, and pumpkin seeds). Minerals are essential for maintaining good health. For example, a deficiency of calcium can lead to rickets or osteoporosis, and a deficiency of iron can cause anemia.

## VITAMINS

This food group comprises organic substances that can be found within the foods we eat. We need only minuscule amounts of these substances in order to be healthy, but a deficiency of even one type of vitamin can cause us to be unhealthy. Vitamins range from the "fat-soluble" kind, such as A (found in green leafy vegetables, liver, and dairy products), D (found in fish liver oils, sardines, tuna, and dairy products), and E (found in soybeans, whole-wheat and grains, and eggs), to the "water-soluble" kind, such as C (found in citrus fruits, green leafy vegetables, and tomatoes). Some people think that it is possible to live on vitamins only, but this concept is a myth—vitamins are only one of the five main nutrients necessary for a healthy body. It is always preferable to get your vitamins naturally from the foods you eat, rather than from synthetic materials, such as tablets, because synthetic vitamins can sometimes cause toxic reactions. Natural vitamins are much safer.

## MAKING THE RIGHT CHOICES

It is vital to make good food choices and eat sensibly. Did you know, for example, that a diet high in salt and saturated fat can increase the risk of heart disease, while eating other foods, such as beans, can help to lower cholesterol and prevent heart disease? The message here is that what you absorb into your body plays a crucial role in your health and overall well-being. Eating more of the right foods, and reducing your intake of the potentially harmful ones, can contribute enormously to how well you feel and the state of your physical health.

So which are the right foods to eat and which are the wrong ones? It is not always easy to decide. For example, too much salt can lead to higher blood pressure and depleted adrenal glands, but to cut it out completely would be very unwise because we need a certain amount each day in order to stay healthy. Salt actually helps to keep our fluid levels in balance and our muscles healthy. The amount we need, however, is very low—less than 1 teaspoon/5 g per day. Since many foods we buy have salt added already—for example, cheese or prepared foods such as pizzas—we can usually get the amount we need without having to add extra salt to our meals. It is the habit of adding extra salt to our food that tends to push us over the healthy limit. Basically, a balanced diet should consist of plenty of fruit, vegetables, whole grains and cereals, and smaller quantities of protein foods from animal sources (such as meat, fish, eggs, or dairy products) as well as from nonanimal sources (such as beans, peas, nuts, and seeds). A vegetarian diet is also perfectly healthy, as long as it is balanced and contains all the essential nutrients.

## DOS AND DON'TS FOR A HEALTHY DIET

Here are some tips to help keep your diet healthy and your body in peak physical condition:

DO eat regular meals—never skip them, especially breakfast. Skipping meals will only encourage your body to go into "starvation mode" and store up fat.

DO eat at least five portions of fruit and vegetables each day. They can be fresh, frozen, or canned, but vary them as much as possible. Not all fruits and vegetables contain the same amount of health-giving nutrients, but when in doubt you can estimate that one portion is equal to about 3 oz/ 85 g. Any of the following foods equal one portion:

• ⅔ cup fruit juice
• one orange, apple, nectarine, peach, or banana
• half a grapefruit
• two plums
• one-quarter of a cucumber
• one bell pepper or tomato
• a 3-oz/85-g portion of cauliflower or broccoli
• three heaping tablespoons of any vegetable—for example, peas, carrots, corn, or beans.

DO eat more whole grains, such as oats, barley, rye, and corn. Choose whole-wheat bread and pasta instead of white varieties, and whole-grain brown rice instead of polished white rice.

DO eat oily fish regularly, at least three times a week if you can.

DO choose organic produce wherever possible; organic foods are free from artificial additives and pesticides, and are a much healthier choice.

DO drink eight glasses of water a day. One glass is equal to a generous ¾ cup, so this means at least 6½ cups daily. You need a regular and adequate intake of water in order to flush toxins from the body and replace water lost through urine and sweat.

If you do not drink enough water, you will become dehydrated. Dehydration causes symptoms, such as headaches, tiredness, and loss of concentration. Prolonged dehydration can lead to constipation and kidney stones.

DON'T eat too much saturated fat. Reduce your intake of greasy deep-fried foods and fatty red meat.

DON'T eat too many sugary foods, such as candies, chocolate, puddings, desserts, and sodas.

DON'T buy processed foods. Processed foods are often full of artificial additives, such as preservatives, colors, and sweeteners—even packaged salad greens have undergone chemical processing before they reach the retailers' shelves. Instead, choose foods that are fresh and in their natural state. The benefits in terms of better flavor and more health-giving nutrients far outweigh the convenience of prepared, packaged foods.

DON'T drink too much caffeine. It is a powerful stimulant and can make you feel lively, but in excess it can lead to health problems. Too much caffeine can lead to irritability, insomnia, and feverish symptoms. Very high doses can cause more serious problems. For example, medical research has reported that people who drink five

or more cups of coffee a day have a 50 percent higher risk of a heart attack than people who do not drink coffee. The main sources of caffeine are coffee, tea, cola drinks, and cocoa, so avoid these drinks as much as possible or use decaffeinated varieties. Even better, switch to herbal teas and fruit juices instead. Some medicines also contain caffeine, so check the ingredients before you take them, and use an alternative if possible.

DON'T consume too much alcohol. Keep your consumption to less than one drink per day (for women), or two drinks per day (for men). In the United States a drink is defined as 1½ fl oz/45 ml of (80%-proof) distilled spirits, 5 fl oz/150 ml of wine, or 12 fl oz/350 ml of regular beer.

DON'T add salt to your food, or at least taste the food before you add salt, then keep any added salt to a minimum.

# HEALTH AND SAFETY

THE KITCHEN IS OFTEN THE FOCAL POINT OF THE HOME. HOWEVER, IT IS ALSO THE RISKIEST AREA: FIRES ARE MUCH MORE LIKELY TO BREAK OUT IN THE KITCHEN THAN IN ANY OTHER PART OF THE HOME, AND THERE IS A RISK OF INFESTATION BY PESTS OR POTENTIALLY HARMFUL BACTERIA. ADOPTING GOOD HYGIENE HABITS AND TAKING SENSIBLE PRECAUTIONS WILL PROTECT YOUR HOUSEHOLD FROM UNNECESSARY ACCIDENTS AND ILLNESSES.

## KITCHEN HYGIENE

Cleanliness is essential in the kitchen. Keep all kitchen surfaces scrupulously clean, and wash your hands thoroughly with soap and water when preparing food. Use a separate towel to dry your hands, not a dish towel. Whenever you go out of the kitchen or touch another surface, such as a door handle or a curtain, even if it is only for a few moments, remember that your hands will quickly pick up bacteria hanging around the home, even if you think your home is scrupulously clean, so always wash your hands again before resuming any food preparation.

Make sure you use different cutting boards and utensils for cooked and raw foods to prevent cross-contamination of bacteria, especially when you are preparing meat or poultry. If you can afford it and have the room to store them, it is a good idea to have several different colored cutting boards for different purposes. You can keep one for raw meat, one for cooked meat, one for a pet's food, and so on. Wash cutting boards and utensils well in hot, soapy water before and after each use.

Change and wash all dish cloths and dish towels regularly. Use a covered garbage can and disinfect it on a regular basis.

## FOOD PREPARATION

Make sure that you thoroughly wash any foods that need cleaning, such as soil-covered vegetables, and pat dry with paper towels. You should also thaw thoroughly any frozen food that requires it, especially meat and poultry, and do not refreeze once it has thawed. The best place to defrost food is in the refrigerator. However, if you are short of time, you can thaw it in a cool room as long as it is well covered to prevent any potentially harmful bacteria from contaminating it.

Throw away any thawed juices from meat and poultry—do not use them in your dishes. And remember never to reuse a marinade, especially if it has been used for meat or poultry.

When reheating cooked meat dishes, remember that they may be reheated once only, to a temperature of at least 167°F/75°C.

Do not leave cooked rice uncovered at room temperature for any length of time. Potentially harmful bacteria can multiply quickly on cooked rice, so if you have to store it, cover it with plastic wrap as soon as possible, and keep it in the refrigerator until you are ready to use it. The same goes for any cooked meats or poultry.

**Storing potatoes**
Potatoes should be stored away from the sunlight in a dark place to prevent green patches from forming. The green patches contain a substance called solanine, which can upset stomachs.

## SAFE STORAGE

Always buy food as fresh as possible, and from a reputable supplier. Check any "sell" or expiration dates, because sometimes out-of-date items languish on retailers' shelves and are bought by the unwary. Cover all exposed foods with plastic wrap before refrigerating. If you buy a whole bird, remove any giblets from the cavity, cover with plastic wrap, and refrigerate separately from the bird. Store raw and cooked meat and poultry separately in different parts of your refrigerator.

Store your potatoes in a dark place, away from sunlight, or they will turn green—even fluorescent lighting can make them turn green. Green patches in potatoes contain a chemical called solanine. Solanine tastes bitter, and in large concentrations it can give you an upset stomach, so do not buy any potatoes with green patches. If, despite your best efforts, a potato you have bought or grown has developed a small green patch, you can cut the patch out, then use the rest of the potato. If the green covers a large area, you may be better off discarding the whole potato.

## KITCHEN FIRST AID

Every kitchen should have a basic first-aid kit. Your standard kit should include rubber gloves, antiseptic wipes, burn cream, eye pads, safety pins, different-size dressings, and triangular bandages. Catering establishments use blue adhesive bandages in order to make them easier to see if they fall off. Although you don't have to use this type at home, their deep-blue coloring makes them ideal for home use, too.

A fire blanket is also a good precaution in a kitchen. It can be a very useful item to have at hand in case a fire breaks out, and it can also be used to help keep a shock victim comfortable until help arrives.

## FIRE SAFETY

As an absolute minimum, fit a battery-operated smoke alarm just outside your kitchen, and check the battery regularly. Do not position it in the kitchen itself or over a direct source of smoke or heat, or it may be set off accidentally. Even better, ask a qualified electrician to install smoke and heat detectors throughout your home—for reliability they should be wired up to your main electricity supply.

It is also a good idea to keep a fire extinguisher in the kitchen. Here are some other tips for kitchen fire safety:
• Keep electrical cords, oven mitts, and dish towels away from the stove.
• Keep your stove clean, especially the broiler and oven. A buildup of fat can catch fire.
• Do not let your sleeves or other loose clothing hang over the stove while you are cooking.

• Never leave pans on the stove unattended. If you have to leave them, even for a few seconds, perhaps to answer the telephone, remove them from the heat.
• When you've finished cooking, make sure the stove or oven is turned off.
• If a pan catches fire and you can't put it out easily and quickly, don't take any risks with your safety. Leave the house at once (making sure

that you close all doors behind you as you go), and call the Fire Department immediately. If the fire is small and you are confident you can handle it, put a fire blanket over it, or alternatively run a cloth under the faucet, wring it out, and then cover the pan with it. Do not throw water into the pan because this action could exacerbate the problem. Turn off the heat as soon as you can get to it safely.

# EQUIPMENT

A SELECTION OF CAREFULLY CHOSEN TOOLS IS ESSENTIAL IN THE KITCHEN. IF YOU ARE A BEGINNER, YOU CAN MAKE DO WITH A FEW MULTIPURPOSE UTENSILS, THEN ADD TO THEM AS YOUR CONFIDENCE GROWS. IF YOU ARE AN EXPERIENCED COOK, YOU MAY WANT TO ADD TO THE BASIC TOOLS WITH SOME MORE SOPHISTICATED ITEMS, SUCH AS A PASTA MACHINE.

## Measuring equipment

The items listed here are useful for measuring liquids and solid foods. If you have cups and spoons in imperial, metric, and cups, it is sensible to stick to just one measuring method to avoid confusion.

### Liquid measuring pitcher
Measuring pitchers are available in glass and plastic and are useful for measuring liquid ingredients. It is helpful to choose a measuring pitcher that shows both imperial and metric measurements, and be sure that it is heatproof.

### Measuring spoons
These spoons are ideal for measuring both liquid and dry ingredients accurately.

### Dry measuring cups
These cups usually come in a nesting set of four different sizes: ¼, ⅓, ½, and 1 cup, and are used for measuring the volume of dry ingredients. The rim is usually level with the top measurement specified. Dry measuring cups are usually available in plastic or metal.

### Kitchen scales
If you want to try recipes from other countries that use metric or imperial measurements, invest in kitchen scales with both measurements. Imperial measurements differ slightly from the U.S. standard measurements. It is best to buy scales that show both imperial and metric measurements.

## Knives

Buy the best-quality knives you can afford because they will last longer, and remember to keep them sharp. The first three listed here are the essential knives; the rest can be added later.

### Small paring knife
A paring knife is invaluable for cutting vegetables, fruit, meat, and cheese. It is 2½–3½ inches/ 6–9 cm long.

### Cook's knife
This good, multipurpose knife is 6–12 inches/15–30 cm long, and is essential for slicing and chopping.

### Bread knife
This long serrated knife is ideal for slicing bread.

### Small serrated knife
This knife is most often used for cutting vegetables and fruit. It is usually about 5 inches/13 cm long.

Measuring cup

Measuring spoons

Bread knife

Carving knife

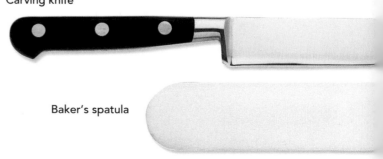
Baker's spatula

### Cleaver
The flat, rectangular blade of this knife is ideal for cutting meat joints.

### Fileting knife
This knife has a flexible blade of about 8 inches/20 cm in length, and is used for vegetables, fruit, and raw fish.

### Carving knife
This knife has a blade about 12 inches/30 cm long, with a point for easy carving around the bones of joints. It usually comes with a carving fork, which has two long prongs and sometimes a guard to protect against accidents.

### Mezzaluna
The mezzaluna has two handles and a curved blade, and is used for chopping herbs and vegetables.

### Baker's spatula
This tool is used for spreading rather than cutting, and it has many uses in the kitchen. It is ideal for frosting cakes.

### Knife sharpener
Although this has a handle like a knife handle, instead of a blade it has a long rod of roughened steel. When the edge of a knife is run along the rod at a 45° angle, it sharpens the blade.

## Other cutting tools and equipment

In addition to a basic set of knives, you will need some other cutting tools. Some of these tools are very specific, such as the zester, while others are for more general use.

### Can opener
This everyday tool comes in many varieties, from hand-operated to wall-mounted automatic devices.

### Zester
A citrus zester has a rectangular metal head with holes along the top edge. The holes are there to help remove fine shavings of zest without picking up the white pith.

### Vegetable peeler
You can buy a swivel-bladed version or one that has a slicing blade in the middle and a sharp tip for coring.

### Grater
There are different graters for different purposes, but a good, multipurpose version to buy is a

hollow box-shaped grater with a handle at the top and different cutting holes on each side.

### Apple corer
This hollow, cylindrical tool is essential for removing cores from apples and pears quickly and easily.

### Pie dough cutters
These round circles are available in metal or plastic and are useful for cutting pie dough circles. They are also ideal for shaping cookies.

### Kitchen scissors
Choose stainless-steel all-purpose scissors and keep them solely for use in the kitchen.

Small paring knife

Cook's knife

Zester

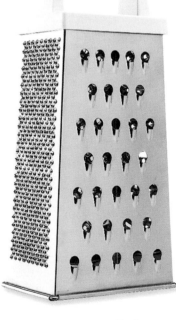

Vegetable peeler

Grater

## Pots and pans

When you are buying pots and pans, choose the best quality you can afford. If cared for properly, they will more than repay the extra cost because they will last for many years.

### Pans

You will need a small, preferably nonstick, milk pan for making sauces and scrambled eggs, and at least three other different-sized pans—small, medium, and large. Choose pans that have secure lids. A large casserole dish or Dutch oven with a lid is useful for casseroles, stews, and whole birds.

### Skillets

You will need a small omelet pan, and a larger skillet for more substantial foods. Nonstick varieties are ideal for cooking low-fat meals, but are not essential. A ridged stove-top grill pan imparts lovely stripes to food, ideal for chargrilling beef and tuna steaks.

### Steamer

Steamers come in different varieties. For example, you can buy a folding metal steamer that adjusts to any size of pan. You can also buy metal and bamboo steamers that are placed on top of the pan—some have more than one tier so that you can steam more than one food at a time. In addition, there are electric steamers, which are useful if you want to save space on the stove.

### Wok

A wok is a deep, rounded, bowl-shaped pan with one or two handles. It is ideal for cooking stir-fries.

## Ovenware and bakeware

Nonstick baking equipment is useful because it will help you to slide out your culinary creations with ease. However, be careful not to scour it, or you will scratch the nonstick coating.

### Baking sheets

Some of these rectangular and square metal sheets are flat and others have a lip around the edges. They are essential for baking a variety of foods, from oven-roasted vegetables and pizzas to meringues and cookies.

### Cake pans

These pans come in different sizes but, to start with, a couple of 8-inch/20-cm diameter shallow pans will come in handy for making sponges, and a deeper 9-inch/23-cm diameter springform cake pan will be useful for making larger cakes.

### Tart pans and dishes

These pans and dishes are usually round, and often have a fluted edge. They are ideal for baking quiches and tarts, and come in a variety of sizes. The best type to buy is the loose-bottom, stainless-steel variety, because it conducts the heat better than ceramic ones and enables food to be lifted out easily.

### Pie pans and dishes

These pans come in a variety of shapes and sizes, and are usually fairly deep with a protruding rim for pie dough edging.

### Roasting pans

These metal pans are deeper than baking sheets, and are ideal for roasting meat and poultry.

### Muffin pans

These rectangular pans usually come with 12 large, round indentations, which are ideal for making savory or sweet muffins, or individual fruit pies.

### Loaf pans

These rectangular pans have deep sides and come in different sizes. They are useful for baking bread or savory nut roasts.

### Ramekins

These small, round dishes have many uses in the kitchen. They are very handy for making individual soufflés and crème caramels. They also double up nicely as serving dishes for butter, olives, and nuts.

Pan

Large pan with lid

Skillet

Ramekins

## Strainers

The following items are useful in any kitchen. In particular, a strainer is essential for sifting dry ingredients, such as flour, while a colander makes light work of draining a variety of foods.

### Strainers
These come in metal or plastic, and are useful for sifting flour and straining liquid ingredients.

### Colander
A colander is a perforated bowl that is used for draining liquid from foods. Colanders are available in different sizes and different materials, usually metal or plastic. They may have one or two handles and a flat bottom so that they can sit steadily on a counter.

### Egg separator
Although this small, round, slotted spoon is not essential, new cooks in particular will find it helpful for separating egg yolks from whites.

### Sifter
This mesh-covered container is especially useful for sprinkling confectioners' sugar or cocoa onto cakes and desserts.

## Bowls

You can buy bowls in a variety of different materials and sizes, but metal will react with acid ingredients, such as lime juice, so you should not use metal bowls for acid-based marinades.

### Mixing bowls
Mixing bowls are available in a variety of materials, including ceramic, glass, plastic, and stainless steel. At least one large mixing bowl is essential, although several bowls of different sizes are even better. For example, you will need a smaller bowl to whip cream. You can also buy bowls that are sufficiently decorative to double up as serving bowls at the table.

### Ovenproof bowls
These come in different sizes and materials, including metal, ceramic, and glass. A large ovenproof bowl is ideal for making a substantial summer dessert or Christmas pudding for a large household, while a set of smaller bowls is useful for making individual chilled or steamed desserts. It is often worth recycling bowls from store-bought desserts, too.

Strainer

Colander

Large mixing bowl

Ovenproof bowl

Slotted spatula

Draining spoon

Serving/basting spoon

Ladle

## Spoons and spatulas

Spoons and spatulas are very helpful for lifting, turning, shaping, draining, and serving a variety of foods. Here are some of the utensils you will find most useful.

### Slotted spatula
This slotted lifting tool is essential when lifting floppy food, such as omelets, fried eggs, or fish fillets from skillets.

### Draining spoon
This large, slotted spoon is ideal for lifting solid foods out of liquids so that the liquid drains away, and for skimming foam from the surface of simmering liquids, such as stock, and from jellies, preserves, and marmalade.

### Serving/basting spoon
This large spoon is useful for serving food onto plates. It has a groove on one side to direct the flow of juices and sauces.

### Ladle
This is helpful for ladling soups into bowls or punch into glasses.

### Tongs
A set of tongs is handy for turning hot food on a griddle or a barbecue grill.

### Wooden spoon
This type of spoon is available in different sizes and is handy for mixing ingredients evenly, without scratching the delicate surfaces of pans and bowls.

### Spatula
This utensil is available in wood or plastic, and is used for folding mixtures such as egg whites. The plastic type is also ideal for scraping down the sides of mixing bowls to get all the mixture out.

## HOT HANDLES

Do not leave spoons and spatulas with metal handles to stand in the pan while cooking on a hot stove. Metal handles can get very hot, and are likely to cause burns.

Wooden spoons

Spatula

Hand balloon whisks

Potato masher

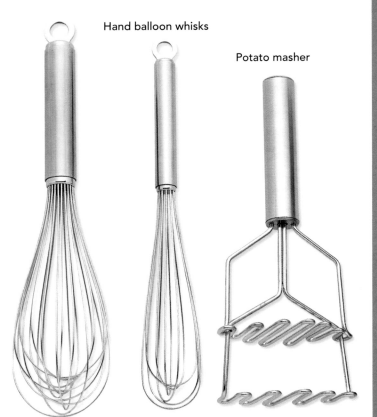

## Other useful utensils

You can add to your cooking utensils as and when you need them. Here are some of the items you are likely to find most useful and will want to buy sooner rather than later.

### Lemon squeezer
These usually come in plastic or glass. They have a strainer to catch any pips, and a bowl underneath to catch the lemon juice.

### Corkscrew and bottle opener
You can buy these individually or combined into one utensil. The lever-action corkscrew is the easiest kind to use.

### Pie dough brush
A brush is useful for sealing pies with water and for glazing.

### Garlic press
A garlic press is not essential but is handy for crushing garlic cloves cleanly and efficiently. Some have a detachable grille for easy cleaning.

### Hand whisks
Whisks are available in a variety of shapes and sizes. The most common is the balloon whisk, which is useful for whisking egg whites and cream.

### Rolling pin
This long, cylindrical utensil comes in wood, glass, or ceramic, and is essential for rolling out pie dough.

### Potato masher
This utensil is essential for mashing boiled potatoes and other cooked vegetables, such as rutabaga.

### Mortar and pestle
These two utensils come as a pair in a variety of sizes and materials, such as marble and porcelain. They are used for crushing herbs and spices. It is a good idea to buy the largest and sturdiest you can afford.

### Cutting boards
If you can, buy several different colored boards so that you can keep one for raw meat and poultry, one for cooked meats, and so on.

### Wire cooling racks
These metal racks can be round or rectangular, and are ideal for cooling cakes, cookies, and bread. It is often essential to have two racks to accommodate larger batches.

### Skewers
Long stainless-steel skewers are a good choice, although other materials, such as wood, are also available. Skewers are essential for cooking kabobs. They are also useful for inserting into cakes and joints of meat to test if they are cooked all the way through.

### Pie funnel
This little funnel is available in a variety of shapes and materials, and is used to hold up the pie dough in pies. It also prevents the pie dough from becoming soggy by allowing the steam to escape.

### Ice-cream scoop
This tool is useful for scooping neat domes of ice cream or mashed potato onto plates.

### Decorative molds
These molds are available in many shapes and sizes, and in plastic or metal. They can be used for shaping mousses, ice creams, gelatin-based desserts, and creamy desserts.

### Pastry bags and tips
These come in various sizes and shapes and are useful for creating piped decorations in frosting or cream on cakes and desserts.

### Thermometers
You can buy thermometers to test the temperature of your refrigerator and oven, and for meat, sugar, and deep-fat frying.

### Kitchen timers
Timers are available in different designs and sizes, and are useful for monitoring the cooking times of dishes. Many ovens also come with a handy built-in timer.

Lemon squeezer

Garlic press

Pie dough brushes

### Machines and electric utensils

There is a wide variety of machines and electrical devices for the kitchen, and these make quick and easy work of preparing food—especially useful when catering for families or parties.

#### Food processor
This multipurpose machine has metal blades that chop, shred, and grate foods. Usually, it also comes with a selection of other attachments that mix and knead ingredients, such as sponge mixes and pie dough.

#### Blender
A blender is useful for pureeing foods and mixing drinks, such as soups, batters, milk shakes, and smoothies. It is also known as a liquidizer.

#### Pasta machine
This machine is not essential because store-bought pasta is excellent these days. But if you prefer to make your own fresh pasta, you will find a machine indispensable for rolling and cutting pasta into noodles, ribbons, and various decorative shapes.

#### Grinder
This very useful machine is essential for grinding nuts and coffee beans. It is also ideal for making fresh bread crumbs, as are food processors.

#### Freestanding mixer
This machine, which is also called a food mixer, has a large bowl and a selection of mixing tools, such as a whisk and a dough kneader. It enables you to beat and whisk foods much faster than you can by hand.

#### Handheld electric mixer
This tool, which you can hold over a bowl or pan, is more portable than a freestanding mixer. It is suitable for light mixtures, such as eggs and cream, but for more substantial mixtures you will find a freestanding mixer easier to use.

#### Handheld blender
This portable version of the blender lets you puree food in a pan while it is cooking on the stove.

#### Deep-fryer
This heavy-bottom machine usually comes with a wire basket that can be hooked onto the side of the machine for easy draining of the cooking oil.

#### Pressure cooker
This deep, heavy electric pan is not essential, but it is useful for steaming food, such as rice, in about half the normal cooking time.

#### Slow cooker
This small appliance is very useful for cooking stews and casseroles slowly, and saves you having to use the oven. It also uses less electricity than an oven does. Simply add the food, cover, plug it in, and wait for the lovely aromas to emerge.

Freestanding mixer

Pasta machine

# CONVERSION CHARTS

## OVEN TEMPERATURES

| Fahrenheit | Celsius | Oven heat |
|---|---|---|
| 225° | 110° | very slow |
| 250° | 120° | very slow |
| 275° | 140° | slow |
| 300° | 150° | slow |
| 325° | 160° | moderate |
| 350° | 180° | moderate |
| 375° | 190° | moderately hot |
| 400° | 200° | moderately hot |
| 425° | 220° | hot |
| 450° | 230° | very hot |
| 475° | 240° | extremely hot |

## SPOON MEASUREMENTS

1 teaspoon of liquid = 5 ml

1 tablespoon of liquid = 15 ml

## OTHER MEASUREMENTS

### Liquid volume

| U.S. standard | Metric |
|---|---|
| 2 fl oz | 50 ml |
| 3½ fl oz | 100 ml |
| 4 fl oz | 125 ml |
| ½ cup | 125 ml |
| 5 fl oz | 150 ml |
| 7 fl oz | 200 ml |
| 8 fl oz | 225 ml |
| 1 cup | 225 ml |
| 10 fl oz | 300 ml |
| 16 fl oz | 475 ml |
| 18 fl oz | 525 ml |
| 2½ cups | 600 ml |
| 3 cups | 700 ml |
| 4 cups | 1.3 liters |

### Weight

| U.S. standard | Metric |
|---|---|
| ⅛ oz | 5 g |
| ¼ oz | 10 g |
| 1 oz | 25 g |
| 1¾ oz | 50 g |
| 2¾ oz | 75 g |
| 3 oz | 85 g |
| 3½ oz | 100 g |
| 5½ oz | 150 g |
| 8 oz | 225 g |
| 10½ oz | 300 g |
| 1 lb | 450 g |
| 1 lb 2 oz | 500 g |
| 2 lb 4 oz | 1 kg |
| 3 lb 5 oz | 1.5 kg |

### Linear

| U.S. standard | Metric |
|---|---|
| 1/16 inch | 2 mm |
| ⅛ inch | 3 mm |
| ¼ inch | 5 mm |
| ⅜ inch | 8 mm |
| ½ inch | 1 cm |
| ¾ inch | 2 cm |
| 1 inch | 2.5 cm |
| 2 inches | 5 cm |
| 3 inches | 7.5 cm |
| 4 inches | 10 cm |
| 8 inches | 20 cm |
| 12 inches/1 foot | 30 cm |
| 18 inches/1½ feet | 46 cm |
| 20 inches/1⅔ feet | 50 cm |

# PREPARATION TECHNIQUES

YOU WILL FIND THIS SECTION A VALUABLE SOURCE OF REFERENCE FOR ALL THE BASIC PREPARATION TECHNIQUES YOU ARE LIKELY TO NEED IN EVERYDAY COOKING. THERE ARE ALSO SOME ADVANCED TECHNIQUES FOR THE MORE EXPERIENCED COOK.

### Grind

To crush food, such as nuts or coffee beans, to a powder or into very small pieces. For this job, you can use a mortar and pestle for a coarser result, or a coffee grinder or food processor.

### Infuse

To steep flavorful ingredients, such as herbs or spices, in a liquid in order to flavor it.

### Bard

This means to wrap pieces of fat, such as bacon, around lean cuts of meat and poultry to keep them moist and impart more flavor. For example, you can wrap chicken or turkey breasts with slices of bacon before baking. You can also wrap a meatloaf with bacon slices to keep it moist during baking.

### Crush

This technique is useful for bringing out the flavor of garlic and herbs, and can be done by pressing the flat side of a knife blade down onto the garlic or herbs. You can also adapt this technique to make cookie crumbs for cheesecakes. Simply place the cookies in a plastic bag, tie the end, then use a rolling pin to crush the cookies inside the bag.

### Fold

This technique involves mixing a light mixture into a heavier one using a spoon or spatula in a figure-eight movement. This is done to keep the air within the mixture.

### Baste

When you spoon juices or fat over food during cooking, it is known as "basting." It helps to keep the food moist and seal in the flavor.

### Beat

This technique involves using a fork, spoon, or electric mixer in a vigorous stirring motion to remove any lumps from sauces and incorporate air into omelets and cake batters.

### Rub in

This technique is mainly used when making pie dough. Using the fingertips, rub the fat into the flour, lifting it high over the bowl in order to trap air in the mixture, making it lighter and giving a better result.

Grind

Crush

Fold

Beat

Rub in

Shred

### Marinate

This term means to soak food in a marinade for a few hours or days to tenderize it and give it more flavor. You can marinate meat, poultry, fish, and vegetables. Marinades usually consist of oil and perhaps alcohol or vinegar, and are flavored with different mixtures of herbs and spices.

### Deglaze

This technique is used after sautéeing food (normally meat). After the food and excess fat have been removed from the pan, a small amount of liquid—such as stock or wine—is stirred in to loosen browned bits of food in the pan. This mixture often forms the base for a sauce to accompany the food.

### Punching down

This entails punching the air out of bread dough after it has risen.

### Clarify

You can clarify butter or a liquid. To clarify butter, heat it slowly to separate the milk solids, which sink to the bottom of the pan, skimming any foam off the top. Clarified butter, such as Indian ghee, has a higher smoke point than ordinary butter, so you can cook with it at higher temperatures. To clarify a liquid, such as a stock, add egg whites and/or egg shells to it and simmer for 10 minutes, then cool and strain it. The egg whites or shells draw out the impurities.

### Shred

This technique involves using a small, sharp knife or grater to cut food into very thin lengths.

### Line

To line a pan with something to prevent food from sticking during cooking. The most common method is to rub butter or oil over the surface of the pan, then cover with parchment paper before adding the food. You can also use bacon slices as a lining for savory nonvegetarian dishes.

### Marble

This technique is used to combine two differently colored ingredients in order to create a marbled effect. For example, you can mix melted white chocolate into melted semisweet chocolate to create a marbled pattern.

**Butterfly**

**Score**

To make light incisions on the surface of a food, particularly meat, poultry, and fish, in order to facilitate cooking, allow fat to drain, and create a decorative effect.

**Blend**

Blending involves combining two or more ingredients together by stirring with a spoon or pureeing with an electric blender. It is a useful technique for soups, milk shakes, and smoothies.

**Butterfly**

To butterfly a leg of lamb, insert the knife into the cavity of the leg bone and cut to one side to open out the meat; then make a shallow surface cut down the center to keep the meat open flat. You can also butterfly other foods, such as chicken breasts or large shrimp.

**Knead**

This technique uses the heel of the hand to pull and stretch bread dough in order to develop the gluten in the flour, so that the bread will keep its shape when it has risen. You can also knead dough in a food processor that has a dough hook.

**Skim**

To remove foam or fat from the surface of a simmering liquid with a large slotted spoon or ladle.

**Whisk**

Whisking involves beating a light mixture, such as cream and eggs, vigorously with a whisk to incorporate more air. You can use a balloon whisk (but it takes a lot of effort), a handheld electric mixer, a freestanding mixer, or a food processor with a whisk attachment.

**Zest**

To remove the outer layer of citrus fruit. A zester shaves off the zest without picking up the bitter white pith underneath.

**Chiffonade**

A French term meaning "made of rags." It refers to the effect you get when you roll leafy vegetables together, then slice them crosswise into ribbons with a sharp knife.

**Whisk**

**Chiffonade**

Emulsify

Tenderize

Mash

### Enrich
To add a rich ingredient to a dish in order to create a richer texture or flavor. For example, you can add butter to a dough, or cream to a sauce.

### Glaze
This involves brushing water, beaten egg, or sugar and water onto pie dough before baking to give it a glossy shine (and make it crunchy if sugar is added). To glaze a ham, remove the skin from the partly cooked meat then coat the outer surface with sugar and mustard and continue cooking. You can glaze sweet dishes with melted jelly or chocolate.

### Lard
To lard means to insert strips of pork fat into a lean cut of meat to flavor it and keep it moist.

### Emulsify
Emulsifying means adding one liquid to another in a slow, gradual stream while stirring or blending rapidly. This is how mayonnaise is made, by adding oil in a slow stream to a beaten egg mixture while whisking or blending vigorously.

### Tenderize
This involves pounding meat, such as a beef steak, with a mallet in order to break down the tough fibers. You can also tenderize meat by marinating it.

### Chop
To cut food into small pieces using a sharp knife. For example, to chop a herb, hold the tip of the knife blade down with one hand, then use your other hand to raise the handle of the knife up and down as you chop the herb. You can chop food coarsely or finely, depending on your requirements. Coarsely chopped means that the food will be left in larger pieces than when finely chopped.

### Mash
To reduce food, usually cooked potatoes and other root vegetables, to a pulp using a potato masher or a freestanding mixer.

### Steep
Steeping means to soak an ingredient in hot liquid in order to release its flavor into the liquid.

### Julienne
This technique involves cutting food, such as carrots and celery, into fine sticks or strips.

### Cut

To use a sharp knife to make an incision or separate a food into smaller pieces.

### Dress

This can mean to add a dressing to a salad, to decorate a dish before serving, or to pluck and truss poultry.

### Grease or oil

To rub a little butter or oil over the surface of a pan to prevent food from sticking to it during cooking.

### Truss

To pull poultry or game into shape, then secure with string or skewers before cooking. This technique is particularly useful for preventing dressing from falling out of a bird.

### Cream

Creaming is similar to beating, in that you use a fork, spoon, or electric mixer to beat ingredients together until they are smooth. This technique is usually associated with something rich and creamy, such as butter.

### Spatchcock

To remove the backbone from a bird and secure it so that it can be cooked flat and therefore more rapidly. To remove the backbone, first tuck under the wings and remove the wishbone. Then turn the bird over and cut along each side of the backbone to remove it. Use your hands to push down on the bird's breast and flatten it. Finally, push a metal skewer through the thighs and another through the wings and breast to secure the bird.

### Puree

To reduce food to a smooth pulp. You can do this by pushing food through a strainer or using a blender.

### Macerate

To soak a food in a liquid, often alcohol, to soften it.

### Open freeze

This technique means to freeze foods, uncovered, in a single layer. For example, you can cut fruit, such as mango, into small pieces, spread them out on a tray, and freeze them uncovered. Then transfer individually to a freezer bag and use as required.

### Cure

To preserve a food by salting or smoking it.

Truss

Puree

Crimp

Sift

Crosshatch

Sieve

### Degorge

This is soaking meat, poultry, or fish in a solution of cold water and salt to remove impurities. It also means salting eggplants to remove their bitter juices.

### Grind

To grind food, such as meat, into small pieces using a knife or grinder.

### Dredge

To sprinkle flour onto a counter when rolling out pie dough, or to sprinkle confectioners' sugar or cocoa over desserts.

### Crimp

This technique means to use the finger and thumb of one hand and the index finger of the other hand to "pinch" pie dough together around the edge of a pie or other pastry. This gives it a decorative effect.

### Sift

This technique involves shaking dry ingredients, such as flour, through a strainer to remove lumps and introduce more air into the mixture.

### Dice

To cut food into small, regular-shape cubes. You can use a sharp knife or a special dicing utensil.

### Grate

To shred food into small pieces. You can use a box-shaped grater or food processor.

### Peel

Peeling involves removing the outer skin or zest from foods, such as oranges, avocados, or potatoes. Depending on the food, you can use your hands, a sharp knife, or a vegetable peeler.

### Shuck

This is how we remove the husks from corn, the shells from peas, and the shells from oysters.

### Crosshatch

To score crisscross patterns on the surface of foods to let them absorb marinades or be removed from their skins. You can crosshatch the outer layer of fat on a pork joint before cooking to let the fat drain and create a decorative effect.

### Snip

This means using kitchen scissors to cut green leafy vegetables or herbs into very small pieces.

### Sieve

This involves pushing food through a strainer in order to create a puree.

# COOKING METHODS

IN THIS SECTION, YOU WILL FIND ALL THE TRADITIONAL COOKING TECHNIQUES, FROM BOILING TO ROASTING, AS WELL AS THE INCREASINGLY POPULAR HEALTH-CONSCIOUS METHODS, SUCH AS STEAMING AND STIR-FRYING.

## Fry

This method involves cooking food in hot fat, usually oil, in a skillet. Frying food gives it a delicious flavor. You can shallow-fry or deep-fry food. Deep-frying needs a lot more oil and can be dangerous, so it is always better to shallow-fry food if possible. However, for some foods, such as tempura (a Japanese dish of batter-coated pieces of fish and vegetables), or Scotch eggs, deep-frying is unavoidable. You can also stir-fry food. This method needs only a little oil and is a very healthy way to cook.

## Deep-fry

This technique involves immersing food completely in very hot oil and cooking it at a high temperature. It is important to choose the correct oil. Peanut and soybean oil have the highest smoke points (the temperature at which the oil begins to emit smoke) and are, therefore, the most suitable for deep-frying. Canola and corn oil have the next highest, and are also suitable. Sunflower-seed oil has a lower smoke point and should not be used for deep-frying. Deep-frying food is dangerous because it is possible to spill the hot oil or the pan can catch fire, so you must be careful and should never leave the pan unattended. A thermostatically controlled deep-fryer is a safer and easier option, but still needs care and attention during use. The oil should be heated to a high temperature in order to allow rapid cooking; the high temperature will also help to seal the food and prevent it from absorbing too much oil. When the food is cooked, lift it out carefully using a spatula or slotted spoon, or the wire basket if using a deep-fryer. Let any excess oil drain away from the food on paper towels.

## Dry-fry

This method involves cooking food or spices in a skillet without using fat or oil. For example, you can cook Indian spices, flat breads, or Mexican tortillas in a dry skillet. You can also dry-fry pumpkin seeds or pine nuts until they are golden and lightly toasted.

Fry

Deep-fry

Dry-fry

Pan-fry

Shallow-fry

Stir-fry

### Pan-fry

This is another quick and healthy way of cooking food. It involves cooking food quickly in a skillet with either no fat at all (as in dry-frying) or with the absolute minimum amount of fat necessary. Some foods, such as bacon, have enough fat content of their own, and, therefore, do not need any added fat. In fact, the fat they emit during cooking can be enough to pan-fry other foods at the same time—in this way, the dish has a minimum amount of fat yet maximum flavor.

### Shallow-fry

This method of cooking is suitable for foods that will not burn easily—for example, foods that are protected in some way, such as foods coated with flour, bread crumbs, or batter. You will need to add enough oil so that the food will not stick to the pan or burn. Be careful to heat the oil to a high temperature because this will help to seal the food when it is added and prevent it from absorbing too much oil. (Food cooked in oil that has not reached the right temperature will be soggy and laden with oil.) Cook the food in the oil for the required time, then turn it over and cook on the other side. Use a slotted spatula to lift out the food, and let any excess oil drain away from the hot food on paper towels. Where this

method differs from sautéing is that the food is not moved around the pan, and generally a little more oil is used.

### Stir-fry

This method comes from Asia and is another very healthy way to cook because of the small amount of oil needed. Foods such as meat, poultry, and vegetables are cut into small, similar-size pieces and cooked rapidly, while being tossed constantly, in a wok. You can also use a large skillet for stir-frying, but a wok is better because the food cooks more rapidly as it comes into contact with the hot sides of the wok. Chinese cooking distinguishes between four or five different methods of stir-frying, but two are the most common. The first is a very rapid technique, where the food is fried in a little oil at the highest heat while being tossed constantly. Foods cooked in this way are often marinated first. The other technique is less vigorous and more moist. The food is cooked in a little liquid, such as a stock, and constantly turned and moved around the pan. Noodles and sauce are often added toward the end of the cooking time. It is important not to overfill the wok, or the food will steam instead of fry.

Boil

### Boil

To cook food in a liquid (usually water, milk, or stock) in a pan at boiling point (212°F/100°C). Not all foods are boiled continually. Sometimes they are "brought to a boil," then the temperature is reduced and the food is left to simmer (bubble gently). You can cook many foods in this way, such as vegetables, rice, pasta, meat, and eggs. You can also boil a liquid rapidly for a period of time in order to evaporate excess moisture (see Reduce).

### Simmer

To cook food in liquid that is just below boiling point; there will be very gentle bubbles on the surface of the liquid. This method is often combined with the boiling technique, where a food is first brought to a boil, then the heat is reduced and the food is allowed to simmer for a period of time.

### Blanch

Blanching is a useful technique for loosening skins on foods such as tomatoes, preserving the color of vegetables, reducing any bitterness in ingredients, and preparing foods for freezing. Blanching also helps to reduce the salt content in cured meats. To blanch a food, simply immerse it in boiling water for a few seconds, then plunge it into cold water to prevent additional cooking.

### Reduce

Although this is not a complete cooking method in its own right, it is a useful technique, especially for sauces. To reduce a liquid, simply boil it down rapidly in an uncovered pan. This evaporates the liquid and makes the sauce thicker.

Simmer

Reduce

Steam

Sauté

Caramelize

### Steam

Steaming is a very healthy way to cook, because the food does not come into direct contact with the liquid and, therefore, more of the nutrients are preserved. Steaming is suitable for a wide range of foods, from poultry and fish to vegetables and puddings. If you use a folding metal steamer, simply bring a small amount of water to a boil in the bottom of the pan, place the steamer inside, add the food, cover the pan, and steam until cooked to your taste. Bamboo steamers are used in a similar way. You can also steam puddings: Bring enough water to a boil to come halfway up the side of the ovenproof bowl, then place the bowl inside the pan and steam the pudding for the recommended time (being careful to top up with boiling water if necessary during cooking).

### Sauté

This is similar to frying, but involves moving the food around the skillet to prevent it from browning too rapidly. Usually a small amount of oil or butter is used to grease the pan and prevent the food from burning.

### Caramelize

This term most often refers to the method of caramelizing sugar or onions. To caramelize sugar, heat it until it melts into a syrup. The color varies from light golden to dark brown, depending on the cooking time. A candy thermometer is useful to get the sugar to the required temperature. When the sugar is removed from the heat, it quickly sets and becomes brittle but retains its caramelized appearance. You can also sprinkle sugar over a food and caramelize it under a preheated hot broiler or by heating its surface with a kitchen blowtorch. To caramelize onions, cook them gently in butter for 30 minutes, or until they turn a rich golden brown.

### Sear

To sear means to brown meat, poultry, and fish rapidly over high heat. This process helps to seal in the juices and keeps the center of the food moist.

### Poach

To poach means to cook food in a liquid at just below boiling point; it is a very gentle method of cooking. The liquids commonly used for poaching are water and alcohol. You can poach poultry, fish, eggs (as long as they are very fresh), and fruit.

### Sweat

To cook food (often vegetables, such as onions) gently in water or fat until they are softened but not brown.

### POACHING FRUIT

Pour enough wine or sugar syrup into a pan to cover the fruit. Bring to a simmer, add the pitted fruit, and simmer for 15 minutes, or until tender. Lift out the fruit, reduce the liquid by boiling it down, then pour it over the fruit.

### Flambé

Strictly speaking, to flambé is more food presentation than cooking method, but since it involves warming an ingredient it is included here. Flambé is a French word meaning "flamed." It involves sprinkling liqueur over a food, such as a Christmas pudding, then setting the alcohol alight just before serving. It makes a dramatic spectacle at the table, and also burns off the alcohol content.

### Toast

This process uses dry heat to cook foods. For example, you can toast nuts by baking them dry in the oven or cooking them under a hot broiler. You can also toast bread under the broiler, or you can spear marshmallows on forks and toast them over a fire.

### Bake

To bake means to cook food in an oven using dry heat at the correct temperature. For example, you can bake potatoes, cakes, cookies, breads, and custards.

Sear

Poach

Sweat

Flambé

Bake blind

Roast

## Bake blind

To bake a pastry shell without a filling. To bake blind, first line a pie pan or tart dish with rolled-out pie dough, prick it with a fork, place a layer of parchment paper over the pie dough, and weight it down with ceramic or metal baking beans. Then bake it. If you don't have any baking beans, you can use dried beans instead. Baking blind helps to ensure that the pie pastry stays crisp after the filling is added, and is especially necessary if the filling does not need to be cooked, or needs only a very short time to cook.

## Roast

Roasting is similar to baking in that food is cooked in the oven using dry heat. In this case, however, the process is often used for meat, poultry, and vegetables. It is usually necessary to add a little fat when roasting foods to keep them moist. Roasting can really bring out the flavor of a food—for example, bell peppers that have been roasted are extra sweet and flavorful. You can also roast a wide variety of other vegetables, not just potatoes and parsnips, but also garlic, onions, carrots, fennel, sweet potatoes, eggplants, and rutabaga.

## Braise

This is a long, slow way to cook food. It is especially useful for tough cuts of meat, and for poultry and vegetables. To braise foods, first brown them in oil, then cook them very slowly in a small amount of flavored liquid, such as stock or wine, in a dish with a tight-fitting lid. You can cook them on a stove or in an oven.

### Casserole

This method is similar to braising; you can use a large, heavy-bottom casserole dish or a Dutch oven with a tight-fitting lid. First brown the food in oil, add a small amount of flavored liquid, cover with a lid, then cook very slowly in the oven. Sometimes a casserole can be likened to a stew, where the food is cut into smaller pieces and more cooking liquid is added. After cooking, you can serve the food directly from the casserole dish.

### Stew

Stewing is a very slow method of cooking. It is similar to braising, except that the food is cut into smaller pieces and more liquid is used. This technique is suitable for meat (especially tough cuts because the long cooking process helps to tenderize the meat), poultry, fish, vegetables, grains, such as barley, and certain fruits, such as apples, pears, peaches, and nectarines.

### CHARGRILLED VEGETABLES

To add some variety to chargrilled vegetables, mix 1 tablespoon olive oil, 1 teaspoon lemon juice, 1 teaspoon each chopped fresh rosemary and thyme, and season to taste with salt and pepper. Brush the mixture over the vegetables, and chargrill as required.

### Pot roast

This technique is very similar to braising in that it involves cooking food (usually meat, especially beef) very slowly in a covered pot in the oven. Only a very little liquid is used.

### Griddle

Traditionally, a griddle is a flat, usually rimless, pan, which is used to cook crêpes and drop scones with the minimum of oil. Griddles usually have a long handle and are often made of a heavy metal that conducts heat well, such as cast iron. Nowadays, the term "griddle" is often confused with chargrill.

### Chargrill

Chargrilling enables you to cook food in the minimum amount of fat; it also gives the food attractive charred stripes. You can cook meat, poultry, fish, and vegetables in this way. Simply heat a ridged stove-top grill pan on the stove, brush the food with a little oil (never brush the oil onto the pan directly), then place the food on the heated pan. Cook according to the recipe, turning the food over once to cook on the other side. You can also chargrill food on a metal grille set over hot coals.

Stew

Pot roast

Griddle

Chargrill

Barbecue

Broil

## Barbecue

With this method the food is usually cooked on a mesh over hot coals. The barbecue apparatus can range from a simple portable tray consisting of a mesh with flammable, slow-burning coals underneath, to an elaborate electric barbecue. Foods are often marinated first, in order to give them more flavor and to aid the cooking process. Always barbecue your food outdoors in the open air in order to waft away any carbon monoxide fumes given off by the lit charcoal. Also, in order to prevent burns, use long-handled utensils to lift and turn the food.

## Broil

Broiling is a quick and healthy way to cook food. Modern ovens usually have an integral broiler; they also come with a broiler pan with a wire mesh to let excess fat drain away. A broiler should always be preheated before use. Broiling is a very versatile method of cooking. You can cook meat, poultry, fish, and vegetables under a broiler, and toast other foods, such as bread or nuts. Broiling food involves cooking it directly under the heat source, which ensures that the outside of the food is browned quickly, while the inside stays moist.

## Blowtorch

One of the cook's best-kept secrets is blowtorching food. This method of cooking is simple, quick, and effective. You can buy a kitchen blowtorch from any reputable kitchen equipment store, and you will find it inexpensive and convenient. It has a variety of uses. For example, to make a crunchy, caramelized topping for crème brûlées, simply sprinkle them generously with white sugar until the surfaces are completely covered. Now ignite your blowtorch and adjust the air for a blue flame.

Apply the flame to the sugar until it caramelizes and turns golden brown. You can also peel a bell pepper by blow torching instead of roasting it. This method is especially suitable if you are short of time or have only one or two bell peppers to peel. Spear the bell pepper with a fork, then turn it over the flame of the blowtorch until the skin is charred and black. Transfer the bell pepper to a plastic bag, leave for 15 minutes, then peel off the skin in the usual way.

# PANTRY

A GOOD STORE OF NONPERISHABLE FOOD STUFFS IS AN ESSENTIAL PART OF EVERY COOK'S KITCHEN. WELL-STOCKED KITCHEN CUPBOARDS, AND PERHAPS A PANTRY, ENSURE THAT YOU ALWAYS HAVE A GOOD SELECTION OF STAPLE ITEMS ON HAND FOR EVERY OCCASION. MAKE SURE YOU CHECK THE EXPIRATION DATES OF YOUR STORED ITEMS REGULARLY, AND DISCARD ANY THAT HAVE BECOME OUT OF DATE.

### Oils

There are many different varieties of oil available these days, but it is not necessary to buy them all. You simply need oil that is suitable for drizzling and for cooking at high temperatures.

**Olive oil**
This mildly fruity oil is ideal for drizzling over salads. It can range from a champagne color to bright green. The best oils are cold-pressed—this is a chemical-free process that uses only pressure and produces a low level of acidity. You can also flavor it with different ingredients—for example, try adding some herbs, such as basil leaves, or some garlic to it—after a day or two the oil will become infused with their flavor. Its smoke point (the temperature at which it begins to smoke) is 410°F/210°C.

**Extra virgin olive oil**
Produced from the first cold-pressing of the olives, this oil has a very low acid level. It is the most expensive type of olive oil, and has a peppery, fruity flavor. You can use it for drizzling over salads and hot dishes, such as pizzas. Its smoke point is 410°F/210°C.

**Sunflower oil**
This is a good multipurpose oil that can be used for most cooking purposes. However, it is not recommended for deep-frying because this method needs an oil with a higher smoke point. The smoke point of sunflower oil is 390°F/199°C. Sunflower oil has a very light flavor and is, therefore, ideal in dressings.

**Sesame oil**
This oil comes in two varieties: one has a light color and a nutty flavor, the other is darker and has a stronger flavor. The darker one is most often used in Asian dishes.

This oil is excellent for frying and stir-frying. Its smoke point is 410°F/210°C.

**Vegetable oil**
A blend of various oils, mainly canola, soybean, coconut, and palm. It is best used for frying instead of in salads because it is greasy.

**Peanut oil**
A combination of a very mild flavor and a high smoke point of 450°F/232°C makes peanut oil extremely versatile. It is, therefore, suitable for dressings and mayonnaise, and for drizzling over dishes, as well as for all forms of cooking, including deep-frying.

**Corn oil**
This oil is economical to buy, and, therefore, is a good choice for cooking. However, it has a strong, distinctive flavor that makes it unsuitable for dressings and drizzling over dishes. Its smoke point is 410°F/210°C.

Olive oil

Extra virgin olive oil

Sunflower oil

### Canola oil
This oil is gaining in popularity because it contains less saturated fat than other oils. It also contains the omega-3 essential fatty acid, which is now widely believed to help reduce cholesterol levels. It has a mild flavor and so is suitable for salad dressings as well as for cooking. Its smoke point is 444°F/229°C.

### Soybean oil
This economical oil is extracted from soybeans and has a light yellow color. Like canola oil, its popularity is growing because it is low in saturated fat. Its smoke point is 450°F/232°C, which makes it ideal for all types of cooking, including deep-frying. However, it has a strong taste and is, therefore, not suitable for dressings or for drizzling over finished dishes.

Nut oil

Corn oil

## Vinegars
Vinegar adds a pungent kick to dressings, marinades, sauces, and a wide range of dishes. It is available in different varieties, and here are some of the most popular types.

### Distilled white vinegar
Made from a grain-alcohol mixture, this popular vinegar has a sharp taste.

### Cider vinegar
This vinegar is made from apples and has a strong, sharp taste. It is best used with meats and in pickles and chutneys.

### Wine vinegars
These are available in different varieties, mainly red, white, and sherry. They can be used in dressings, marinades, and sauces, and can be sprinkled over food.

### Malt vinegar
A dark brown variety, malt vinegar is used in chutneys and on traditional British fish and french fries. This vinegar is not suitable for dressings.

### Balsamic vinegar
This delicious vinegar is thick, dark and slightly sweet. It is made from grape juice that is aged in barrels over a period of years.

### Specialty vinegars
These vinegars can be made with fruits, such as berries, nuts, or a wide variety of herbs. Other popular favorites are rice vinegar (used in Asian cooking) and cane vinegar, which has a rich, slightly sweet taste.

Vegetable oil

Basil-flavored olive oil

Malt vinegar

Red wine vinegar

Balsamic vinegar

## ■ Flour

Keep your flour fresh by storing it in an airtight container with a tight-fitting lid in a cool, dry place. You can store white flours for 6–8 months, and whole-wheat flours for up to 2 months.

### Cornstarch
This powdery flour is made from corn and is used for thickening sauces, soups, and desserts. It is usually mixed with a small quantity of cold liquid to make a smooth paste before being added to hot dishes.

### All-purpose flour
This flour is used for thickening sauces as well as for making batters and pie dough.

### Self-rising flour
All-purpose flour that has had baking powder and salt added is known as self-rising flour. It is used for making cakes and cookies.

### Whole-wheat flour
This flour has a stronger flavor than white flour and contains wheat germ, which means it has a higher fiber, fat, and nutrient content. However, since it has a higher fat content, it should be stored in the refrigerator to stop it from going rancid.

### White bread flour
This flour is used for making bread. It contains a high level of gluten, which helps to give the bread dough its elasticity. If you are using a whole-wheat variety, keep it in an airtight container in the refrigerator.

### Rice flour
This powdery flour is made from white rice, and is used mainly in baked foods and to make Asian rice-flour noodles.

### Malted brown flour
This is a brown flour that has had malted wheat grains added for a distinctive nutty flavor.

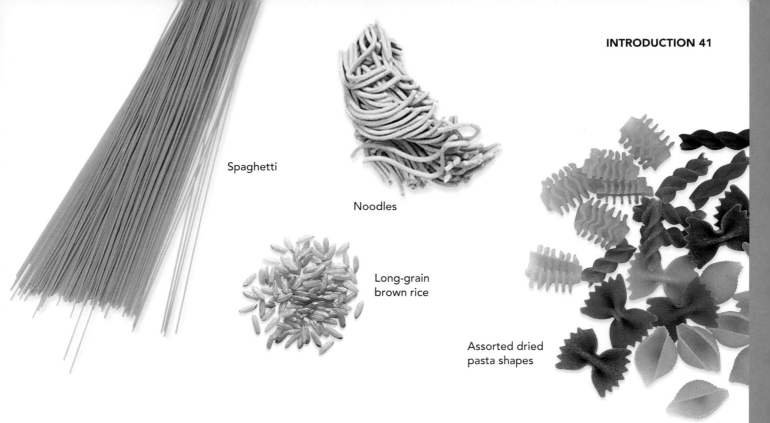

Spaghetti

Noodles

Long-grain
brown rice

Assorted dried
pasta shapes

## Pasta, noodles, and grains

All these different dried pasta shapes, noodles, and grains keep well in the pantry. They are ideal for cooking quick, satisfying meals at short notice.

### Long-shaped pasta

There are different varieties of dried long-shaped pastas, including spaghetti, fettuccine (narrow ribbons), tagliatelle (slightly wider ribbons), and vermicelli (very fine, hairlike lengths). These pastas are usually made with durum wheat or whole-wheat flour, and may be colored using ingredients, such as spinach (green), beet juice (red), tomatoes (orange-red), or even squid ink (black).

### Short-shaped pasta

Dried short shapes of pasta include conchiglie (shells), fusilli (spirals), farfalle (bows), and tubular varieties, such as penne and macaroni. These shapes are particularly good for holding chunky sauces.

### Other shapes of dried pasta

Other favorite shapes to keep in your pantry include lasagna (rectangular sheets) and cannelloni (large tubes).

### Dried noodles

Most noodles are associated with Asian cooking. The main difference between noodles and long-shaped pasta is that noodles usually have egg added, such as Chinese egg noodles. Alternatively, sometimes they are made from rice flour. Noodles are very popular in stir-fries and soups. Many varieties need no cooking—you simply soak them in hot water for a few minutes before adding to the dish of your choice.

### Long-grain rice

You can buy white and brown varieties of long-grain rice. When cooked, the grains stay dry and separate and do not clump together. This rice is used in savory dishes.

### Medium-grain rice

These grains are a little shorter than long-grain rice, and more moist. They tend to clump together

when cooked. This rice is used in savory dishes, such as Spanish paella and Japanese sushi.

### Short-grain rice

This rice has short, fat grains that are more starchy and moist than medium- and long-grain rice. There are different varieties, including pearl rice (used in Asian cooking) and risotto rice.

### Instant rice

The grains in instant, or quick, rice are polished and partly boiled so that they are quick and easy to cook and stay fluffy and separate. Easy-cook rice is a convenient alternative to white or brown rice, but does not have as much flavor.

### Wild rice

Despite its name, wild rice is not actually a rice—it is a marsh grass that is cultivated in the United States and Canada. The grains are long and black and have a nutty flavor. Wild rice is expensive, so for economic reasons it is often mixed with less-expensive brown long-grain rice.

### Bulgur wheat

This comprises wheat kernels that have had the bran removed. They

are then steamed, dried, and ground into different degrees of coarseness. The result is a golden-brown grain that has a nutty flavor. It can be cooked like rice and is also excellent in salads.

### Couscous

This is not a true grain, but pieces of semolina dough that have been rolled, dampened, and coated with a fine wheat flour. It makes a fine accompaniment to savory dishes.

### Cornmeal

This yellow grain is also known as polenta and is very popular in Italian cooking. It can be eaten hot or cold. It can also be cooked in a slab, then cut into squares and broiled or fried.

### Beans

All beans except lentils and split peas need soaking for at least 8 hours, then boiling rapidly for 10 minutes before cooking for around 45 minutes. The exception is soybeans, which need even longer.

#### Cannellini beans
A type of haricot bean, these long, creamy white beans are excellent in soups and salads.

#### Red kidney beans
These red, kidney-shaped beans can be added to soups, salads, stews, and other savory dishes, such as chili con carne.

#### Aduki beans
These beans are small and red and are popular in Japanese cooking, especially coated with sugar. They are also good in savory dishes, such as soups and salads.

#### Lima beans
These white, kidney-shaped beans are excellent in soups and salads.

#### Black-eyed peas
These beans are small and beige and have a circular black "eye." They are commonly found in Chinese cooking, and are particularly popular in sauces, stir-fries, and soups.

#### Cranberry beans
These oval-shaped beans have pale pink to maroon streaked skin. They are creamy when cooked and are excellent in soups, dips, and other savory dishes.

#### Soybeans
Although most soybeans are yellow, they can also be black, brown, or green. They are much richer in nutrients than the other legumes, and are particularly full of protein, as well as iron and calcium. Soybeans are used to make cooking oils and margarine, flour, soymilk, and cheeses, soy sauce, tofu, miso, and textured vegetable protein. They are good in soups and other savory dishes, particularly curries. They should be soaked for at least 12 hours, drained, and rinsed, then covered with fresh water and brought to a boil. Boil them for the first hour of cooking, then simmer them for the remaining 2–3 hours that it takes to cook them.

#### Chickpeas
These round, beige beans have a nutty flavor and are excellent in soups, stews, and salads, as well as ground up in dips, such as hummus. Like soybeans, they need a longer soaking and cooking time than many beans, so it is good to keep some canned chickpeas at hand for when you are short of time.

#### Lentils
These tiny, disk-shaped beans are available in different varieties and colors. Red and orange lentils become mushy when cooked, and are, therefore, ideal pureed and used in soups and sauces. The green and European brown varieties (Puy lentils) keep their shape when cooked and are ideal in warm winter salads, sauces, stews, and other savory dishes.

#### Split peas
These small peas are disk-shaped and split along a natural seam. They can be yellow or green, and are excellent cooked and pureed. They are also good in soups, bakes, and other savory dishes.

Red kidney beans

Red lentils

Aduki beans

Chickpeas

Cannellini beans

Almonds

Pistachios

Hazelnuts

Pine nuts

Walnuts

Peanuts

Cashews

## Nuts and seeds

Nuts and seeds have a high oil content, and can quickly go rancid. If they have shells, store them in a cool, dry place. If they do not have shells, refrigerate them in airtight containers.

### Almonds
These lozenge-shaped nuts have a thin brown covering and a cream center. They come in two types, sweet and bitter, but it is the sweet variety that is normally used. Available whole, blanched, chopped, and candied, they are excellent in both savory and sweet dishes, from salads and savory bakes to cakes, cookies, and marzipan.

### Hazelnuts
These small, round nuts have a brown covering, a cream interior, and a rich, sweet flavor. They are especially popular in granola and cereals, savory dishes, and bakes, such as nut loaf, as well as sweet dishes, including cakes and cookies.

### Walnuts
These nuts have a large, round, wrinkled shell and two double lobes inside. The nuts have a delicious creamy taste and are good in salads and savory bakes, as well as sweet dishes and cakes. They also make a very flavorful oil.

### Pecans
These nuts are golden brown with a beige interior. They have a very high fat content. They are used in a variety of savory dishes and desserts, such as pecan pie.

### Cashews
These creamy, butter-flavored, kidney-shaped nuts have a high fat content and are delicious roasted and added to stir-fries and bakes.

### Pistachios
These pale green nuts have a delicate flavor. They are often used in dressings and also to decorate desserts.

### Pine nuts
These small, oval nuts are creamy in color and in flavor. They are excellent toasted or dry-fried, and are used in salads and rice dishes, sauces, such as pesto, and also savory and sweet dishes.

### Peanuts
Despite their name, peanuts are not nuts but legumes, and are very versatile. They are used to make oil and also peanut butter, which in turn makes a delicious satay sauce. They are also good in salads, side dishes, and stir-fries.

### Seeds
A selection of seeds can be very useful in your pantry. Sunflower seeds, for example, are rich in essential fatty acids and are delicious sprinkled into granola and salads. Pumpkin seeds are also nutritious and make a good snack. Sesame seeds are popular in Asian cooking and are delicious toasted and in stir-fries. Dill seeds have an anise flavor and are good with fish and vegetables. Caraway seeds have a pungent flavor and are used in soups, stews, vegetable dishes, and in bread. Poppy seeds are slightly sweet and make an attractive decoration sprinkled over salads and bread rolls.

## Dried herbs

It is always worthwhile having a collection of dried herbs. They are especially useful for dishes that require a long cooking time, such as casseroles. Use half the recommended fresh quantity.

### Oregano
This herb has a strong flavor and is perfect sprinkled on pizzas and in pasta sauces.

### Basil
This popular herb is delicious in sauces and is particularly good with tomatoes.

### Sage
This herb is good in egg, cheese, poultry, and meat dishes.

### Dill
This is an excellent herb with vegetables and fish.

### Rosemary
A pungent herb that goes well with poultry and meat, and also root vegetables, especially potatoes.

### Mixed herbs
This combination usually consists of oregano, rosemary, and thyme, plus one or two other herbs. Mixed herbs can be used in a variety of savory dishes, including sauces and Italian dishes, such as pizza and pasta.

## Spices and seasonings

A selection of spices in your pantry is extremely useful for enhancing the flavor of dishes. Some spices, such as ginger and turmeric, are also said to aid digestion.

### Ginger
This hot, pungent spice has a lemony flavor when fresh, but a sweeter flavor when dried. It is particularly used in Indian cooking, as well as in chutneys, desserts, and baked goods, such as cakes, notably gingerbread, and cookies.

### Turmeric
A peppery spice with a distinctive yellow color. Turmeric is often used instead of the more expensive saffron. It is especially good in curries and rice dishes, such as paella.

### Saffron
This yellow spice has a slightly bitter flavor and a pungent aroma. It is sold in strands and is used in dishes to color and flavor them.

### Coriander
This spice has an aromatic flavor and is excellent with meat, poultry, and vegetables.

### Cumin
This spice has a strong, slightly bitter flavor, and is particularly good with poultry and vegetables.

### Cloves
A sweet spice with a strong flavor. Use whole cloves to stud hams and fruits, and ground cloves to add flavor to desserts.

### Nutmeg
This spice has a sweet flavor and is used in savory and sweet dishes.

Paprika

Basil

Cumin

Sage

Oregano

Rosemary

Cloves

Confectioners' sugar

Brown sugar

Superfine sugar

Raw brown sugar

Granulated sugar

## Mace
This spice has a sweet flavor and is excellent in soups and sauces.

## Cinnamon
This is a very popular spice. It is sweet and fragrant and used in desserts and baked foods, such as cakes, sweet pies, and cookies.

## Curry powder
This is a blend of spices, and the flavor varies from mild to hot. It adds a distinctive flavor to sauces and savory dishes.

## Allspice
A mixture of sweet spices, such as cinnamon, cloves, mace, and nutmeg, plus one or two others. It gives a delicious flavor to desserts, cakes, cookies, and drinks.

## Chili powder
This is a blend of dried chiles. It adds a kick to sauces and savory dishes.

## Five-spice powder
This blend of five spices usually contains cinnamon, cloves, fennel seeds, Szechuan peppercorns, and star anise. It is very popular in Chinese cooking, and gives a marvelous flavor to stir-fries.

## Paprika
This has a hot flavor and an attractive red color. It is ideal as a garnish.

## Peppercorns
These come in different varieties. Ground black or white peppercorns are an extremely popular seasoning for a wide variety of savory foods and also some sweet dishes such as balsamic strawberries. You can also buy green peppercorns.

## Salt
This is a great favorite as a seasoning, but be careful that you don't to overuse it or it will overpower the food it will also be bad for health.

Turmeric

Ground ginger

Peppercorns

## ■ Sugars and syrups
Store your sugar in a dry place at room temperature. Syrups should be kept in tightly sealed containers at room temperature or in the refrigerator.

## Granulated sugar
This basic, cheap sugar is essential in your pantry. Use it to sweeten drinks and cereals and to sprinkle on desserts.

## Superfine sugar
This sugar is finer than granulated sugar and dissolves quickly, so it is ideal for meringues and cakes.

## Confectioners' sugar
This very fine sugar is ideal for making frosting and for dusting cakes and desserts.

## Brown sugar
This stronger-flavored sugar comes in various shades, from pale gold to chocolate brown.

## Raw brown sugar
This crunchy brown sugar is delicious sprinkled over desserts and cakes before being broiled or baked.

## Honey
This comes in a variety of flavors and colors, as either clear, liquid honey or opaque, set honey. It has many uses, from glazing ham and flavoring vegetables to sweetening desserts and drinks.

## Corn syrup
Clear corn syrup is made from evaporated sugar cane juice. It is used in a variety of dishes, and to top crêpes and ice cream.

## Maple syrup
This syrup has a delicious sweet flavor and can be used in a wide variety of savory and sweet dishes. It is very popular on crêpes.

## Sauces, pastes, and condiments

A good selection of sauces and condiments is invaluable in the kitchen, and will ensure you always have the right ingredient at hand to add exciting and interesting flavors to your dishes.

### Ketchup
This sauce is popular in cooking and is added to cooked foods, such as french fries and hamburgers. It is also good as an ingredient in dressings and relishes.

### Brown sauce
Also known as espagnole sauce, this strongly flavored sauce is used as a base for a number of other sauces.

### Soy sauce
This popular sauce is essential for stir-fries and other Asian dishes. You can buy the Chinese version, which is salty, or the Japanese type, which is slightly sweeter.

### Worcestershire sauce
This strongly flavored sauce is made with onions, molasses, and anchovies, and is used to season meats, gravies, and soups, and occasionally cocktails.

### Pesto
Pesto is made from basil, garlic, pine nuts, Parmesan cheese, and olive oil. It is ideal for quick pasta meals.

### Tabasco sauce
This very hot chili sauce is used in dishes to give them a kick, such as Mexican salsas. It is also used to season certain cocktails.

### Hoisin sauce
This sweet soy-based sauce with a sticky texture is very popular in Chinese cooking. It is known by various names, such as Peking sauce.

### Thai fish sauce (nam pla)
This salty sauce is made from fermented fish and has a very strong taste and smell. It is used to flavor Thai dishes and as a table condiment.

### Horseradish sauce
Horseradish is a root with a very hot flavor. It makes an excellent creamy white sauce, which is very good with meat, poultry, fish, and egg dishes.

### Plum sauce
This fruity sauce is popular in Chinese cooking and is traditionally served with egg rolls and also Peking duck.

### Harissa
This North African condiment is made from oil, garlic, herbs, and spices, and is served with soups and couscous.

### Sesame seed paste
A thick paste made from finely ground sesame seeds. It is used to flavor Middle Eastern dishes.

### Thai curry paste
This is available in different varieties: green is the hottest, yellow is the mildest, and red varies in the amount of heat. It is a popular ingredient in Thai dishes.

### Miso
A paste made from fermented soybeans. It is used in Japanese cooking to thicken and flavor soups and other dishes.

### Tomato paste
This is a concentrate that is useful in sauces and soups because of its intense flavor.

### Strained canned tomatoes
The juice strained from canned tomatoes is ideal for soups and sauces, and for spreading over pizzas.

### Mustards
You can buy different types of mustard. Dijon mustard has a strong flavor and is used in dips and dressings. English mustard is very hot and is useful in dips and dressings. Coarse-grain mustard is usually milder, and is good with a variety of savory dishes, especially meats.

Soy sauce

Coarse-grain mustard

Tabasco sauce

Thai fish sauce

Pesto sauce

Horseradish sauce

## Canned and bottled foods

Keep a selection of canned and bottled foods at hand, such as beans, fish, vegetables, and pickled items, and you will never be short of ingredients for delicious meals at short notice.

### Canned beans
You can buy a wide variety of canned beans, such as red kidney beans and chickpeas, which will save you time because you do not have to soak them or cook them. Cans of baked beans in tomato sauce are indispensable for quick meals.

### Canned fish
Canned fish, such as tuna, salmon, crab, anchovies, sardines, and pilchards, are versatile items to have in the pantry. They are particularly useful when added to pastas and salads.

### Canned tomatoes
Canned tomatoes can be used in a wide variety of dishes, from sauces and soups to stews and casseroles.

### Coconut milk
Canned coconut milk is very useful for cooking Thai dishes, particularly creamy curries and desserts.

### Corn
Canned corn is deliciously sweet and ideal in salads, soups, bakes, and casseroles.

### Water chestnuts
These are popular in Chinese cooking, and are particularly good in stir-fries.

### Olives
It is always useful to keep a can or bottle of olives at hand. They make ideal tapas for unexpected guests and are delicious in salads and pastas and on pizzas.

### Sun-dried tomatoes
These are very good in Italian recipes, particularly salads, pastas, and bread.

### Pickled foods
Onions, gherkins, and capers make perfect accompaniments and garnishes for meat and vegetable dishes.

## Dried fruits and berries

A selection of dried fruits and berries is very useful to keep at hand. They make ideal snacks and can be used in a wide variety of savory and sweet dishes, from granola, vegetable curries, and meat dishes to desserts and sweet pies. Dried fruits and berries include currants, raisins, apricots, prunes, figs, dates, mangoes, pears, apples, bananas, cranberries, and blueberries.

## Other items

Here is a selection of other items you will find useful to keep in your pantry.

### Bouillon cubes
These are very convenient for soups, casseroles, and other dishes, particularly if you do not have enough time to make fresh stock.

### Gelatin
You need gelatin to set mousses and gelatin-based desserts. You can also buy a vegetarian equivalent, such as agar agar.

### Chocolate and cocoa
These are useful for desserts and baked goods, and also for some savory dishes.

### Vanilla
You can buy vanilla in bean or liquid form (extract) as a flavoring. Vanilla is particularly delicious in desserts.

### Alcohol
White wine, red wine, and sherry are handy for a variety of savory and sweet dishes. Although not essential, flavored liqueurs are also useful, such as orange, coffee, and almond.

## Refrigerator and freezer essentials

Your chilled essentials should include eggs, milk, and yogurt. You should also keep some butter, including an unsalted variety for baking and desserts. Bread is another essential, not just as an accompaniment, but for making bread crumbs and recipes such as crostini. Cheeses should include an all-purpose firm variety, such as cheddar, and also Parmesan, as well as cream cheese. You may find bacon useful. Tofu is full of protein. It is good in stir-fries and is useful for vegetarian meals. In the freezer, you might want to keep frozen shrimp and fish fillets, vegetables, berries, and ice cream.

Vanilla beans

# PART TWO

# MAIN COMMODITIES AND RECIPES

# CHAPTER 1

# EGGS AND DAIRY

EGGS AND DAIRY PRODUCTS, SUCH AS MILK, BUTTER, AND CHEESE, ARE EXCELLENT SOURCES OF PROTEIN. THEY ARE ALSO VERY VERSATILE FOODS AND CAN BE USED TO ENRICH A WIDE RANGE OF SWEET AND SAVORY DISHES. IN THIS SECTION YOU WILL FIND A MOUTHWATERING ARRAY OF EGG AND DAIRY RECIPES TO DELIGHT EVERY MEMBER OF YOUR HOUSEHOLD.

# INTRODUCTION

NOWADAYS, WE CAN BUY A WIDE RANGE OF DELICIOUS EGGS, FROM FACTORY-PRODUCED WHITE AND BROWN TO FREE-RANGE AND ORGANIC. LIKEWISE, MORE DAIRY PRODUCTS ARE AVAILABLE THAN BEFORE, AND WE CAN CHOOSE FROM AN EVER-INCREASING ARRAY OF MILK, YOGURT, CREAM, BUTTER, AND CHEESE, WHICH ARE FULL OF PROTEIN AND VERY EASY TO PREPARE AND COOK.

### Buying and storing eggs

Always buy your eggs from a reputable supplier, and do not buy any with cracked shells. Ensure the eggs are as fresh as possible by checking the "sell by" and expiration, or "EXP," dates on the carton. Choose ones that are marked Grade AA or A. You can also check an egg's freshness by floating it in water. If it sinks to the bottom of the bowl horizontally, it is very fresh; if it stays vertical with its tip on the bottom, it is less fresh; if it floats to the top, it is stale and should be discarded. Store your eggs, pointed ends down, in their carton in the door of your refrigerator or in a cool place in your kitchen. Separated egg whites will keep in the refrigerator in a lidded container for a week, and in the freezer for three months. Egg yolks or whole beaten eggs will keep in the refrigerator for up to 2 days, or in the freezer for up to 3 months (add a little salt to them before freezing). When freezing eggs, or indeed any food, always label the container with the date of freezing and what it contains. Eggs are best cooked at room temperature, so get them out of the refrigerator 2–3 hours before they are needed, if possible.

### Whisking egg whites

Eggs that are 3–5 days old are best for whisking. Make sure that everything is clean and that your bowl is free from grease. Place the egg whites in the bowl. If you are whisking by hand, use a large balloon whisk in an upward, circular movement. Alternatively, use a hand-held electric mixer or freestanding food mixer. If the recipe calls for a "soft peaks" consistency, the mixture should form peaks that are soft and will flop over. If you need "firm peaks," the peaks should stand rigid.

### Scrambling eggs

Allow 2 eggs and 1 tablespoon of milk per person. Whisk together the eggs and milk in a bowl, then season with salt and pepper. Melt 1 tablespoon of butter in a nonstick pan, then pour in the egg mixture. Stir constantly over low heat for 5–7 minutes, until almost set, then remove from the heat. Stir for 1 more minute, then serve.

### Boiling eggs

To boil eggs, bring a small pan of water to a boil. Reduce the heat to a simmer, add a pinch of salt, then carefully add the eggs (if they have been refrigerated, bring them out about an hour beforehand to let them reach to room temperature). Simmer gently for 4–5 minutes for soft-cooked, and 9–10 minutes for hard-cooked (no longer, or a dark ring will appear around the yolk). Remove with a

## SAFETY

Eggs can carry harmful bacteria and may cause food poisoning if not thoroughly cooked, so do not give dishes with raw or lightly cooked eggs to people who may be particularly vulnerable, such as pregnant or breastfeeding women, babies and infants, the elderly, people who are ill, or convalescents.

Small duck egg

Goose egg

Quail egg

Free-range hen egg

Medium duck egg

Large duck egg

slotted spoon and plunge into cold water to prevent the eggs from cooking any further. Serve as required.

### Frying eggs

Heat 1–2 tablespoons of oil in a skillet until hot (but not smoking). Break the eggs carefully into the skillet so that the yolks remain intact. Cook over medium heat, occasionally basting with the hot oil to help the yolk set, for 3–4 minutes. Use a slotted spatula to lift out the eggs and let the oil drain away. Serve immediately.

### Poaching eggs

Eggs need to be very fresh for poaching or they will break up in the water. You can use a nonstick egg poacher for this, or alternatively you can use the following method.

Take a small skillet and fill it with enough water to cover an egg. Bring the water to a boil, then reduce the heat to a simmer. Add a pinch of salt. Break the egg carefully into a cup, then pour it gently into the boiling water so that the yolk does not break. Cook for 3–4 minutes, depending on how you like your eggs; you may find it helpful to baste the egg with a little of the cooking liquid to ensure it is cooked. Lift it out with a slotted spoon and serve.

### Separating eggs

There are some clever devices available for separating yolks from egg whites—for example, you can buy a spoon-shaped implement that has holes in to let the egg white pass through, leaving the egg yolk intact. If you don't have a separating gadget, you can use the shell method (using cold eggs makes this method easier).
**1** Crack the egg shell gently on the edge of a bowl.
**2** Open the shell slowly, letting the white drip into the bowl. **3** Being careful not to break the yolk, pass it from one shell half to the other. **4** Repeat until the yolk and white are fully separated. Alternatively, open the egg into your hand and let the white drip through your fingers to separate.

### Buying and storing milk

Milk is a good source of protein and calcium. The most commonly available is fresh cow's milk, which comes in whole (3½% fat), low-fat (between 1% and 2% fat), and skim, or nonfat, (less than ½ % fat). Other varieties include homogenized, which has the fat spread throughout the milk so that there is no creamy layer on top, and ultrapasteurized milk, which has been heated quickly to around 300°F/149°C, then cooled and vacuum-packed to ensure a shelf life without refrigeration of around six months. You can also buy sweetened condensed milk, which is very thick and sweet; evaporated milk, which is sterilized in cans and often used to replace whole milk; buttermilk, which tastes like yogurt or thickened lowfat milk; and dry milk, which you can reconstitute with water and use in place of fresh milk. If you are sensitive to cow's milk, you can buy goat milk or sheep's milk, or milk made from soy or rice instead.

These days most fresh milk is pasteurized (heated then quickly cooled) in order to kill off any harmful bacteria, although some unpasteurized milk is available, often straight from the farm (see Safety box, opposite). Always check the expiration date on milk before you buy it, and store fresh milk in the refrigerator. Keep it covered to prevent contamination.

### Buying and storing yogurt

Yogurt is made by fermenting milk with healthy bacteria. It has a slightly tangy taste and is a healthy choice because it is thick and creamy yet low in fat. Strained plain yogurt is the thickest and has the creamiest consistency. You can also freeze yogurt for a healthy lowfat alternative to ice cream. Check the expiration date before buying, and store it in the refrigerator. Keep it covered when not in use.

### Buying and storing butter

Butter is made by churning cream until it separates into semisolids. It comprises at least 80% fat and the other 20% is made up of milk solids and water. Sometimes it is colored with annatto (a natural color made from the paste of seeds). Butter is available in salted and unsalted varieties: unsalted is essential for sweet dishes. You can also buy "spreadable" butter. This has been blended with oil so that it will stay soft and can be spread more easily. Make sure your butter is always tightly wrapped to prevent it from absorbing odors. Check the expiration date on the packaging. Butter also freezes well. It will keep for up to 6 months in the freezer.

Fresh milk

Clotted cream

Yogurt

Butter

## Buying and storing cream

Cream is made from the fattiest part of milk. Therefore, it has a higher fat content than milk and a milder flavor. Half-fat and light cream have the lowest fat contents. The former is useful for pouring into drinks, such as coffee, and the latter is ideal for sauces and soups. Sour cream (around 18–20% fat) has a slightly tangy taste and is ideal in savory dishes, as is the higher fat crème fraîche (up to 50% fat). Light whipping cream has a high fat content (30–36%) and, as its name suggests, is ideal for whipping and piping into decorative shapes. Heavy cream has a very high fat content of between 36% and 40% and should, therefore, be used sparingly. It is a delicious luxury for special occasions, perhaps to enrich a sauce or accompany a dessert. Clotted cream has the highest fat content of all (around 60%) and is very thick. In Great Britain it is used on biscuits or as an accompaniment for special desserts. All cream should be kept covered and stored in the refrigerator. Use it by the expiration date on the container.

## Buying and storing cheese

Cheese is made from milk that is allowed to thicken and then separate into curds (semisolids) and whey (a liquid). Fresh cheeses are rindless and vary in consistency. Typical cheeses in this category are cream cheese and cottage cheese. Soft and semihard cheeses are firmer, and range from creamy soft cheeses with rinds, such as Brie, to firmer cheeses, such as Port Salut. Generally, the harder the cheese, the higher the fat content, and hard cheeses have the highest fat of all. They are often easy to grate, and range from cheddar cheese to Parmesan. Blue cheeses are also available. These have blue veins running through them and a strong flavor and aroma (the veins are made by a friendly bacteria). Blue cheese varieties include Gorgonzola and Stilton. You can also buy cheese made from goat milk and sheep's milk.

Keep your cheese tightly wrapped. Store fresh cheese in the coldest part of the refrigerator, and the other cheeses in the warmest part. Hard cheeses can be grated ready for use and kept in the refrigerator for up to one week. Use cheeses by the expiration date. You can also freeze hard cheeses, but they will have a crumblier texture when they are defrosted. Grated cheese also freezes well but is suitable only for cooking, not for adding to salads.

Cheddar

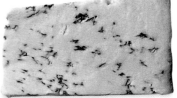
Stilton

Parmesan

Curd cheese

### SAFETY

Unpasteurized milk is available from specialty suppliers, but there is still a risk of disease and, therefore, this milk should not be given to vulnerable people, especially pregnant or breastfeeding women, babies and toddlers, the elderly, people who are ill, or convalescents.

# EGGS BENEDICT WITH QUICK HOLLANDAISE SAUCE

**SERVES 4**

**PREPARATION
20 MINUTES
COOKING
10 MINUTES**

THIS DELICIOUS RECIPE IS QUICK AND EASY TO PREPARE. IT MAKES AN EXCELLENT BREAKFAST, LUNCH, OR SUPPER, OR A TASTY SNACK AT ANY TIME OF DAY. YOU CAN ALSO SUBSTITUTE BACON FOR THE HAM, OR USE SPINACH IF YOU ARE CATERING FOR VEGETARIANS.

## INGREDIENTS
• 1 TBSP WHITE WINE VINEGAR
• 4 EGGS
• 4 ENGLISH MUFFINS
• 4 SLICES GOOD-QUALITY HAM

QUICK HOLLANDAISE SAUCE
• 3 EGG YOLKS
• SCANT 1 CUP BUTTER
• 1 TBSP LEMON JUICE
• PEPPER

**1** Fill a wide skillet three-quarters full with water and bring to a boil over low heat. Reduce the heat to a simmer and add the vinegar. When the water is barely simmering, carefully break the eggs into the skillet. Leave for 1 minute, then, using a large spoon, gently loosen the eggs from the bottom of the skillet. Cook for an additional 3 minutes, or until the white is cooked but the yolk is still soft, basting the top of the egg with the water from time to time.

**2** Meanwhile, to make the hollandaise sauce, place the egg yolks in a blender or food processor. Melt the butter in a small pan until bubbling. With the motor still running, gradually add the hot butter in a steady stream until the sauce is thick and creamy. Add the lemon juice, and a little warm water if the sauce is too thick, then season to taste with pepper. Remove from the blender or food processor and keep warm.

**3** Split the muffins and toast them on both sides. To serve, top each muffin with a slice of ham, a poached egg, and a generous spoonful of hollandaise sauce.

## COOK'S TIP
FOR BEST RESULTS WHEN POACHING EGGS, BREAK THEM INTO A CUP FIRST, THEN SLIDE THEM INTO THE HOT WATER. IF YOU PREFER FIRMER YOLKS, POACH FOR A LITTLE LONGER THAN THE SUGGESTED TIME IN THIS RECIPE.

# EGGS FLORENTINE

THIS TASTY DISH IS RICH IN PROTEIN AND MINERALS, INCLUDING IRON, CALCIUM, AND ZINC. IT ALSO WORKS VERY WELL FOR VEGETARIANS, AS LONG AS YOU USE A CHEDDAR THAT IS MADE FROM NONANIMAL RENNET. IF NECESSARY, YOU CAN REPLACE THE WHOLE-WHEAT FLOUR WITH WHITE FLOUR.

**SERVES 2–4**
(2 AS A LIGHT SNACK OR 4 AS PART OF A BRUNCH)
**PREPARATION**
**20 MINUTES**
**COOKING**
**45–55 MINUTES**

**INGREDIENTS**
- 1 LB/450 G FRESH SPINACH LEAVES, THOROUGHLY WASHED
- 4 TBSP UNSALTED BUTTER
- 1 CUP WHITE MUSHROOMS, SLICED
- ⅜ CUP PINE NUTS, TOASTED
- 6 SCALLIONS, CHOPPED
- 4 EGGS
- ¼ CUP WHOLE-WHEAT FLOUR
- 1¼ CUPS MILK, WARMED
- 1 TSP ENGLISH MUSTARD
- ¾ CUP SHARP CHEDDAR CHEESE, GRATED
- SALT AND PEPPER

**VARIATION**
TRY REPLACING THE CHEDDAR CHEESE WITH A SMOKED CHEDDAR CHEESE. IT WILL BRING OUT THE FLAVOR OF THE PINE NUTS BEAUTIFULLY.

**1** Preheat the oven to 375°F/190°C. Shake off any excess water from the spinach, place in a large pan with the water clinging to the leaves, and sprinkle with a little salt. Cover and cook over medium heat for 2–3 minutes, or until wilted. Drain, pressing out any excess liquid, then chop.

**2** Heat 1 tablespoon of the butter in a small pan over medium heat. Add the mushrooms and cook for 2 minutes, stirring frequently. Add the pine nuts and scallions and cook for an additional 2 minutes. Remove, season to taste with salt and pepper, and sprinkle over the spinach. Set aside until required.

**3** Meanwhile, fill a skillet with cold water and bring to a boil, then reduce the heat to a gentle simmer. Carefully break an egg into a cup and slip it into the water. Add the remaining eggs and cook for 4–5 minutes, or until set. Carefully remove the eggs with a slotted spoon and arrange on top of the spinach mixture.

**4** Melt the remaining butter in a pan and stir in the flour. Cook for 2 minutes, then remove from the heat and gradually stir in the milk. Return to the heat and

cook, stirring constantly, until the mixture comes to a boil and has thickened. Stir in the mustard, then ½ cup of the cheese. Continue stirring until the cheese has melted. Add salt and pepper to taste, then pour over the eggs, completely covering them. Sprinkle with the remaining cheese.

**5** Cook in the preheated oven for about 20–25 minutes, or until piping hot and the top is golden brown and bubbling. Serve immediately.

# CRÊPES

YOU CAN SERVE THESE CRÊPES WITH LEMON AND SUGAR OR WITH WARMED HONEY OR JELLY. THEY CAN ALSO BE SERVED WITH ICE CREAM AND CHOCOLATE SAUCE OR WITH STEWED FRUIT. FOR SAVORY DISHES, USE THEM LIKE CANNELLONI AND STUFF THEM WITH MEAT, CHEESE, OR VEGETABLE FILLINGS.

**MAKES 10**

**PREPARATION**
**5 MINUTES**
**COOKING**
**15–20 MINUTES**

**INGREDIENTS**
- HEAPING ¾ CUP ALL-PURPOSE FLOUR
- PINCH OF SALT
- 1 EGG, BEATEN
- 1¼ CUPS MILK
- SCANT ¼ CUP BUTTER OR OIL

**1** Place the flour and salt in a mixing bowl. Make a well in the center, and add the egg and half of the milk. Using a whisk, beat the egg and milk together and gradually incorporate the flour. Continue beating until the mixture is smooth and there are no lumps. Gradually beat in the remaining milk. Pour the batter into a pitcher.

**2** Heat the skillet over medium heat and add 1 teaspoon of the butter or oil, depending on what you are going to eat with the crêpes. If you are cooking traditional Mardi Gras crêpes to serve with sugar and lemon, then butter is best, but if you are doing something else, for example filling them with broiled vegetables, the oil would be a better choice.

**3** Pour in enough batter just to cover the bottom, then swirl the batter around the skillet while tilting it so that you have a thin, even layer. Cook for about half a minute, then lift up the edge of the crêpe and see if it is brown. Loosen the crêpe around the edges and flip it over with a spatula. Alternatively, try tossing it by shaking the pan quickly with a deft flick of the wrist and catching the crêpe carefully.

**4** Cook on the other side for 1 minute, until golden brown. Turn out onto a warm plate. Cover with baking foil and keep warm. Use all the remaining butter or oil, a teaspoon at a time, until all the crêpes have been cooked. Layer them with wax paper so that you have a separated stack at the end.

# QUICHE LORRAINE

THIS ELEGANT VERSION OF THE CLASSIC FRENCH TART IS DELICIOUS AS IT IS, OR IT CAN FORM THE BASIS OF AN EVEN MORE ELABORATE QUICHE. YOU CAN, FOR EXAMPLE, ARRANGE COOKED OR CANNED ASPARAGUS SPEARS ON THE TOP, OR SMOTHER IT WITH A LAYER OF SAUTÉED MUSHROOMS.

**MAKES ONE 9-INCH/23-CM QUICHE**

**PREPARATION**
**30 MINUTES, PLUS 45 MINUTES' CHILLING AND COOLING**
**COOKING**
**40–50 MINUTES**

**INGREDIENTS**
FOR THE PIE DOUGH
• 1¼ CUPS ALL-PURPOSE FLOUR, PLUS EXTRA FOR DUSTING
• PINCH OF SALT
• ½ CUP BUTTER, DICED
• ¼ CUP ROMANO CHEESE, GRATED
• 4–6 TBSP ICE WATER

FOR THE FILLING
• 4 OZ/115 G GRUYÈRE CHEESE, THINLY SLICED
• ½ CUP ROQUEFORT CHEESE, CRUMBLED
• 6 OZ/175 G RINDLESS LEAN BACON, BROILED UNTIL CRISP
• 3 EGGS
• ⅔ CUP HEAVY CREAM
• SALT AND PEPPER

**1** To make the pie dough, sift the flour with the salt into a bowl. Add the butter and rub it in with your fingertips until the mixture resembles bread crumbs. Stir in the grated cheese, then stir in enough of the water to bind. Shape the dough into a ball, wrap in foil, and chill in the refrigerator for 15 minutes.

**2** Preheat the oven to 375°F/190°C. Unwrap and roll out the dough on a lightly floured counter. Use to line a 9-inch/23-cm tart pan. Place the pan on a baking sheet. Prick the bottom of the pastry shell all over with a fork, line with foil or parchment paper, and fill with baking beans. Bake in the preheated oven for 15 minutes, until the edges are set and dry. Remove the beans and lining and bake the pastry shell for an additional 5–7 minutes, or until golden. Cool slightly.

**3** For the filling, arrange the cheese over the bottom of the pastry shell, then crumble the bacon evenly on top. Place the eggs and cream in a bowl and beat together until thoroughly combined. Add salt and pepper to taste. Pour the mixture into the pastry shell and return to the oven for 20 minutes, or until the filling is golden and set.

**4** Remove from the oven and cool the quiche in the pan for 10 minutes. Transfer to a wire rack to cool completely. Cover with plastic wrap and store in the refrigerator, but return to room temperature before serving.

**VARIATION**
TO MAKE A MEAT-FREE VERSION OF THIS QUICHE, REPLACE THE BACON WITH 2 MEDIUM TOMATOES, THINLY SLICED. YOU CAN ALSO ADD A THINLY SLICED RED ONION, BUT YOU WILL NEED TO SAUTÉ IT FOR 3 MINUTES IN A LITTLE BUTTER FIRST.

# GARLIC CHEESE MELT

THIS EASY-TO-MAKE SAVORY DISH HAS A DELICIOUS BASE OF GARLIC-FLAVORED BAKED BREAD AND A MOUTHWATERING GOLDEN TOPPING OF MELTED PARMESAN CHEESE. IT MAKES A SATISFYING LUNCH OR SUPPER, AND YOU CAN SERVE IT WITH A FRESH GREEN SALAD OR SOME LIGHTLY COOKED VEGETABLES.

**SERVES 4**

**PREPARATION**
**15 MINUTES, PLUS
15 MINUTES' STANDING**
**COOKING**
**25–40 MINUTES**

**INGREDIENTS**
- 6 THICK SLICES DAY-OLD WHITE BREAD
- 4 TBSP BUTTER, SOFTENED
- 1 TBSP OLIVE OIL
- 3 EXTRA LARGE EGGS
- 1¼ CUPS MILK
- ⅔ CUP STRAINED PLAIN YOGURT
- 1 GARLIC CLOVE
- 1½ CUPS GRATED CHEDDAR OR DOUBLE GLOUCESTER CHEESE
- 4–8 SCALLIONS
- 1 TBSP CHOPPED FRESH PARSLEY OR MINT
- 2 TBSP GRATED PARMESAN
- SALT AND PEPPER
- GREEN SALAD, TO SERVE

**1** Preheat the oven to 325°F/160°C. Spread the bread slices with butter on one side only. Brush a large baking sheet with a little of the olive oil and lay out the bread on it. Bake in the preheated oven for 5–10 minutes, until the bread is nearly dry and slightly brown. Remove the bread from the oven but leave the oven switched on.

**2** In a separate bowl, beat the eggs and add the milk and yogurt. Season generously with salt and pepper.

**3** Use the remaining oil to brush an ovenproof dish. Cut the crisp bread into thick fingers and rub them with the garlic clove. Lay half the pieces in the dish and sprinkle with the cheese, scallions to taste, and chopped parsley or mint.

**4** Cover with the remaining bread and pour in the egg mixture. Let the dish stand for about 15 minutes to absorb the liquid.

**5** Sprinkle over the Parmesan and bake in the preheated oven for 20–30 minutes, until almost set and golden brown. Serve warm for lunch or supper with a green salad.

# CHEESE SOUFFLÉ

SOUFFLÉS HAVE A REPUTATION FOR BEING DIFFICULT TO GET RIGHT BECAUSE THEY TEND TO SINK AFTER BAKING MAKING THEM AN UNPOPULAR CHOICE FOR A DINNER PARTY. HOWEVER, THEY ARE ACTUALLY VERY EASY TO MAKE. THE KEY TO PRODUCING A REALLY GOOD, LIGHT SOUFFLÉ IS TO SERVE IT STRAIGHT FROM THE OVEN BEFORE IT HAS TIME TO SINK.

**SERVES 3–4**

**PREPARATION
20 MINUTES
COOKING
30–35 MINUTES**

**INGREDIENTS**
- 1 TBSP BUTTER, MELTED
- 1 TBSP FINELY GRATED PARMESAN
- 2 TBSP BUTTER
- ¼ CUP ALL-PURPOSE FLOUR
- 1¼ CUPS MILK
- 1 CUP CHEDDAR CHEESE, FINELY GRATED
- 1 TSP GRAINY MUSTARD
- A GOOD GRATING OF NUTMEG
- 4 LARGE EGGS, SEPARATED
- SALT AND PEPPER

**TO SERVE**
- GREEN SALAD
- FRESH CRUSTY BREAD

**1** Preheat the oven to 400°F/200°C. Grease the bottom and sides of a soufflé dish with the melted butter. Then sprinkle the dish with the Parmesan, turning the dish in your hands so that all the surface is covered with the cheese. Alternatively, use ramekins instead of the soufflé dish.

**2** Melt the remaining 2 tablespoons of butter in a pan (preferably nonstick) over medium heat. Add the flour, mix well using a wooden spoon, and cook for 1 minute, stirring constantly. Remove from the heat and gradually stir in the milk until you have a smooth consistency.

**3** Return the pan to low heat and continue to stir while the sauce comes to a boil and thickens. Simmer gently, stirring constantly, for about 3 minutes until the sauce is creamy and smooth.

**4** Remove from the heat and stir in the cheese, mustard, and nutmeg. Taste, then season well. Set aside to cool a little.

**5** Whisk the egg whites until soft peaks have formed but are not too dry.

**6** Beat the egg yolks into the sauce mixture and then carefully stir in a little of the beaten egg white to slacken the mixture. Then carefully fold in the remaining egg whites.

**7** Turn into the prepared dish or ramekins. Place on a baking sheet and cook in the preheated oven for 25–30 minutes, until well risen and golden brown. Serve immediately, perhaps with a light green salad and crusty bread.

# PENNE WITH MUSHROOMS & DOLCELATTE

THIS IS A DELICIOUS PASTA DISH, WHICH USES PENNE (TUBE PASTA) AND RICH ITALIAN BLUE DOLCELATTE CHEESE. IT IS QUICK AND EASY TO MAKE, AND, THEREFORE, IDEAL WHEN YOU ARE PRESSED FOR TIME OR CATERING FOR UNEXPECTED GUESTS. IT IS ALSO SUITABLE FOR VEGETARIANS IF YOU USE VEGETARIAN CHEESES.

**SERVES 4**

**PREPARATION**
**5 MINUTES**
**COOKING**
**10–15 MINUTES**

**INGREDIENTS**
- 3½ CUPS PENNE (TUBE PASTA)
- 1 TBSP OLIVE OIL
- 3⅔ CUPS CRIMINI MUSHROOMS, SLICED
- 8 OZ/225 G DOLCELATTE, CRUMBLED
- 1 CUP HALF-FAT CRÈME FRAÎCHE OR SOUR CREAM
- 5½ OZ/150 G ARUGULA LEAVES OR SPINACH
- SALT AND PEPPER

**1** Cook the pasta over medium heat in a large pan of salted boiling water, according to the instructions on the package.

**2** Meanwhile, heat the oil in a skillet over low heat and gently sauté the mushrooms for 3–4 minutes, until they start to soften.

**3** Stir in the dolcelatte and let it melt, then add the crème fraîche or sour cream.

**4** Add the arugula or spinach and heat for 1–2 minutes, until just wilted. Taste, and add salt and pepper.

**5** Drain the cooked pasta in a colander and serve in hot bowls with the sauce poured over the top. Serve immediately.

## VARIATION

FOR A MORE LUXURIOUS SAUCE, REPLACE THE CRÈME FRAÎCHE WITH THE SAME QUANTITY OF HEAVY CREAM, AND SCATTER OVER 1–2 TABLESPOONS OF TOASTED PINE NUTS.

# HOT GOAT CHEESE SALAD

**SERVES 2**

**PREPARATION**
**5 MINUTES**
**COOKING**
**25 MINUTES**

**INGREDIENTS**
- 8 OZ/225 G CHERRY VINE TOMATOES
- 4 GARLIC CLOVES, UNPEELED
- 1 TBSP OLIVE OIL
- 7 OZ/200 G SOFT RIND GOAT CHEESE, SUCH AS PYRAMID
- 2 CUPS ARUGULA
- 2 TBSP BALSAMIC VINEGAR
- SALT AND PEPPER
- A FEW FRESH BASIL LEAVES, TO GARNISH

THIS SALAD MAKES A GOOD LUNCH OR LIGHT SUPPER DISH AND WILL DELIGHT MEAT EATERS AND VEGETARIANS ALIKE. ALL IT NEEDS TO MAKE IT INTO A MORE SATISFYING MEAL IS THE ADDITION OF SOME FRESH CRUSTY BREAD. TO SERVE FOUR PEOPLE, SIMPLY DOUBLE THE QUANTITY OF THE INGREDIENTS.

**1** Preheat the oven to 350°F/180°C. Put the tomatoes and garlic in a small roasting pan. Sprinkle them with the oil and season well. Cook at the top of the preheated oven for 20 minutes.

**2** Remove the top and bottom rinds from the goat cheese and cut in half horizontally. If you are using two smaller cheeses, cut them both in half horizontally.

**3** Place the cheese pieces in a heatproof dish and cook under a hot broiler for 3–4 minutes, until they begin to melt and turn golden.

**4** Arrange the arugula on two plates. Remove the tomatoes and garlic from the oven. Use a slotted spoon to remove them, and reserve the roasting juices. Arrange the tomatoes and garlic around the plates and put the cheese in the center.

**5** Add the balsamic vinegar to the juices in the roasting pan and mix well to make a dressing. Drizzle the dressing over the cheese and salad and serve garnished with the basil leaves.

# MERINGUES

THESE ARE JUST AS MERINGUES SHOULD BE—AS LIGHT AS AIR AND AT THE SAME TIME CRISP, WITH A MELT-IN-THE-MOUTH QUALITY. MAKE SURE THAT THE BOWL YOU USE TO THE WHISK EGG WHITES IS COMPLETELY CLEAN AND GREASE-FREE, OR YOUR MERINGUE MIXTURE WILL COLLAPSE.

**MAKES 13**

**PREPARATION**
**15 MINUTES, PLUS 8 HOURS' COOLING**
**COOKING**
**1½ HOURS**

**INGREDIENTS**
- 4 EGG WHITES
- PINCH OF SALT
- ⅔ CUP GRANULATED SUGAR
- ⅔ CUP SUPERFINE SUGAR
- 1¼ CUPS HEAVY CREAM, LIGHTLY WHIPPED, TO SERVE

1 Preheat the oven to 250°F/120°C. Line 3 baking sheets with sheets of parchment paper.

2 Place the egg whites and a pinch of salt in a large clean bowl and, using a handheld electric mixer or balloon whisk, whisk until stiff. (You should be able to turn the bowl upside down without any movement from the whisked egg whites.)

3 Whisk in the granulated sugar, a little at a time; the meringue should begin to look glossy at this stage.

4 Sprinkle in the superfine sugar, a little at a time, and continue whisking until all the sugar has been incorporated and the meringue is thick, white, and forms peaks.

5 Transfer the meringue mixture to a pastry bag with a ¾-inch/2-cm star tip attached. Pipe about 26 small whirls of the mixture onto the prepared baking sheets.

6 Bake in the preheated oven for 1½ hours, or until the meringues are pale golden in color and can be easily lifted off the paper. Let them cool overnight in the turned-off oven.

7 Just before serving, sandwich the meringues together in pairs with the cream and arrange on a serving plate.

## VARIATION

FOR A FINER TEXTURE, REPLACE THE GRANULATED SUGAR WITH SUPERFINE SUGAR.

# LEMON MERINGUE PIE

IN THIS RECIPE, A SWEET, TANGY FILLING AND A MELT-IN-THE-MOUTH TOPPING CONTRAST SUPERBLY WITH A CRISP PASTRY SHELL. THIS POPULAR DESSERT LOOKS EVERY BIT AS LOVELY AS IT TASTES. IT'S USUALLY SERVED HOT AND THERE'S RARELY ANY LEFT OVER BUT, IF THERE IS, IT'S ALSO DELICIOUS COLD.

**SERVES 4**

**PREPARATION**
**25 MINUTES, PLUS**
**30 MINUTES' RESTING**
**COOKING**
**1 HOUR**

**INGREDIENTS**
**FOR THE PIE DOUGH**
- HEAPING 1⅜ CUPS ALL-PURPOSE FLOUR, PLUS EXTRA FOR DUSTING
- ¾ CUP BUTTER, DICED, PLUS EXTRA FOR GREASING
- ⅜ CUP CONFECTIONERS' SUGAR, SIFTED
- FINELY GRATED RIND OF 1 LEMON
- 1 EGG YOLK, BEATEN
- 3 TBSP MILK
- LIGHT CREAM, TO SERVE

**FOR THE FILLING**
- 3 TBSP CORNSTARCH
- 1¼ CUPS COLD WATER
- JUICE AND GRATED ZEST OF 2 LEMONS
- ¾ CUP SUPERFINE SUGAR
- 2 EGGS, SEPARATED

**COOK'S TIP**
TO PRODUCE A PERFECTLY SMOOTH MERINGUE, WHISK IN THE SUGAR A TABLESPOON AT A TIME.

**1** To make the pie dough, sift the flour into a large bowl. Add the butter and rub it in until the mixture resembles bread crumbs. Mix in the remaining ingredients. Knead briefly on a lightly floured counter. Let the dough rest for 30 minutes.

**2** Preheat the oven to 350°F/180°C. Grease an 8-inch/20-cm ovenproof tart pan with butter.

**3** Roll out the dough to a thickness of ¼ inch/5 mm and line the dish with it. Prick with a fork, then line with parchment paper and fill with baking beans. Bake for 15 minutes. Remove from the oven, then reduce the oven temperature to 300°F/150°C.

**4** To make the filling, mix the cornstarch with a little water to form a paste. Pour the remaining water into a pan. Stir in the lemon juice and zest and the cornstarch paste. Bring to a boil, stirring, and cook for 2 minutes.

**5** Remove from the heat, cool slightly, then stir in 5 tablespoons of the sugar, and the egg yolks, and pour into the pastry shell. Whisk the egg whites in a separate bowl until stiff.

**6** Gradually whisk in the remaining sugar and spread over the pie. Bake in the oven for 40 minutes, or until the meringue is light brown. Remove the pie from the oven and serve.

# RICH VANILLA ICE CREAM

**SERVES 4–6**

**PREPARATION**
**20 MINUTES, PLUS**
**30 MINUTES' INFUSING**
**AND 4–6 HOURS' COOLING**
**AND FREEZING**
**COOKING**
**15–20 MINUTES**

**INGREDIENTS**
- 1¼ CUPS LIGHT CREAM
- 1¼ CUPS HEAVY CREAM OR 2½ CUPS WHIPPING CREAM
- 1 VANILLA BEAN
- 4 LARGE EGG YOLKS
- GENEROUS ½ CUP SUPERFINE SUGAR

THIS RICH ICE CREAM PROVIDES A DELICIOUS FINISH TO A MEAL. YOU CAN SERVE IT EITHER AS IT IS, OR WITH A TOPPING OF YOUR CHOICE, SUCH AS A CHOCOLATE OR FRUIT SAUCE, AND/OR SOME CHOPPED TOASTED MIXED NUTS. IT ALSO MAKES AN EXCELLENT ACCOMPANIMENT TO FRUIT DESSERTS AND SWEET PIES.

**1** Pour the light and heavy cream into a large heavy-bottom pan. Split open the vanilla bean and scrape out the seeds into the cream, then add the whole vanilla bean. Bring almost to a boil, then remove the pan from the heat and let the mixture infuse for 30 minutes.

**2** Place the egg yolks and sugar in a large bowl and whisk together until pale and the mixture leaves a trail when the whisk is lifted. Remove the vanilla bean from the cream, then slowly add the cream to the egg mixture, stirring constantly with a wooden spoon. Strain the mixture into the rinsed-out pan or a double boiler and cook over low heat for 10–15 minutes, stirring constantly, until the mixture thickens enough to coat the back of the spoon. Do not let the mixture boil or it will curdle. Remove the custard from the heat and cool for at least 1 hour, stirring occasionally to prevent a skin from forming.

**3** If using an ice-cream machine, churn the cold custard in the machine following the manufacturer's instructions. Alternatively, freeze the custard in a freezerproof container, uncovered, for 1–2 hours, or until it begins to set around the edges. Turn the custard into a bowl and stir with a fork or beat in a food processor until smooth. Return to the freezer and freeze for an additional 2–3 hours, until firm or until required. Cover the container with a lid for storing.

# CHOCOLATE CHIP ICE CREAM WITH HOT CHOCOLATE FUDGE SAUCE

**SERVES 4–6**

**PREPARATION**
**20 MINUTES, PLUS 30 MINUTES' INFUSING AND 4–6 HOURS' COOLING AND FREEZING COOKING 15–20 MINUTES**

**INGREDIENTS**
- 1¼ CUPS MILK
- 1 VANILLA BEAN
- SCANT ½ CUP SUPERFINE SUGAR
- 3 EGG YOLKS
- 1¼ CUPS WHIPPING CREAM
- 4 OZ/115 G MILK CHOCOLATE, BROKEN INTO PIECES

**FOR THE CHOCOLATE FUDGE SAUCE**
- 1¾ OZ/50 G MILK CHOCOLATE, BROKEN INTO PIECES
- 2 TBSP BUTTER
- 4 TBSP MILK
- HEAPING 1 CUP PACKED BROWN SUGAR
- 2 TBSP CORN SYRUP

THE ADDITION OF CHOCOLATE PIECES AND THE CHOCOLATE FUDGE SAUCE IN THIS RECIPE PROVIDE A PERFECT COUNTERPOINT TO THE CREAMINESS OF THE ICE CREAM. THIS IS A POPULAR DESSERT WITH CHILDREN AND ADULTS ALIKE.

**1** Put the milk and vanilla into a heavy-bottom pan and bring almost to a boil. Remove from the heat and let infuse for 30 minutes.

**2** Whisk the sugar and egg yolks in a bowl until pale and the mixture leaves a trail when the whisk is lifted. Discard the vanilla. Stir the milk into the eggs, strain into a clean saucepan or double boiler, and stir over low heat for 10–15 minutes until thick enough to coat the back of the spoon. Do not boil or it will curdle. Remove from the heat. Cool for 1 hour, stirring occasionally to prevent a skin from forming. Meanwhile, whip the cream until it holds its shape. Chill until required.

**3** If using an ice-cream machine, fold the cold custard into the whipped cream, then churn in the machine following the manufacturer's instructions. Just before it freezes, add the chocolate pieces. Alternatively, freeze the custard in a freezerproof container, uncovered, for 1–2 hours, or until it begins to set around the edges. Turn into a bowl and stir with a fork or beat in a food processor until smooth. Fold in the whipped cream and chocolate pieces. Freeze for 2–3 hours, or until required. Cover with a lid for storing.

**4** Make the sauce just before serving the ice cream. Place the chocolate, butter, and milk in a heatproof bowl set over a saucepan of simmering water and heat gently, stirring occasionally, until the chocolate has melted and the sauce is smooth. Transfer the mixture to a heavy-bottom pan and stir in the sugar and corn syrup. Heat gently until the sugar has dissolved, then bring to a boil and boil, without stirring, for 5 minutes. Serve the hot sauce poured over the ice cream.

# TIRAMISU

LITERALLY MEANING "PICK ME UP," THIS SOPHISTICATED DESSERT HAS A REPUTATION FOR DOING EXACTLY THAT. IT'S NOT A TRADITIONAL DISH, BUT SINCE ITS INVENTION ABOUT THIRTY YEARS AGO, IT HAS BECOME A FIRM FAVORITE ACROSS THE GLOBE.

**SERVES 4**

**PREPARATION**
**20 MINUTES, PLUS**
**2 HOURS' CHILLING**
**COOKING**
**NONE**

**INGREDIENTS**
- 1 CUP STRONG BLACK COFFEE, COOLED TO ROOM TEMPERATURE
- 4 TBSP ORANGE LIQUEUR, SUCH AS COINTREAU
- 3 TBSP ORANGE JUICE
- 16 ITALIAN LADYFINGERS
- HEAPING 1 CUP MASCARPONE CHEESE
- 1¼ CUPS HEAVY CREAM, LIGHTLY WHIPPED
- 3 TBSP CONFECTIONERS' SUGAR
- GRATED ZEST OF 1 ORANGE
- 2¼ OZ/60 G SEMISWEET CHOCOLATE, GRATED

**TO DECORATE**
- CHOPPED TOASTED ALMONDS
- CANDIED ORANGE PEEL
- CHOCOLATE SHAVINGS

**1** Pour the cooled coffee into a pitcher and stir in the orange liqueur and orange juice. Place 8 of the ladyfingers in the bottom of a serving dish, then pour over half of the coffee mixture.

**2** Place the mascarpone in a separate bowl together with the cream, confectioners' sugar, and orange zest and mix well. Spread half of the mascarpone mixture over the coffee-soaked ladyfingers, then arrange the remaining ladyfingers on top. Pour over the remaining coffee mixture, then spread over the remaining mascarpone mixture. Sprinkle over the grated chocolate and chill in the refrigerator for at least 2 hours. Serve decorated with chopped toasted almonds, candied orange peel, and chocolate shavings.

## COOK'S TIP

YOU CAN DECORATE THIS DESSERT WITH CHOPPED MIXED NUTS INSTEAD OF CHOPPED TOASTED ALMONDS. ALTERNATIVELY, TRY REPLACING THE ORANGE LIQUEUR WITH THE SAME QUANTITY OF ALMOND-FLAVORED LIQUEUR, SUCH AS AMARETTO.

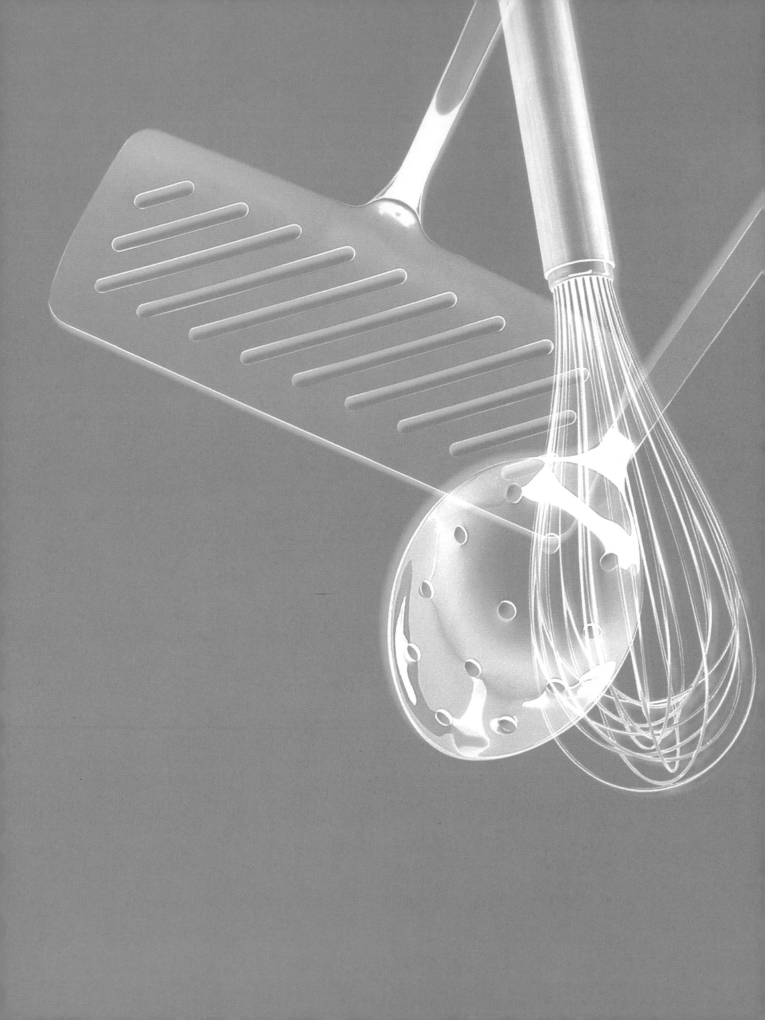

# CHAPTER 2

# FISH AND SHELLFISH

WHO CAN RESIST THE AROMA AND FLAVOR OF FRESH FISH AND SHELLFISH, LOVINGLY PREPARED? YOU CAN COOK AND SERVE SEAFOOD IN A MULTITUDE OF WAYS, FROM STIR-FRIES AND CHARGRILLS TO BAKES AND BARBECUES. THIS SECTION PRESENTS A STUNNING COLLECTION OF DISHES THAT YOU WILL WANT TO MAKE AGAIN AND AGAIN.

# INTRODUCTION

FISH AND SHELLFISH ARE VERY GOOD FOR YOU: THEY ARE FULL OF PROTEIN, IODINE, AND MAGNESIUM, WHICH ARE ESSENTIAL FOR BUILDING TISSUE, REGULATING THE METABOLISM, AND KEEPING THE BOWEL HEALTHY. OILY FISH IN PARTICULAR ARE RICH IN ESSENTIAL FATTY ACIDS, WHICH HELP TO LOWER CHOLESTEROL AND SUPPORT THE IMMUNE SYSTEM.

## Buying and storing fresh fish

Nowadays, there is a wide variety of fish available. You can buy fresh flatfish, such as flounder, sole, or halibut, or roundfish, such as cod, haddock, salmon, or trout. You can also buy preserved fish, which have been smoked, dried, or salted. When buying fresh whole fish, choose those that smell fresh or that smell of the sea. Avoid any that smell of ammonia. They should have moist, full eyes and shiny, firm bodies. You can ask your fish supplier to skin, gut, and fillet whole larger fish for you. Refrigerate the fish as soon as you get home. Fresh fish is best eaten on the day of purchase, but it will keep for a day or two if necessary. Frozen fish will keep for up to six months in the freezer, but will need thawing in the refrigerator for at least 8 hours before use. Oily fish, such as mackerel, should be wrapped well in clean damp cloths and stored in the refrigerator. Lower-fat white fish, such as cod and haddock, can be covered with plastic wrap. Use it by the expiration date on the packaging.

## Smoked fish

You can buy a wide variety of smoked fish. Smoked salmon is very popular and is usually served cold with slices of lemon. Smoked trout has a mild flavor and is best partnered with horseradish or slices of lemon. Smoked mackerel has a rich flavor and needs a sharp sauce, such as dill or mustard. Smoked haddock is delicious served with a creamy sauce or in kedgerees, while smoked cod is popular in pies. Kippered herring are best broiled or poached. Fresh smoked fish should be wrapped well in plastic wrap and stored in the refrigerator. Smoked fish is often bought vacuum-packed. Store it in the refrigerator and use by the expiration date.

Brown trout

Sole

## Preparing and cooking fresh fish

There is a wide range of white fish available these days. Some are low in fat, such as cod and haddock, while other types of fish are rich in healthy essential fatty acids, such as sardines.

### Cod
This roundfish has firm, white, flaky flesh and a mild flavor. It can be baked, broiled, poached, pan-fried, or deep-fried in batter or bread crumbs.

### Haddock
Like cod, this roundfish has firm, white flesh and a mild flavor. It can be baked, broiled, poached, pan-fried, or deep-fried, and in many recipes is interchangeable with cod.

### Hake
Milder-flavored than cod, this roundfish can be fried, baked, or steamed and is also useful in soups.

### Trout
This roundfish is available farmed or wild, but the wild variety is rare. It can be pan-fried, broiled, poached, steamed, barbecued, or baked. This is an oily fish, which means that it is rich in essential fatty acids.

### Halibut and turbot
These are large flatfish that have firm flesh and an excellent flavor. They are interchangeable in many recipes. You can fry, poach, steam, broil, or bake both these fish.

### Sole
In the United States, sole usually refers to the flatfish found in the Pacific Ocean, from California to Alaska. It has less flavor than the true sole found in European waters and needs a little added flavoring to bring out its best qualities. It can be pan fried, baked, steamed, or broiled.

### Herring, sardines, sprats, and whitebait
These small fish have plenty of bones, so it is best to ask your fish supplier to remove the innards and as many bones as possible. They can be barbecued, deep-fried, baked, or broiled. They are also oily fish, and, therefore, rich in essential fatty acids.

### Mackerel
This is a roundfish with a delicious flavor. It is at its best when simply broiled, but can also be fried or barbecued. It is another oily fish, so is good for your health.

### Flounder
This flatfish needs extra flavoring but is very good when pan-fried or deep-fried, baked, broiled, poached, or steamed.

### Salmon
This roundfish is available farmed or wild. Salmon is a popular fish, and it can be pan-fried, broiled, poached, steamed, barbecued, or baked. Salmon en croûte or en papillote (salmon baked in pie dough or in parchment) are particularly popular dishes. This is another oily fish.

### Tuna
This is a round oily fish with firm, "meaty" flesh that makes marvelous steaks with only a very mild fish flavor. The steaks are excellent chargrilled for 2–3 minutes each side (do not overcook). You can also bake, barbecue, broil, braise, or stew fresh tuna.

Herring

Mackerel

## Buying and storing shellfish

Shellfish can cause food poisoning, so always buy them as fresh as possible from a reputable supplier. Shellfish should smell fresh or sweet—avoid any that smell of chlorine or sulfur.

If you are buying mussels, clams, or oysters, the shells should be tightly closed and not cracked or damaged. Refrigerate shellfish in a covered container as soon as you get home and use on the day of purchase. If you buy live lobster or crabs, place something heavy on top of the container to stop them escaping. Handle shellfish as little as possible and prepare with thoroughly clean equipment and hands.

## Preparation and cooking techniques

Preparation techniques vary greatly, depending on the type of shellfish you are using. If you are in any doubt, your local fish supplier will be able to give you advice. Shellfish does not need to cook for long periods of time, so stick to the recommended cooking times. Do not overcook it or you could impair the texture and/or taste. Squid, for example, becomes unpleasantly rubbery if cooked for too long.

Crab

## Fresh and frozen shellfish

You can buy fresh shellfish from fish suppliers and many stores and supermarkets. In some cases, shrimp for example, you can also buy them prepared, cooked, and frozen.

### Crab and lobster

You can buy crabs and lobsters live or cooked. If you buy them live, make sure the claws are tied with string to keep them still. Put them in the freezer for 1 hour before cooking to desensitize. To cook, take a large pan and pour in enough water or stock to cover the crab or lobster. Bring it to a boil, add the crab or lobster, cover the pan, and boil until it turns red. Allow 5 minutes of cooking for every 1 lb/ 450 g of crab. For a lobster, allow 5 minutes for the first 1 lb/450 g, plus an extra 3 minutes for each additional 1 lb/450 g. To remove the cooked meat from the crab, crack the claws and remove and set aside the white meat. Snap off the tail, then use your hands to break the shell. Lift out the body, cut it in half lengthwise, and scoop out the meat. Then lift out the brown meat from the shell. The edible parts of a lobster are the meat in the tail and claws, the liver, and the roe if the lobster is female. Cooking a lobster and removing the meat can be awkward, however, so it is usually best to ask your fish supplier to do this for you.

Mussels

### Mussels

Use mussels on the day of purchase and keep them in lightly salted water before use. To clean them, use a small knife to scrape off any barnacles from the shells, then pull out and discard any clumps of hair (these are usually called "beards.") Use a stiff brush to scrub the shells under cold running water, then tap them all with the handle of the knife and discard any that do not close tightly. To steam them, heat a little liquid (water, stock, or wine) in a large saucepan, add the cleaned mussels, cover with the lid, and steam them, shaking the pan occasionally, for 5–6 minutes. Remove the saucepan from the heat and discard any mussels that remain closed. You can also broil or bake them half shelled, or stew them shelled.

## Oysters

These shellfish are usually eaten raw. Use a stiff brush to scrub the shells under cold running water, and discard any that are open. To open an oyster, insert a knife blade between the two shell halves and twist it to pry them open. Use a spoon to lift out the oyster inside (you will need to cut it from the muscle underneath). Serve it on a half shell. You can also bake or broil oysters in their half shells, or stew them shelled.

## Shrimp

These come in different sizes and you can buy them shelled or unshelled, cooked or raw. Cooked, shelled shrimp are also available frozen. To shell and devein a raw shrimp, carefully peel off the shell (you can remove the tail or leave it on for decorative effect). Using a small knife, make a shallow cut along the dark vein to reveal it, then remove it with the knife's tip. Discard the vein, then rinse the shrimp under cold running water and pat dry with paper towels. Shrimp require very little cooking—for example, you need to stir-fry them for only 2–3 minutes, until they turn pink. You can pan-fry, stir-fry, broil, bake, barbecue, or steam them.

## Scallops

These have a delicate flavor and are becoming increasingly popular. They should be creamy-white with pink corals. They need a minimal amount of cooking, usually 1–2 minutes on each side if you are pan-frying them shelled. You can also broil or bake them in their half shells.

## Squid

You can buy squid whole or already prepared. The edible parts are the tentacles, fins, pouch, and the ink. Sauté the squid for 2–3 minutes only—do not overcook it or it will be rubbery. You can also deep-fry, bake, poach, and stew it.

## Clams

Use a stiff brush to scrub the shells under cold running water, and discard any that open. To open a clam, insert a knife blade between the two shell halves and twist it to pry them open. Use a spoon to lift out the soft flesh inside. You can eat clams raw, or you can steam them in their shells for 4 minutes, or until they have opened. You can also bake or broil them in their half shells, or stew them shelled.

Shrimp

Lobster

Squid

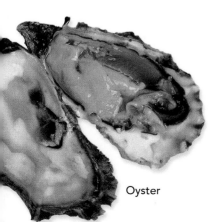

Oyster

# FISH CAKES

THIS RECIPE MAKES 4 LARGE FISH CAKES. YOU CAN MAKE 8 SMALLER FISH CAKES IF YOU PREFER, BUT THEY ARE A LITTLE MORE FUSSY TO PREPARE. SERVE THEM WITH FRIES, SALAD, AND BREAD ROLLS TO MAKE A DELICIOUS LUNCH OR SUPPER.

**SERVES 4**

**PREPARATION**
**30 MINUTES, PLUS**
**30 MINUTES' CHILLING**
**COOKING**
**10 MINUTES**

**INGREDIENTS**
- 1 LB/450 G POTATOES, PEELED
- 1 LB/450 G MIXED FISH FILLETS, SUCH AS COD, HADDOCK, AND SALMON, SKINNED
- 2 TBSP CHOPPED FRESH PARSLEY OR TARRAGON
- GRATED ZEST OF 1 LEMON
- 1 TBSP ALL-PURPOSE FLOUR
- 1 EGG, BEATEN
- 2 CUPS WHITE OR WHOLE-WHEAT BREAD CRUMBS, MADE FROM ONE-DAY-OLD BREAD
- 4 TBSP VEGETABLE OIL, FOR FRYING
- SALT AND PEPPER

**1** Cut the potatoes into chunks. Cook in a large saucepan of boiling, salted water for 15 minutes. Drain well and mash with a potato masher until smooth.

**2** Place the fish in a skillet and just cover with water. Bring to a boil over medium heat, then cover and simmer gently for 5 minutes, until just cooked. Remove from the heat and transfer the fish to a plate, draining it well. When cool enough to handle, flake the fish and make sure that there are no bones.

**3** Mix the potatoes with the fish, parsley or tarragon, and lemon zest in a bowl. Season well and shape into four round, flat cakes.

**4** Dust the cakes with flour, dip them into the beaten egg, then coat thoroughly in the bread crumbs. Place on a baking sheet and chill for at least 30 minutes.

**5** Heat the oil in the skillet and cook the cakes over medium heat for 5 minutes on each side. Use a metal spatula to turn them carefully.

# POACHED SALMON

A WHOLE SALMON CAN OFTEN BE BOUGHT IN SUPERMARKETS AND IT MAKES A GOOD CENTERPIECE FOR A BUFFET OR LARGE PARTY. THIS ONE IS COOKED IN A FISH KETTLE AND SERVED HOT OR COLD. IF YOU DON'T WANT TO GO TO THE EXPENSE OF BUYING A KETTLE, YOU CAN IMPROVISE (SEE COOK'S TIP, BELOW).

**SERVES 12**

**PREPARATION
15 MINUTES
COOKING
2–8 MINUTES, PLUS
15 MINUTES–2 HOURS'
STANDING/COOLING**

**INGREDIENTS**
- 1 WHOLE SALMON (HEAD ON), ABOUT 6–8 LB/2.7–3.6 KG PREPARED WEIGHT
- 3 TBSP SALT
- 3 BAY LEAVES
- 10 PEPPERCORNS
- 1 ONION, PEELED AND SLICED
- 1 LEMON, SLICED

**1** Wipe the salmon thoroughly inside and out with paper towels, then use the back of a cook's knife to remove any scales that might still be on the skin. Remove the fins with a pair of scissors and trim the tail. Some people prefer to cut off the head but it is traditionally served with it on.

**2** Place the salmon on the two-handled rack and place in the kettle. Fill the kettle with enough cold water to cover the salmon adequately. Sprinkle in the salt, bay leaves, and peppercorns and add the onion and lemon slices.

**3** Place on the stovetop, over two low burners, and bring just to a boil very slowly.

**4** Put on the lid and simmer very gently. To serve cold, simmer for 2 minutes only, remove from the heat, and cool in the cooking liquid for about 2 hours with the lid on. To serve hot, simmer for 6–8 minutes and let the kettle stand in the hot water for 15 minutes before removing.

**COOK'S TIP**
TO POACH FISH WITHOUT A KETTLE, LINE A LARGE ROASTING PAN WITH FOIL, PUT IN THE FISH, COVER WITH THE WATER AND OTHER INGREDIENTS, AND TOP WITH ANOTHER LAYER OF FOIL. COOK AS ABOVE.

# BROILED TROUT FILLETS

THESE LIGHTLY BROILED TROUT FILLETS HAVE A DELICIOUS CRISPY COATING OF TOASTED NUTS AND MELTED CHEESE. THEY ARE RICH IN PROTEIN, AND ARE DELICIOUS SERVED WITH RICE AND TWISTS OF LEMON, OR FRESHLY BAKED WEDGES OF POTATO AND OTHER ROOT VEGETABLES.

**SERVES 4**

PREPARATION
**20 MINUTES**
COOKING
**5 MINUTES**

**INGREDIENTS**
- 2 TBSP CHOPPED TOASTED HAZELNUTS
- 2 TBSP GROUND ALMONDS
- 1 CUP CHEDDAR CHEESE, GRATED
- 4 TBSP FRESH BREAD CRUMBS, WHITE OR WHOLE-WHEAT
- 1 EGG
- 1 TBSP MILK
- 4 BROWN TROUT FILLETS, ABOUT 6 OZ/175 G EACH
- 2 TBSP ALL-PURPOSE FLOUR
- SALT AND PEPPER
- FRESH FLAT-LEAF PARSLEY SPRIGS, TO GARNISH
- FRESHLY COOKED RICE, TO SERVE

**1** Preheat the broiler to medium. Place the hazelnuts and almonds in a large bowl. Add the cheese and bread crumbs and mix together. Place the egg and milk in a separate bowl and beat together. Season to taste with salt and pepper.

**2** Rinse the fish fillets and pat dry with paper towels. Coat the fillets in the flour, then dip them into the egg mixture. Transfer them to the bowl containing the nuts and cheese, and turn the fillets in the mixture until thoroughly coated.

**3** Cook the fish under the hot broiler for 5 minutes, turning once during the cooking time, or until golden and cooked through. Remove from the broiler and transfer to warmed plates. Garnish with parsley sprigs and serve immediately with freshly cooked rice.

# BROILED HALIBUT WITH GARLIC BUTTER

THIS DISH IS DELICIOUS, AND VERY QUICK AND SIMPLE TO MAKE. IT IS ALSO VERY NUTRITIOUS: THE FISH IS RICH IN PROTEIN AND OTHER MINERALS, AND THE PARSLEY AND LIME WEDGES ARE EXCELLENT SOURCES OF VITAMIN C. YOU CAN SERVE THIS FOR LUNCH, BUT IT ALSO MAKES A TASTY LIGHT SUPPER.

**SERVES 4**

**PREPARATION
5 MINUTES
COOKING
7–8 MINUTES**

**INGREDIENTS**
- 4 HALIBUT FILLETS, ABOUT 6 OZ/175 G EACH
- 6 TBSP BUTTER, PLUS EXTRA FOR GREASING
- 2 GARLIC CLOVES, FINELY CHOPPED
- SALT AND PEPPER
- SPRIGS OF FRESH FLAT-LEAF PARSLEY, TO GARNISH
- COOKED GREEN BEANS, AND LIME WEDGES, TO SERVE

**1** Preheat the broiler to medium. Rinse the fish fillets under cold running water, then pat dry with paper towels.

**2** Grease a shallow, heatproof dish with butter, then arrange the fish in it. Season with salt and pepper.

**3** In a separate bowl, mix together the remaining butter with the garlic. Dot pieces of the garlic butter all over the fish, then transfer to the broiler. Cook for 7–8 minutes, turning once, until the fish is cooked through.

**4** Remove the dish from the broiler. Using a spatula, remove the fillets from the dish and arrange on individual serving plates. Pour over the remaining melted butter from the dish, and garnish with the parsley sprigs. Serve with the green beans and the lime wedges.

# BROILED SEA BASS WITH STEWED ARTICHOKES

IN THIS IDEAL DISH FOR A LUNCH OR LIGHT SUPPER, BABY GLOBE ARTICHOKES ARE SLOWLY COOKED WITH OLIVE OIL, GARLIC, THYME, AND LEMON TO CREATE A SOFT BLEND OF FLAVORS THAT HARMONIZE VERY WELL WITH THE FISH, WITHOUT BEING OVERPOWERING.

**SERVES 6**

**PREPARATION
30 MINUTES
COOKING
20–30 MINUTES**

**INGREDIENTS**
- 4 LB/1.8 KG BABY GLOBE ARTICHOKES
- 2½ TBSP FRESH LEMON JUICE, PLUS THE CUT HALVES OF THE LEMON
- ⅔ CUP OLIVE OIL
- 10 GARLIC CLOVES, FINELY SLICED
- 1 TBSP CHOPPED FRESH THYME, PLUS EXTRA TO GARNISH
- 6 SEA BASS FILLETS, 4 OZ/115 G EACH
- 1 TBSP OLIVE OIL
- SALT AND PEPPER
- CRUSTY BREAD, TO SERVE

**1** Peel away the tough outer leaves of each artichoke until the yellow-green heart is revealed. Slice off the pointed top at about halfway between the point and the top of the stem. Cut off the stem and pare off what is left of the dark green leaves around the bottom of the artichoke.

**2** Submerge the prepared artichokes in water containing the cut halves of the lemon to prevent them browning. When all the artichokes have been prepared, turn them choke side down and slice thickly.

**3** Heat the oil in a large saucepan. Add the artichoke pieces, garlic, thyme, lemon juice, and seasoning, cover, and cook the artichokes over low heat for 20–30 minutes, without coloring, until tender.

**4** Meanwhile, preheat a ridged stove-top broiler pan or light a barbecue. Brush the sea bass fillets with the 1 tablespoon olive oil and season well. Cook on the broiler pan or over hot coals for 3–4 minutes on each side, until just tender.

**5** Divide the stewed artichokes between plates and top each with a fish fillet. Garnish with chopped thyme and serve with crusty bread.

**VARIATION**
ARTICHOKES COOKED THIS WAY ALSO SUIT COD, HALIBUT, OR SALMON.

# DOVER SOLE À LA MEUNIÈRE

USE FLOUNDER OR DOVER SOLE, WHICH IS IMPORTED FROZEN INTO THE UNITED STATES FROM NORTHERN EUROPEAN COUNTRIES. IT IS DELICATELY FLAVORED, SO THE COMBINATION OF CHOPPED FRESH PARSLEY, LEMON, AND MELTED BUTTER COMPLEMENTS THE FISH PERFECTLY.

**SERVES 4**

**PREPARATION**
**10 MINUTES**
**COOKING**
**15 MINUTES**

**INGREDIENTS**
- 4 TBSP ALL-PURPOSE FLOUR
- 1 TSP SALT
- 4 DOVER SOLE, 14 OZ/ 400 G EACH, CLEANED AND SKINNED
- HEAPING ⅔ CUP BUTTER
- 3 TBSP LEMON JUICE
- 1 TBSP CHOPPED FRESH PARSLEY
- ¼ OF A PRESERVED LEMON, FINELY CHOPPED (OPTIONAL)
- FRESH PARSLEY SPRIGS, TO GARNISH
- LEMON WEDGES, TO SERVE

**1** Preheat the broiler to medium. Mix the flour with the salt and place on a large plate or tray. Drop the fish into the flour, one at a time, and shake well to remove any excess. Melt 3 tablespoons of the butter in a small pan and use to brush the fish liberally all over.

**2** Place the fish under the hot broiler and cook for 5 minutes on each side.

**3** Meanwhile, melt the remaining butter in a pan. Pour cold water into a bowl that is large enough to take the bottom of the pan. Keep nearby.

**4** Heat the butter until it turns golden brown and begins to smell nutty. Remove at once from the heat and immerse the bottom of the pan in the cold water to stop cooking.

**5** Place the fillets on individual plates, drizzle with the lemon juice, and sprinkle with the parsley and preserved lemon, if using. Pour over the browned butter, garnish with parsley sprigs, and serve immediately with lemon wedges for squeezing over.

**COOK'S TIP**
IF YOU HAVE A LARGE ENOUGH SKILLET (OR TWO) YOU CAN PAN-FRY THE FLOURED FISH IN BUTTER, IF YOU PREFER.

# PAELLA

**SERVES 4**

**PREPARATION
20 MINUTES
COOKING
25 MINUTES**

PAELLA IS A RUSTIC SPANISH DISH OF SHELLFISH, SAUSAGE (CHORIZO), POULTRY, VEGETABLES, AND RICE, SEASONED WITH GOLDEN SAFFRON. IT IS BEST TO USE STARCHY RICE, SUCH AS RISOTTO RICE, TO ENSURE YOU RECREATE THE TRADITIONAL CREAMINESS THAT IS THE HALLMARK OF THIS DISH.

## INGREDIENTS
- 3 TBSP OLIVE OIL
- 2 TBSP BUTTER
- 2 GARLIC CLOVES, CHOPPED
- 1 ONION, CHOPPED
- 2 LARGE TOMATOES, SEEDED AND DICED
- ¾ CUP FROZEN PEAS
- 1 RED BELL PEPPER, SEEDED AND CHOPPED
- 1 CUP RISOTTO RICE
- 2 TSP DRIED MIXED HERBS
- 1 TSP SAFFRON POWDER
- 2 CUPS CHICKEN STOCK
- 4 SKINLESS, BONELESS CHICKEN BREASTS
- 5½ OZ/150 G LEAN CHORIZO, SKINNED
- 7 OZ/200 G COOKED LOBSTER MEAT
- 7 OZ/200 G SHRIMP, SHELLED AND DEVEINED
- 1 TBSP CHOPPED FRESH FLAT-LEAF PARSLEY
- SALT AND PEPPER

TO GARNISH
- PINCH OF CAYENNE PEPPER
- RED BELL PEPPER STRIPS

1 Heat the oil and butter in a large skillet over medium heat. Add the garlic and onion and cook, stirring, for 3 minutes, or until slightly softened.

2 Add the tomatoes, peas, red bell pepper, rice, mixed herbs, and saffron and cook, stirring, for 2 minutes. Pour in the stock and bring to a boil. Reduce the heat to low and cook, stirring, for 10 minutes.

3 Chop the chicken into bite-size pieces and add to the skillet. Cook, stirring occasionally, for 5 minutes. Chop the chorizo, add to the skillet, and cook for 3 minutes. Chop the lobster meat and add to the skillet with the shrimp and parsley. Season with salt and pepper and cook, stirring, for an additional 2 minutes.

4 Remove the skillet from the heat, transfer the paella to a large serving platter or individual plates, garnish with cayenne pepper and red bell pepper strips, and serve.

## COOK'S TIP
SAFFRON GIVES THE RICE A LOVELY GOLDEN COLOR, BUT IT IS EXPENSIVE. IF YOUR BUDGET IS TIGHT, YOU CAN REPLACE THE SAFFRON WITH THE SAME AMOUNT OF TURMERIC.

# MEDITERRANEAN FISH CASSEROLE

THIS COLORFUL CASSEROLE IS FULL OF THE DELICIOUS FLAVORS OF THE MEDITERRANEAN. IT IS ALSO VERY NUTRITIOUS. BE CAREFUL YOU DON'T OVERCOOK THE SQUID. IT NEEDS ONLY 2 MINUTES TO COOK—ANY LONGER AND IT WILL GO RUBBERY.

**SERVES 6**

**PREPARATION**
**25 MINUTES**
**COOKING**
**38–40 MINUTES**

**INGREDIENTS**
- 2 TBSP OLIVE OIL
- 1 RED ONION, PEELED AND SLICED
- 2 GARLIC CLOVES, PEELED AND CHOPPED
- 2 RED BELL PEPPERS
- 14 OZ/400 G CANNED CHOPPED TOMATOES
- 1 TSP CHOPPED FRESH OREGANO OR MARJORAM
- A FEW SAFFRON THREADS SOAKED IN 1 TBSP WARM WATER FOR 2 MINUTES
- 1 LB/450 G WHITE FISH (COD, HADDOCK, OR HAKE), SKINNED AND BONED
- 1 LB/450 G PREPARED SQUID, CUT INTO RINGS
- 1¼ CUPS FISH STOCK OR VEGETABLE STOCK
- 1 CUP COOKED SHELLED SHRIMP
- SALT AND PEPPER
- CHUNKY BREAD, TO SERVE

**TO GARNISH**
- 6 COOKED WHOLE SHRIMP IN THEIR SHELLS
- 2 TBSP CHOPPED FRESH PARSLEY

**1** Heat the oil in a skillet and cook the onion and garlic over medium heat for 2–3 minutes, until it begins to soften.

**2** Seed and thinly slice the bell peppers and add to the skillet. Continue to cook over low heat for 5 minutes more. Add the tomatoes with the herbs and saffron and stir well.

**3** Preheat the oven to 400°F/200°C. Cut the white fish into 1¼-inch/3-cm pieces and place with the squid in the casserole dish. Pour in the cooked vegetable mixture and the stock, stir well, and season to taste.

**4** Cover and cook in the center of the preheated oven for about 30 minutes, until the fish is tender and cooked. Add the shrimp at the last minute and just heat through.

**5** Serve in hot bowls garnished with the whole shrimp and the parsley. Provide plenty of chunky bread to soak up the casserole juices.

# TEMPURA WHITEBAIT

**SERVES 4**

**PREPARATION
20 MINUTES
COOKING
10 MINUTES**

TEMPURA IS A CLASSIC JAPANESE BATTER MADE WITH EGG, FLOUR, AND WATER. THE BATTER IS VERY COLD AND LUMPY, WHICH GIVES THE FINISHED DISH ITS CHARACTERISTIC APPEARANCE. IDEALLY, IT SHOULD BE EATEN STRAIGHT AFTER COOKING WHILE STILL HOT.

## INGREDIENTS
- 1 LB/450 G FRESH WHITEBAIT
- ¾ CUP ALL-PURPOSE FLOUR
- 1¾ CUPS CORNSTARCH
- ½ TSP SALT
- 1 CUP COLD WATER
- 1 EGG
- A FEW ICE CUBES
- VEGETABLE OIL, FOR FRYING
- LEMON WEDGES, TO SERVE

CHILI AND LIME MAYONNAISE
- 1 FRESH RED CHILE
- 1 EGG YOLK
- 1 TBSP LIME JUICE
- 2 TBSP CHOPPED FRESH CILANTRO
- SCANT 1 CUP LIGHT OLIVE OIL
- SALT AND PEPPER

**1** To make the mayonnaise, seed and finely chop the chile and place in a food processor with the egg yolk, lime juice, cilantro, and seasoning. Process until foaming. With the machine still running, gradually add the olive oil, drop by drop, until the mixture begins to thicken. Continue adding the oil in a steady stream until all the oil has been incorporated. Taste and adjust the seasoning and add a little hot water if the mixture is too thick. Set aside.

**2** Rinse the whitebait and pat dry. Set aside on paper towels. Sift together the all-purpose flour, cornstarch, and salt into a large bowl. In a separate bowl, whisk together the water, egg, and ice, then pour onto the flour mix. Whisk briefly until the mixture is runny but still lumpy with dry bits of flour still apparent.

**3** Meanwhile, fill a deep pan about one-third full with vegetable oil and heat to 375°F/190°C, or until a cube of bread browns in 30 seconds.

**4** Dip the whitebait, a few at a time, into the batter and carefully drop into the hot oil. Deep-fry for 1 minute until the batter is crisp but not browned. Drain on paper towels and keep warm while you cook the remaining fish. Serve hot with the mayonnaise and lemon wedges.

## COOK'S TIP
USE LIGHT OLIVE OIL FOR THE MAYONNAISE. YOU CAN USE FROZEN WHITEBAIT INSTEAD OF FRESH FOR THIS DISH, BUT YOU WILL NEED TO THAW IT FIRST.

# FISH & CHIPS

**SERVES 4**

**PREPARATION
30 MINUTES, PLUS 1 HOUR
RESTING
COOKING
40–50 MINUTES**

THIS IS THE GENUINE ARTICLE—A CRUNCHY, DEEP GOLDEN BATTER SURROUNDING PERFECTLY COOKED FISH, SERVED WITH GOLDEN CRISPY FRENCH FRIES (OR CHIPS). IF YOU'VE NEVER HAD FRIES WITH MAYONNAISE, TRY THEM WITH THIS LOVELY MUSTARDY VERSION AND YOU'LL BE CONVERTED.

**INGREDIENTS**
- 2 LB/900 G POTATOES
- 4 THICK PIECES COD FILLET, PREFERABLY FROM THE HEAD END, 6 OZ/175 G EACH
- VEGETABLE OIL, FOR DEEP-FRYING
- SALT AND PEPPER
- FRESH PARSLEY SPRIGS, TO GARNISH
- LEMON WEDGES, TO SERVE

**FOR THE BATTER**
- ½ OZ/15 G FRESH YEAST
- 1¼ CUPS BEER
- SCANT 1⅔ CUPS ALL-PURPOSE FLOUR
- 2 TSP SALT

**FOR THE MAYONNAISE**
- 1 EGG YOLK
- 1 TSP WHOLE-GRAIN MUSTARD
- 1 TBSP LEMON JUICE
- 1 CUP LIGHT OLIVE OIL
- SALT AND PEPPER

**1** For the batter, cream the yeast with a little of the beer to a smooth paste. Gradually stir in the rest of the beer. Sift the flour and salt into a bowl, make a well in the center, add the yeast, and whisk to a smooth batter. Cover and let the batter stand at room temperature for 1 hour.

**2** For the mayonnaise, process all the ingredients except the oil in a food processor for 30 seconds until frothy. With the machine still running, gradually add the oil, drop by drop, until the mixture begins to thicken. Continue adding in a steady stream until it has been incorporated. Adjust the seasoning. Thin with a little hot water if too thick, and chill.

**3** Cut the potatoes into fries about ⅝ inch/1.5 cm thick. Heat a large pan half-filled with vegetable oil to 275°F/140°C, or until a cube of bread browns in 1 minute. Cook the fries in 2 batches for 5 minutes, or until they are cooked through but not browned. Place the fries to drain on paper towels and set aside.

**4** Increase the heat to 325°F/160°C, or until a cube of bread browns in 45 seconds. Season the fish, then dip them into the batter. Deep-fry 2 pieces at

a time for 7–8 minutes, until deep golden brown and cooked through. Drain on paper towels and keep warm while you cook the remaining fish and the fries.

**5** Increase the heat to 375°F/190°C, or until a cube of bread browns in 30 seconds. Deep-fry the fries again, in 2 batches, for 2–3 minutes, until crisp and golden. Drain on paper towels and sprinkle with salt. Garnish the fish with parsley and serve with the french fries, mayonnaise, and lemon wedges.

# SMOKED FISH PIE

THIS IS A CLASSIC VERSION OF A FISH PIE WITH BEAUTIFULLY FLAVORED SMOKED FISH, AND SHRIMP AND VEGETABLES. IT IS VERY EASY TO PREPARE AND COOK, AND THE TANTALIZING AROMAS AND FLAVORS WILL HAVE EVERY MEMBER OF YOUR HOUSEHOLD CLAMORING FOR MORE.

**SERVES 6**

PREPARATION
**20 MINUTES, PLUS
20 MINUTES' COOLING**
COOKING
**1½ HOURS**

**INGREDIENTS**
- 2 TBSP OLIVE OIL
- 1 ONION, FINELY CHOPPED
- 1 LEEK, THINLY SLICED
- 1 CARROT, DICED
- 1 CELERY STALK, DICED
- 4 OZ/115 G WHITE MUSHROOMS, HALVED
- GRATED ZEST OF 1 LEMON
- 12 OZ/350 G SKINLESS, BONELESS SMOKED COD OR HADDOCK FILLET, CUBED
- 12 OZ/350 G SKINLESS, BONELESS WHITE FISH, CUBED
- 8 OZ/225 G COOKED SHELLED SHRIMP
- 2 TBSP CHOPPED FRESH PARSLEY
- 1 TBSP CHOPPED FRESH DILL, PLUS SPRIGS TO GARNISH
- COOKED VEGETABLES, TO SERVE

FOR THE SAUCE
- 4 TBSP BUTTER
- 4 TBSP ALL-PURPOSE FLOUR
- 1 TSP MUSTARD POWDER
- 2½ CUPS MILK
- ¾ CUP GRUYÈRE CHEESE, GRATED

FOR THE TOPPING
- 1 LB 8 OZ/675 G POTATOES, UNPEELED
- 4 TBSP BUTTER, MELTED
- ¼ CUP GRUYÈRE CHEESE, GRATED
- SALT AND PEPPER

**COOK'S TIP**
WHITE FISH SUCH AS HADDOCK, MONK FISH, OR HAKE WOULD BE SUITABLE TO USE IN THIS DISH.

**1** For the sauce, heat the butter in a large pan and when melted add the flour and mustard powder. Stir until smooth and cook over very low heat for 2 minutes, without coloring. Slowly beat in the milk until smooth. Simmer gently for 2 minutes, then stir in the cheese until smooth. Remove from the heat and place some plastic wrap over the surface of the sauce to prevent a skin from forming. Set aside.

**2** Meanwhile, to make the topping, boil the whole potatoes in plenty of salted water for 15 minutes. Drain the potatoes well and let stand until they are cool enough to handle.

**3** Preheat the oven to 400°F/200°C. Heat the oil in a clean saucepan. Add the onion and cook for 5 minutes, until softened. Add the leek, carrot, celery, and mushrooms and cook for an additional 10 minutes, or until the vegetables have softened. Stir in the lemon zest and cook briefly.

**4** Add the softened vegetables to the sauce, along with the fish, shrimp, parsley, and dill. Season to taste with salt and pepper and transfer to a greased 2-quart casserole dish.

**5** Peel the cooled potatoes and grate them coarsely. Mix with the melted butter. Cover the filling with the grated potato and sprinkle with the grated Gruyère cheese.

**6** Cover loosely with foil and bake in the preheated oven for 30 minutes. Remove the foil and bake for an additional 30 minutes, or until the topping is tender and golden and the filling is bubbling. Garnish with dill sprigs and serve with a selection of your favorite vegetables.

# CHARGRILLED TUNA WITH CHILI SALSA

A FIRM FISH, SUCH AS TUNA, IS AN EXCELLENT CHOICE FOR BARBECUES BECAUSE IT IS MEATY AND DOES NOT BREAK UP DURING COOKING. HERE, IT IS SERVED WITH A COLORFUL AND SPICY CHILI SALSA. IT MAKES AN EXCELLENT CHOICE FOR PEOPLE ON A LOW-FAT DIET.

**SERVES 4**

**PREPARATION**
**20 MINUTES, PLUS**
**1 HOUR'S MARINATING**
**COOKING**
**20 MINUTES**

**INGREDIENTS**
- 4 TUNA STEAKS, ABOUT 6 OZ/ 175 G EACH
- GRATED ZEST AND JUICE OF 1 LIME
- 2 TBSP OLIVE OIL
- SALT AND PEPPER
- FRESH CILANTRO SPRIGS, TO GARNISH

**FOR THE CHILI SALSA**
- 2 ORANGE BELL PEPPERS
- 1 TBSP OLIVE OIL
- JUICE OF 1 LIME
- JUICE OF 1 ORANGE
- 2–3 FRESH RED CHILES, SEEDED AND CHOPPED
- PINCH OF CAYENNE PEPPER

**1** Rinse the tuna thoroughly under cold running water and pat dry with paper towels, then place in a large shallow nonmetallic dish. Sprinkle the lime zest and juice and the oil over the fish. Season to taste with salt and pepper, cover with plastic wrap, and marinate in the refrigerator for up to 1 hour.

**2** Preheat the barbecue. To make the salsa, brush the bell peppers with the olive oil and cook over hot coals, turning frequently, for 10 minutes, or until the skin is blackened and charred. Remove from the barbecue and cool slightly, then peel off the skins and discard the seeds. Place the bell peppers in a food processor with the remaining salsa ingredients and process to a puree. Transfer to a bowl and season to taste with salt and pepper.

**3** Cook the tuna over hot coals for 4–5 minutes on each side, until golden. Transfer to plates, garnish with cilantro sprigs, and serve immediately with the salsa.

## COOK'S TIP
YOU CAN MAKE THE CHILI SALSA IN ADVANCE. HALVE THE ORANGE BELL PEPPERS AND COOK, SKIN-SIDE UPWARD, UNDER A PREHEATED HOT BROILER. COOK UNTIL BLACKENED AND CHARRED, THEN CONTINUE AS IN STEP 2.

# TRADITIONAL GREEK BAKED FISH

**SERVES 4–6**

**PREPARATION**
**30 MINUTES**
**COOKING**
**1 HOUR 20 MINUTES–**
**1 HOUR 40 MINUTES**

THE TRADITIONAL GREEK WAY OF BAKING FISH IS TO COOK IT WHOLE WITH TOMATOES AND LEMONS (WHICH ARE EATEN WITH THE RIND ON), ALTHOUGH BOTH THE GREEKS AND THE TURKS CLAIM TO HAVE ORIGINATED THE METHOD. A VARIETY OF FISH CAN BE COOKED THIS WAY, SO TAKE YOUR PICK.

**INGREDIENTS**
- 5 TBSP OLIVE OIL
- 2 ONIONS, THINLY SLICED
- 2 GARLIC CLOVES
- 2 CARROTS, THINLY SLICED
- 2 CELERY STALKS
- ⅔ CUP DRY WHITE WINE
- 14 OZ/400 G CANNED CHOPPED TOMATOES
- PINCH OF SUGAR
- 1 LARGE LEMON
- 2 TBSP CHOPPED FRESH FLAT-LEAF PARSLEY
- 1 TSP CHOPPED FRESH MARJORAM
- 2–3 LB/1–1.3 KG ROUND WHOLE FISH (SEE COOK'S TIP)
- SALT AND PEPPER

**1** Preheat the oven to 350°F/180°C. Heat 4 tablespoons of the oil in a large pan. Add the onions and garlic and cook for 5 minutes, until softened. Add the carrots and celery and fry for 5–10 minutes, until slightly softened.

**2** Add the wine and bring to a boil. Thinly slice the lemon and add half to the pan with the tomatoes and their juice, the sugar, and salt and pepper, and simmer for 20 minutes. Add the herbs.

**3** Place the fish in a greased, shallow ovenproof dish. Arrange the vegetables around the fish, putting some of the lemon slices on top. Sprinkle with the remaining oil and season to taste with salt and pepper.

**4** Bake the fish, uncovered, in the preheated oven for 45 minutes– 1 hour, depending on the thickness of the fish, until tender. Serve immediately, straight from the oven.

## COOK'S TIP
YOU CAN USE DIFFERENT FISH FOR THIS RECIPE, SUCH AS SEA BREAM, SEA BASS, TILAPIA, RED SNAPPER, OR RED OR GRAY MULLET.

# SEAFOOD GRATIN

A DISH THAT IS COOKED "AU GRATIN" IS TRADITIONALLY TOPPED WITH BREAD CRUMBS AND/OR CHEESE, AND THEN BAKED UNTIL GOLDEN BROWN. USUALLY IT IS THEN SERVED IN THE BAKING DISH. THIS SEAFOOD GRATIN IS MADE WITH A MARVELOUS COMBINATION OF FRESH FISH AND SHELLFISH.

**SERVES 4**

**PREPARATION
20 MINUTES
COOKING
1 HOUR**

**INGREDIENTS**
- 1 LB/450 G COD FILLETS
- 8 OZ/225 G SHRIMP, SHELLED AND DEVEINED
- 8 OZ/225 G SCALLOPS
- 3 TBSP EXTRA VIRGIN OLIVE OIL
- 1 GARLIC CLOVE, CHOPPED
- 4 SCALLIONS, CHOPPED
- 1 ZUCCHINI, SLICED
- 15 OZ/425 G CANNED PLUM TOMATOES
- 2 TBSP CHOPPED FRESH BASIL
- 1 CUP FRESH BREAD CRUMBS
- ⅔ CUP CHEDDAR CHEESE, GRATED
- SALT AND PEPPER
- FRESHLY COOKED BROCCOLI AND CAULIFLOWER, TO SERVE

**1** Preheat the oven to 375°F/190°C. Bring a large saucepan of water to a boil, then reduce the heat to medium. Rinse the cod, pat dry with paper towels, and add to the saucepan. Cook for 5 minutes. Add the shrimp and cook for 3 minutes, then add the scallops and cook for 2 minutes. Drain, refresh under cold running water, and drain again.

**2** Heat 2 tablespoons of the oil in a skillet over low heat. Add the garlic and scallions and cook, stirring, for 3 minutes. Add the zucchini and cook for 3 minutes, then add the tomatoes with their juice, and the basil. Season to taste with salt and pepper and then simmer for 10 minutes.

**3** Brush a shallow baking dish with the remaining oil and arrange the seafood in it. Remove the pan from the heat and pour the sauce over the fish. Sprinkle over the bread crumbs and top with cheese. Bake in the oven for 30 minutes until golden. Serve with freshly cooked broccoli and cauliflower.

# BREADED FISH STRIPS

THESE DELICIOUS MORSELS OF FRIED FISH HAVE A MARVELOUS CRISP, GOLDEN COATING OF BREAD CRUMBS AND FINELY CHOPPED FRESH PARSLEY. THEY MAKE IDEAL PARTY FARE OR A MOUTHWATERING SNACK TO ENJOY AT ANY TIME OF THE DAY.

**SERVES 2**

PREPARATION
**20 MINUTES, PLUS
30 MINUTES' CHILLING**
COOKING
**5–6 MINUTES**

**INGREDIENTS**
- 2 LEMON SOLE FILLETS, ABOUT 6 OZ/175 G EACH, SKINNED
- 2 TBSP ALL-PURPOSE FLOUR
- 1 EGG, BEATEN
- 2 CUPS WHITE OR WHOLE-WHEAT BREAD CRUMBS, MADE FROM ONE-DAY-OLD BREAD
- 1 TBSP FINELY CHOPPED FRESH PARSLEY
- 1 GARLIC CLOVE, PEELED AND CRUSHED (OPTIONAL)
- 1 CUP VEGETABLE OIL, FOR FRYING
- SALT AND PEPPER
- 1 LEMON, HALVED, AND AÏOLI, TO SERVE

**1** Cut the fillets across diagonally into thin strips, about ½ inch/1 cm wide.

**2** Season the flour well and put onto a plate. Roll the strips of fish in the flour until well covered.

**3** Place the beaten egg in a shallow dish and then dip the fish into it.

**4** Mix the bread crumbs with the parsley, and garlic if using, and season well. Put the mixture into a plastic bag, add the goujons, and toss to coat thoroughly. Chill in the refrigerator for at least 30 minutes.

**5** Heat the oil in a skillet and fry half the goujons over medium heat for 2–3 minutes, turning them with a slotted spoon. Remove from the skillet and drain on paper towels. Keep warm. Repeat using the remaining fish.

**6** Serve at once with a half lemon per portion to squeeze over the goujons, and a bowl of aïoli.

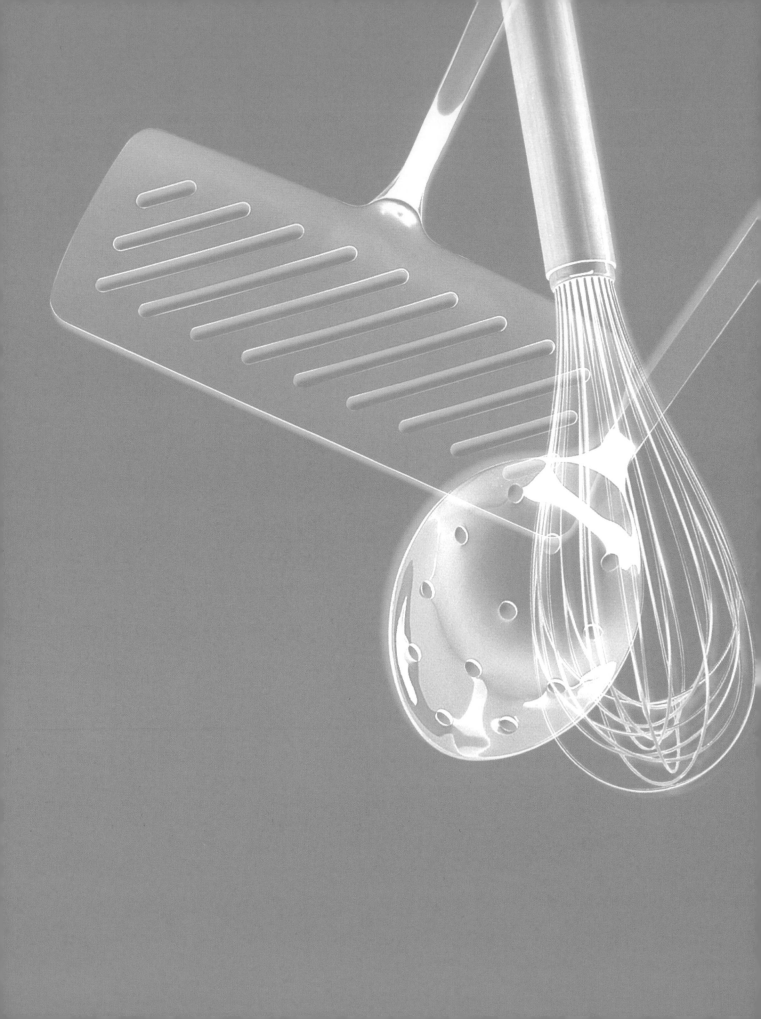

# CHAPTER 3

# MEAT

RED MEAT IS VERY NUTRITIOUS AND CAN PLAY A VALUABLE PART IN A HEALTHY DIET, ESPECIALLY IF YOU CHOOSE LEAN CUTS TO KEEP THE SATURATED FAT LEVELS TO A MINIMUM. IT IS FULL OF VITAMINS AND MINERALS, ESPECIALLY IRON AND PROTEIN. ON THE FOLLOWING PAGES YOU WILL FIND SOME DELICIOUS RECIPES TO MAKE THE MOST OF ANY CUT OF MEAT.

# INTRODUCTION

MEAT IS RICH IN PROTEIN AND EASY TO COOK. IT MAKES AN EXCELLENT CENTERPIECE TO ANY MEAL, AND YOU CAN CHOOSE FROM A WIDE RANGE OF JOINTS AND CUTS, FROM THE ECONOMICAL TO THE INDULGENT, TO SUIT ANY OCCASION.

### Buying and storing meat

Always buy your fresh meat from a reputable supplier. For lamb, choose firm, pinkish, marbled meat; avoid any that looks dark and soggy. The fat should be cream-colored, not yellow. For pork, choose moist, pinkish meat with white fat. Avoid any meat that looks oily or that has yellow fat. For beef, look for meat that is deep burgundy red, not bright red; the fat should be cream-colored, not yellow. Choose beef that has a marbling of fat through it—this will ensure that the meat stays moist during cooking. For veal, the flesh should be a very pale pink and the fat white. If it is turning red, it means that the meat is older than it should be.

If you are buying a joint of meat, allow 6–12 oz/ 175–350 g per person, depending on whether the meat is on or off the bone.

As soon as you get the meat home, unwrap it and transfer it to a clean dish (the dish should have a lip deep enough to catch any juices). Cover it with plastic wrap and store in the refrigerator away from any cooked meats in order to prevent cross-contamination. Leave any prepackaged meat in its wrapping in the refrigerator and use by the expiration date. Unpackaged ground lamb, beef, and pork is best used within 1–2 days of purchase. Fresh cuts of beef and pork will keep in the refrigerator for 2–3 days, and cooked beef and pork can be refrigerated for 4–5 days. Fresh lamb cuts will keep for up to 4 days in the refrigerator. Before cooking, bring out the meat (keep it covered) and let it reach room temperature about 30 minutes before cooking. You can freeze small cuts of beef or pork for up to 6 months, and lamb for up to 3 months. Make sure you thaw the meat thoroughly in a refrigerator or cool room before cooking; allow 6 hours per 1 lb/450 g.

### Preparation techniques

There is a range of techniques you can use to prepare and/or improve your chosen cuts of meat before cooking. Some of them are done purely for presentation, while other techniques help to tenderize the meat or facilitate thorough cooking.

### Lamb chops

Use a sharp knife to remove the excess fat around the edge.

### Pork chops and round steaks

Use a sharp knife to make incisions in the fat at intervals of 1 inch/2.5 cm around the edge.

### Top round steak

Use a sharp knife to remove any excess fat. Slice the meat across the grain, then cut across the slices to form smaller pieces or cubes of meat.

### Tenderize thin cuts of meat

Put them between sheets of wax paper and pound with either a meat mallet or the bottom of a pan.

### Stuff and tie a boneless joint

Put it skin-side down and arrange the dressing evenly over the surface. Roll up the joint from the thick end, tie a piece of clean string lengthwise around the joint, then knot it and trim off the ends. Now tie more pieces of string crosswise around the joint at intervals of about 1 inch/2.5 cm. Knot each one in turn and trim the ends.

### Butterfly a leg of lamb

Push a chef's knife into the cavity of the bone, then cut sideways to part the meat. Open it out and make a light incision down the center of the meat so that it stays open and flat.

### Prepare a rack of lamb

Remove the skin and excess fat, leaving a layer of fat about ⅝-inch/1.5-cm thick. Cut off the bone at the back, then remove the fat from the ends of the bones (to a length of about 2 inches/5 cm). Use a knife to scrape out the meat from between the bones.

### Choosing cuts of meat

There are many different cuts of meat available. Choosing the right cut will help to ensure the perfect result for your chosen recipe. When in doubt, ask your local butcher for advice.

**Beef**
For roasting, choose sirloin, rump, tenderloin, and rib. Tenderloin and steaks are excellent for broiling, pan-frying, or barbecuing. For stewing, use chuck or rump.

**Pork**
For roasting, choose the belly, leg, loin, shoulder, tenderloin, chops, or steaks. For broiling, use the belly, scallops, loin, shoulder, tenderloin, chops, or steaks. The belly, loin, tenderloin, chops, or steaks are good for barbecues. For frying, use the loin, tenderloin, chops, steaks, and bacon. To stew, use the leg or loin.

**Veal**
The breast, loin, and shoulder are best for roasting, while the loin, round, and chops are ideal for broiling and barbecuing. For pan-frying, choose the loin or round, and for stewing or braising use the foreshank, shoulder, or breast.

**Lamb**
The leg is the most popular choice for roasting, but you can also roast the shoulder, saddle, and breast. For broiling, try chops, noisettes, and leg. The leg or chops are ideal for barbecues, and for pan-frying use noisettes. Finally, for stewing, braising, or casseroles, use the shoulder or shank.

Beef

Pork

Lamb

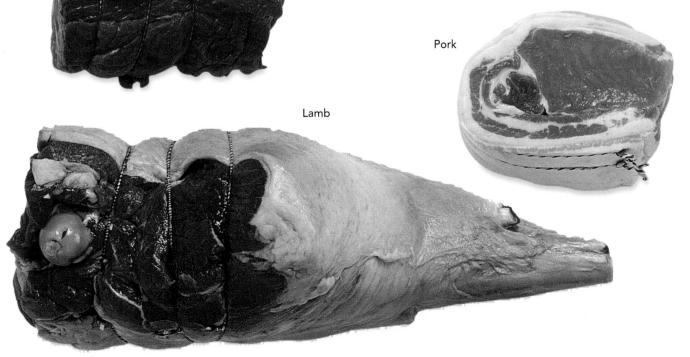

## Cooking and carving techniques

Techniques for cooking and carving joints of meat are not difficult, but they do have to be performed properly in order to get the best out of the meat. Follow the instructions given here for perfect results every time.

### Roasting and carving a boned joint

This technique is suitable for boned joints of lamb, pork, and beef. Rub the surface with a little oil, followed by some salt and some crushed peppercorns (use a mortar and pestle for this). Place on a rack in a roasting pan, then roast in the oven, basting once or twice during cooking. Remove from the oven and cut off the strings. Wrap the meat in foil and let it stand for 15–20 minutes. To carve, steady the meat with a fork, then carve slices downward from one end.

### Roasting and carving a leg of lamb

Using a sharp knife, score a crisscross pattern in the fat, then rub all over the surface with a little oil, followed by some salt and freshly ground black pepper. Place the meat on a rack in a roasting pan and roast in the oven, basting once or twice during cooking.

To test if the meat is cooked all the way through, pierce a skewer or knife into the thickest part. The juices that run out will be clear if the meat is cooked. If not, return the meat to the oven and cook until it is done. Remove from the oven and wrap the meat in foil. Let it stand for 15–20 minutes. To carve, turn the leg meat-side up, then steady the meat with a fork. Start carving from the knuckle end. When you have finished, turn over the leg and carve horizontal slices.

### Using a meat thermometer

A meat thermometer is a useful device for testing whether a joint of meat is cooked thoroughly. Thorough cooking is particularly important in the case of pork, which can carry harmful bacteria and cause food poisoning if not cooked all the way through. Simply insert the thermometer into the thickest part of the meat at the start of cooking. Be careful to ensure that it does not come into contact with any bone, because this could give a false reading. When the thermometer reaches the required temperature, the meat is cooked. The recommended temperatures for different meats are shown below.

### COOKING TEMPERATURES

| Lamb | Medium rare | 167°F/75°C |
|------|-------------|------------|
|      | Well done   | 176°F/80°C |
| Pork | Well done   | 194°F/90°C |
| Beef | Rare        | 149°F/65°C |
|      | Medium rare | 158°F/70°C |
|      | Well done   | 167°F/75°C |

# OVEN TEMPERATURES AND ROASTING TIMES

Please note that individual oven temperatures and cooking times vary, so the following cooking times are approximate only. Remember to preheat the oven before cooking in order to ensure the best results.

| Meat | Joint | Weight | Temperature | Cooking time |
|---|---|---|---|---|
| Lamb | Whole leg | 5 lb 8 oz/2.5 kg | 350°F/180°C | 2¼ hours (medium rare) or 2½ hours (well done) |
| Lamb | Whole shoulder | 5 lb 8 oz/2.5 kg | 350°F/180°C | 2¼ hours (medium rare) or 2½ hours (well done) |
| Pork | Loin (boned) | 5 lb 8 oz/2.5 kg | 350°F/180°C 425°F/220°C | 3 hours at lower temperature, then 20 minutes at higher temperature (well done) |
| Pork | Shoulder (boned) | 5 lb 8 oz/2.5 kg | 350°F/180°C 425°F/220°C | 3 hours at lower temperature, then 20 minutes at higher temperature (well done) |
| Beef | Short loin | 5 lb 8 oz/2.5 kg | 400°F/200°C | 1¾ hours (rare), 2¼ hours (medium rare), or 2½ hours (well done) |
| Beef | Rump | 4 lb 8 oz/2 kg | 350°F/180°C | 1½ hours (rare), 2 hours (medium rare), or 2½ hours (well done) |

# OVEN TEMPERATURES AND HEAT DESCRIPTIONS

You may come across recipes that do not give a specific temperature: instead they will simply recommend cooking in a "moderate" or "hot" oven. Here is a list of these heat descriptions and their correct corresponding temperatures.

| Oven heat description | Fahrenheit | Centigrade |
|---|---|---|
| Very slow | 225–250° | 110–120° |
| Slow | 250–300° | 120–150° |
| Moderate | 300–375° | 150–190° |
| Hot | 375–425° | 190–220° |
| Very hot | 425–475° | 220–240° |
| Extremely hot | 475–525° | 240–274° |

# MEATLOAF

THERE ARE ALMOST AS MANY MEATLOAF RECIPES IN THE WORLD AS THERE ARE COOKS—THIS VERSION IS A VERY TRADITIONAL RECIPE, USING BASIC INGREDIENTS TO CREATE A HEARTY MEATLOAF THAT EVERYONE WILL REMEMBER FONDLY.

**SERVES 4**

**PREPARATION**
**10 MINUTES**
**COOKING**
**45 MINUTES**

**INGREDIENTS**
- 1 THICK SLICE CRUSTLESS WHITE BREAD
- 3 CUPS FRESHLY GROUND BEEF, PORK, OR LAMB
- 1 SMALL EGG
- 1 TBSP FINELY CHOPPED ONION
- 1 BEEF BOUILLON CUBE, CRUMBLED
- 1 TSP DRIED HERBS
- SALT AND PEPPER

**TO SERVE**
- TOMATO SAUCE OR MUSHROOM SAUCE, OR GRAVY
- MASHED POTATOES
- FRESHLY COOKED GREEN BEANS

**1** Preheat the oven to 350°F/180°C.

**2** Put the bread into a small bowl and add enough water to soak. Let it stand for 5 minutes, then drain and squeeze well to get rid of all the water.

**3** Combine the bread and all the other ingredients in a bowl. Shape into a loaf, then place on a baking sheet or in an ovenproof dish. Put the meatloaf in the oven and cook for 30–45 minutes, until the juices run clear when it is pierced with a toothpick.

**4** Serve in slices with your favorite sauce or gravy, mashed potatoes, and freshly cooked green beans.

# BEEF BOURGUIGNON

BEEF BOURGUIGNON USES A TRADITIONAL METHOD OF PREPARATION FROM THE BURGUNDY REGION OF FRANCE. IT CONTAINS SUCCULENT BEEF BRAISED IN RED WINE, COMPLEMENTED BY BACON, ONIONS, AND MUSHROOMS. SERVE IT WITH FRESH CRUSTY BREAD TO SOAK UP THE JUICES.

**SERVES 6**

**PREPARATION
40 MINUTES
COOKING
3¼ HOURS**

## INGREDIENTS

- 2 TBSP OLIVE OIL
- 6 OZ/175 G PIECE UNSMOKED BACON, SLICED INTO THIN STRIPS
- 3 LB/1.3 KG STEWING BEEF, CUT INTO 2-INCH/5-CM PIECES
- 2 CARROTS, SLICED
- 2 ONIONS, CHOPPED
- 2 GARLIC CLOVES, VERY FINELY CHOPPED
- 3 TBSP ALL-PURPOSE FLOUR
- 3 CUPS RED WINE
- 1½–2 CUPS BEEF STOCK
- 1 BOUQUET GARNI SACHET
- 1 TSP SALT
- ¼ TSP PEPPER
- 3 TBSP BUTTER
- 12 OZ/350 G PEARL ONIONS
- 12 OZ/350 G WHITE MUSHROOMS
- 2 TBSP CHOPPED FRESH PARSLEY, TO GARNISH

**1** Heat the oil in a large, ovenproof casserole over medium heat. Add the bacon and brown for 2–3 minutes. Remove with a slotted spoon. Add the beef in batches to the casserole and cook until browned. Drain and keep with the bacon. Add the carrots and chopped onions to the casserole and cook for 5 minutes. Add the garlic and cook until just colored. Return the meat and bacon to the casserole. Sprinkle on the flour and cook for 1 minute, stirring. Add the wine, enough stock to cover, the bouquet garni, and salt and pepper. Bring to a boil, cover, and simmer gently for 3 hours.

**2** Heat half the butter in a skillet. Add the pearl onions, cover, and cook until softened. Remove with a slotted spoon and keep warm. Heat the remaining butter in the skillet. Add the mushrooms and cook briefly. Remove and keep warm.

**3** Strain the casserole liquid into a clean pan. Wipe the casserole with paper towels and tip in the meat, bacon, mushrooms, and onions. Remove the surface fat from the cooking liquid, simmer for 1–2 minutes to reduce, then pour over the meat and vegetables. Serve sprinkled with chopped parsley.

# BEEF STROGANOFF

BEEF STROGANOFF GETS ITS NAME FROM THE 19TH CENTURY RUSSIAN DIPLOMAT COUNT PAUL STROGANOV. THIS DELICIOUS DISH OF BEEF, ONIONS, AND MUSHROOMS HAS A RICH, CREAMY SAUCE, AND THE COMBINATION OF RED WINE AND GARLIC GIVES IT AN UNFORGETTABLE FLAVOR.

**SERVES 4**

**PREPARATION**
**5 MINUTES**
**COOKING**
**12–15 MINUTES**

## INGREDIENTS
- ⅓ CUP ALL-PURPOSE FLOUR
- 1 TSP PAPRIKA
- 1 LB 9 OZ/700 G ROUND STEAK
- 4 TBSP BUTTER
- 1 ONION, FINELY CHOPPED
- 1 GARLIC CLOVE, FINELY CHOPPED
- 8 OZ/225 G WHITE MUSHROOMS
- 1 TBSP LEMON JUICE
- 2 TBSP DRY RED WINE
- 2 TBSP TOMATO PASTE
- 1½ CUPS SOUR CREAM
- SALT AND PEPPER
- 2 TBSP SNIPPED FRESH CHIVES, TO GARNISH

**1** Place the flour and paprika in a plastic bag and season with salt and pepper. Shake to mix, then add a few steak strips at a time and shake to coat.

**2** Melt the butter in a large, heavy-bottom skillet over low heat. Add the onion and garlic and cook, stirring occasionally, for 5 minutes, or until softened. Increase the heat to high, add the steak strips, and cook, stirring constantly, until browned all over. Stir in the mushrooms, lemon juice, and wine, reduce the heat, and simmer for 5 minutes.

**3** Stir in the tomato paste and sour cream and adjust the seasoning, if necessary. Garnish with the chives and serve immediately.

## COOK'S TIP
BEEF STROGANOFF IS TRADITIONALLY SERVED OVER NOODLES, BUT YOU CAN ALSO SERVE IT ON A BED OF FRESHLY COOKED RICE OR PASTA. USE A LIGHT, FLUFFY LONG-GRAIN RICE TO PARTNER THIS DISH.

# CLASSIC BEEF FAJITAS

**SERVES 4–6**

**PREPARATION**
**30 MINUTES, PLUS**
**3–8 HOURS' MARINATING**
**COOKING**
**10–15 MINUTES**

THIS RECIPE CONTAINS SIZZLING MARINATED STRIPS OF MEAT ROLLED UP IN SOFT FLOUR TORTILLAS WITH A TANGY SALSA. IT IS A REAL MEXICAN TREAT, AND PERFECT FOR RELAXED ENTERTAINING. SIMPLY PASS ROUND THE INGREDIENTS AND LET YOUR GUESTS ROLL THEIR OWN FAJITAS.

## INGREDIENTS
- 1 LB 9 OZ/700 G BEEF SKIRT STEAK, CUT INTO STRIPS
- 6 GARLIC CLOVES, CHOPPED
- JUICE OF 1 LIME
- LARGE PINCH OF MILD CHILI POWDER
- LARGE PINCH OF PAPRIKA
- LARGE PINCH OF GROUND CUMIN
- 1–2 TBSP EXTRA VIRGIN OLIVE OIL
- 12 FLOUR TORTILLAS
- BUTTER, FOR GREASING
- VEGETABLE OIL, FOR COOKING
- 1–2 AVOCADOS, PITTED, SLICED, AND TOSSED WITH LIME JUICE
- ½ CUP SOUR CREAM
- SALT AND PEPPER

### FOR THE PICO DE GALLO SALSA
- 8 RIPE TOMATOES, DICED
- 3 SCALLIONS, SLICED
- 1–2 FRESH GREEN CHILES, SUCH AS JALAPEÑO OR SERRANO, SEEDED AND CHOPPED
- 3–4 TBSP CHOPPED FRESH CILANTRO
- 5–8 RADISHES, DICED
- GROUND CUMIN

**1** Combine the beef with the garlic, lime juice, chili powder, paprika, cumin, and olive oil. Add salt and pepper, mix well, and marinate for at least 30 minutes at room temperature, or up to overnight in the refrigerator.

**2** To make the salsa, place the tomatoes in a bowl with the scallions, green chile, cilantro, and radishes. Season to taste with cumin, and salt and pepper. Set aside.

**3** Heat the tortillas one by one in a lightly greased nonstick skillet, wrapping each in foil as you work to keep them warm.

**4** Heat a little vegetable oil in a large, heavy-bottom skillet over high heat. Add the meat and stir-fry until browned and just cooked through.

**5** Serve the sizzling hot meat with the warm tortillas, the salsa, avocado, and sour cream for each person to make his or her own rolled-up fajitas.

## COOK'S TIP
A LETTUCE AND ORANGE SALAD MAKES A REFRESHING ACCOMPANIMENT.

# BROILED STEAK WITH TOMATOES & GARLIC

ORIGINATING IN NAPLES, WHERE IT IS DIFFICULT TO FIND ANY DISH THAT DOES NOT FEATURE THE BRILLIANTLY COLORED, RICH-TASTING TOMATOES OF THE REGION, THIS WAY OF SERVING STEAK IS NOW POPULAR THROUGHOUT ITALY—AND BEYOND.

**SERVES 4**

**PREPARATION
20 MINUTES
COOKING
20 MINUTES**

**INGREDIENTS**
- 3 TBSP OLIVE OIL, PLUS EXTRA FOR BRUSHING
- 1 LB 9 OZ/700 G TOMATOES, PEELED AND CHOPPED
- 1 RED BELL PEPPER, SEEDED AND CHOPPED
- 1 ONION, CHOPPED
- 2 GARLIC CLOVES, FINELY CHOPPED
- 1 TBSP CHOPPED FRESH FLAT-LEAF PARSLEY
- 1 TSP DRIED OREGANO
- 1 TSP SUGAR
- FOUR 6-OZ/175-G ENTRECÔTE (FLESH FROM RIBS) OR ROUND STEAKS
- SALT AND PEPPER
- GREEN BEANS AND NEW POTATOES, TO SERVE

**1** Place the oil, tomatoes, red bell pepper, onion, garlic, parsley, oregano, and sugar in a heavy-bottom saucepan and season to taste with salt and pepper. Bring to a boil, reduce the heat, and simmer for 15 minutes.

**2** Meanwhile, preheat the broiler to high. Snip any fat around the outsides of the steaks. Season each generously with pepper (no salt) and brush with oil. Broil for 1 minute on each side, then reduce the heat to medium and cook according to taste: 1½–2 minutes each side for rare; 2½–3 minutes each side for medium; 3–4 minutes on each side for well done.

**3** Transfer the steaks to warmed individual plates and spoon the sauce over them. Serve immediately with green beans and new potatoes.

# SHEPHERD'S PIE

**SERVES 4–5**

**PREPARATION**
**15 MINUTES**
**COOKING**
**1¼ HOURS**

SHEPHERD'S PIE IS AN OLD ENGLISH DISH, AND WAS ORIGINALLY CREATED TO USE UP LEFTOVERS FROM THE SUNDAY ROAST. IT USUALLY CONTAINS GROUND LAMB OR BEEF COOKED WITH ONIONS, CARROTS, HERBS, AND TOMATOES IN GRAVY, AND IS TOPPED WITH PIPED MASHED POTATOES.

## INGREDIENTS
- 1 LB 9 OZ/700 G FRESH LEAN GROUND LAMB OR BEEF
- 2 ONIONS, CHOPPED
- 8 OZ/225 G CARROTS, DICED
- 1–2 GARLIC CLOVES, CRUSHED
- 1 TBSP ALL-PURPOSE FLOUR
- 1 CUP BEEF STOCK
- 7 OZ/200 G CANNED CHOPPED TOMATOES
- 1 TSP WORCESTERSHIRE SAUCE
- 1 TSP CHOPPED FRESH SAGE
- 2 LB 4 OZ/1 KG POTATOES
- 2 TBSP MARGARINE
- 3–4 TBSP SKIM MILK
- 4½ OZ/125 G WHITE MUSHROOMS (OPTIONAL)
- SALT AND PEPPER

**1** Preheat the oven to 400°F/200°C. Place the meat in a large, heavy-bottom saucepan with no extra fat and cook gently until it begins to brown.

**2** Add the onions, carrots, and garlic and continue to cook gently for 10 minutes. Stir in the flour and cook for 1–2 minutes, then gradually stir in the stock and tomatoes and bring to a boil.

**3** Add the Worcestershire sauce, seasoning, and sage, cover, and simmer gently for 25 minutes, giving an occasional stir.

**4** Cook the potatoes in boiling salted water until tender, then drain thoroughly and mash, beating in the margarine, seasoning, and enough milk to give a piping consistency. Place in a pastry bag with a large star tip attached.

**5** Stir the mushrooms (if using) into the meat and taste and adjust the seasoning if necessary. Turn into a shallow ovenproof dish.

**6** Pipe the potatoes evenly over the meat. Cook in the preheated oven for 30 minutes, or until piping hot and the potatoes are golden brown.

## VARIATION
YOU CAN MIX THE BOILED POTATOES WITH PARSNIPS OR RUTABAGA FOR THE TOPPING. YOU CAN ALSO REPLACE THE SAGE WITH OREGANO. IF USING DRIED HERBS, HALVE THE QUANTITY.

# MOUSSAKA

MOUSSAKA ORIGINATED IN GREECE, BUT ITS POPULARITY IS NOW WIDESPREAD THROUGHOUT THE EASTERN MEDITERRANEAN. THERE ARE MANY VARIATIONS OF THIS DISH, BUT IT USUALLY CONTAINS SLICES OF EGGPLANT, AND GROUND LAMB (OR SOMETIMES BEEF AS AN ALTERNATIVE, WHICH IS USED HERE). IT IS COVERED WITH BÉCHAMEL SAUCE AND CHEESE.

**SERVES 4**

**PREPARATION
15 MINUTES
COOKING
1 HOUR 20 MINUTES**

**INGREDIENTS**
- 2 EGGPLANTS, THINLY SLICED
- 1 LB/450 G FRESH LEAN GROUND BEEF
- 2 ONIONS, THINLY SLICED
- 1 TSP FINELY CHOPPED GARLIC
- 14 OZ/400 G CANNED TOMATOES
- 2 TBSP CHOPPED FRESH PARSLEY
- 2 EGGS
- 1¼ CUPS LOWFAT PLAIN YOGURT
- 1 TBSP FRESHLY GRATED PARMESAN CHEESE
- SALT AND PEPPER

**1** Preheat the oven to 350°F/180°C. Dry-fry the eggplant slices, in batches, in a nonstick skillet on both sides until browned. Remove from the skillet.

**2** Add the beef to the skillet and cook for 5 minutes, stirring, until browned. Stir in the onions and garlic and cook for 5 minutes, or until browned. Add the tomatoes, parsley, and salt and pepper, then bring to a boil and simmer for 20 minutes, or until the meat is tender.

**3** Arrange half the eggplant slices in a layer in an ovenproof dish. Add the meat mixture, then a final layer of the remaining eggplant slices.

**4** Beat the eggs in a bowl, then beat in the yogurt and add salt and pepper to taste. Pour the mixture over the eggplants and sprinkle the grated cheese on top. Bake the moussaka in the oven for 45 minutes, or until golden brown. Serve straight from the dish.

**COOK'S TIP**
TRY EXPERIMENTING WITH YOUR OWN COMBINATIONS OF INGREDIENTS TO VARY THE FLAVOR AND TEXTURE. FOR EXAMPLE, YOU CAN USE GROUND LAMB HERE INSTEAD OF THE BEEF, AND ADD SLICED ARTICHOKES OR POTATOES TO THE EGGPLANTS.

# RACK OF LAMB

IF YOU WANT A ROAST FOR TWO, A RACK OF LAMB IS IDEAL. IT IS SIMPLE TO COOK AND PROVIDES DELICIOUS MEAT, FULL OF FLAVOR. LAMB IS BEST IN SPRING, FROM EASTER ONWARD, WHEN IT IS AT ITS SWEETEST AND MOST SUCCULENT. FRESH MINT IS ALSO AT ITS BEST AROUND THIS TIME.

**SERVES 2**

**PREPARATION**
**20 MINUTES, PLUS**
**3–8 HOURS' MARINATING**
**COOKING**
**15–20 MINUTES**

**INGREDIENTS**
- 1 TRIMMED RACK OF LAMB (ABOUT 9–10½ OZ/250–300 G)
- 1 GARLIC CLOVE, CRUSHED
- ⅔ CUP RED WINE
- 1 FRESH ROSEMARY SPRIG, CRUSHED TO RELEASE THE FLAVOR
- 1 TBSP OLIVE OIL
- ⅔ CUP LAMB STOCK
- 2 TBSP RED CURRANT JELLY
- SALT AND PEPPER

**FOR THE MINT SAUCE**
- SMALL BUNCH OF FRESH MINT LEAVES, CHOPPED
- 2 TSP SUPERFINE SUGAR
- 2 TBSP BOILING WATER
- 2 TBSP WHITE WINE VINEGAR

**1** Place the rack of lamb in a non-metallic bowl and rub all over with the garlic. Pour over the wine and place the rosemary sprig on top. Cover and marinate in the refrigerator for 3 hours, or overnight if possible.

**2** To make the mint sauce, combine the mint leaves with the sugar in a small bowl. Add the boiling water and stir to dissolve the sugar. Add the white wine vinegar and let the sauce stand for 30 minutes before serving with the lamb.

**3** Preheat the oven to 220°C/425°F.

**4** Remove the lamb from the marinade, reserving the marinade, dry the meat with paper towels, and season well with salt and pepper. Place in a small roasting pan, drizzle with the oil, and roast in the oven for 15–20 minutes, depending on whether you like your meat rare or medium. Remove the lamb from the oven and let it rest, covered with foil, in a warm place for 5 minutes.

**5** Meanwhile, place the marinade in a small saucepan, bring to a boil over medium heat, and continue to boil for 2–3 minutes. Add the lamb stock and red currant jelly and simmer until a syrupy consistency is achieved.

**6** Carve the lamb into cutlets and serve on warmed plates with the stock and red currant jelly sauce spooned over the top. Serve the mint sauce separately.

**COOK'S TIP**
RACK OF LAMB IS AN IMPRESSIVE DISH FOR ENTERTAINING, TOO. JUST DOUBLE OR TREBLE THE INGREDIENTS, DEPENDING ON THE NUMBER OF GUESTS.

# LAMB SHANKS WITH ROASTED ONIONS

IN THIS RECIPE, SLOW-ROASTED LAMB IS INFUSED WITH THE FLAVORS OF GARLIC AND ROSEMARY AND SERVED WITH SWEET RED ONIONS AND GLAZED CARROT STICKS. YOU WON'T REQUIRE ANYTHING MORE EXCEPT A BOTTLE OF FRUITY RED WINE.

**SERVES 4**

**PREPARATION
20 MINUTES
COOKING
2–2¼ HOURS**

## INGREDIENTS
- 4 LAMB SHANKS, 12 OZ/350 G EACH
- 6 GARLIC CLOVES
- 2 TBSP EXTRA VIRGIN OLIVE OIL
- 1 TBSP FRESH ROSEMARY, VERY FINELY CHOPPED
- 4 RED ONIONS
- 12 OZ/350 G CARROTS, CUT INTO THIN STICKS
- 4 TBSP WATER
- SALT AND PEPPER

**1** Preheat the oven to 350°F/180°C. Trim off any excess fat from the lamb. Using a small, sharp knife, make 6 incisions in each shank. Cut the garlic cloves lengthwise into 4 slices. Insert 6 garlic slices in the incisions in each lamb shank.

**2** Place the lamb in a single layer in a roasting pan, drizzle with the olive oil, sprinkle with the rosemary, and season with pepper. Roast in the preheated oven for 45 minutes.

**3** Wrap each of the onions in a piece of foil. Remove the roasting pan from the oven and season the lamb with salt. Return to the oven and place the wrapped onions on the shelf next to it. Roast for an additional 1–1¼ hours, until the lamb is very tender.

**4** Meanwhile, bring a large saucepan of water to a boil. Add the carrot sticks and blanch for 1 minute. Drain and refresh in cold water.

**5** Remove the roasting pan from the oven when the lamb is meltingly tender and transfer it to a warmed serving dish. Skim off any fat from the roasting pan and place it over medium heat. Add the carrots and cook for 2 minutes, then add the water, bring to a boil, and simmer, stirring constantly and scraping up the glazed bits from the bottom of the roasting pan.

**6** Transfer the carrots and sauce to the serving dish. Remove the onions from the oven and unwrap. Cut and discard about ½ inch/1 cm off the tops and add the onions to the dish. Serve immediately.

# ROGAN JOSH

THIS INDIAN DISH OF CHUNKS OF LAMB BRAISED IN CREAM AND SPICES IS A KASHMIRI SPECIALTY. THE TURMERIC GIVES IT A LOVELY GOLDEN COLOR. IT IS DELICIOUS SERVED WITH COOKED RICE, BUT IT CAN ALSO BE SERVED WITH NAANS TO SOAK UP THE MARVELOUSLY CREAMY SAUCE.

**SERVES 4**

**PREPARATION**
30 MINUTES, PLUS
15 MINUTES' COOLING
**COOKING**
50–55 MINUTES

**INGREDIENTS**
- ½ CUP GHEE OR VEGETABLE OIL
- 1 LB 2 OZ/500 G BONELESS LAMB, CUT INTO BITE-SIZE CHUNKS
- 4 GARLIC CLOVES, CHOPPED
- 3 FRESH GREEN CHILES, CHOPPED
- 1-INCH/2.5-CM PIECE FRESH GINGER, GRATED
- 1 TSP POPPY SEEDS
- 1 CINNAMON STICK, GROUND
- 1 CARDAMOM POD, GROUND
- 4 CLOVES, GROUND
- 1 TSP CORIANDER SEEDS, GROUND
- 1 TSP CUMIN SEEDS, GROUND
- GENEROUS 1 CUP SOUR CREAM
- ½ TSP TURMERIC
- ½ TSP CHILI POWDER
- 2 LARGE TOMATOES, CHOPPED
- 1 BAY LEAF
- FRESH CILANTRO LEAVES, TO GARNISH
- FRESHLY COOKED RICE, TO SERVE

**1** Heat half of the ghee in a large saucepan over high heat. Add the lamb and cook, stirring, for 5 minutes. Lift out the meat with a slotted spoon and drain on paper towels. Add the garlic, chiles, ginger, poppy seeds, and ground spices to the pan and cook over medium heat, stirring, for 4 minutes. Remove from the heat, let the mixture cool for a few minutes, then transfer it to a food processor. Stir in the sour cream, turmeric, and chili powder and process the mixture until smooth.

**2** Heat the remaining ghee in the pan over low heat. Add the chopped tomatoes and cook, stirring, for 3 minutes. Add the sour cream mixture and cook, stirring, until the oil separates. Remove from the heat and add the lamb. Add the bay leaf, return the pan to the heat, and cover. Simmer gently for 35–40 minutes, or until most of the liquid has been absorbed. Remove from the heat and discard the bay leaf. Garnish with cilantro leaves and serve with freshly cooked rice.

# POT ROAST PORK

BEEF AND CHICKEN ARE THE MOST POPULAR CHOICES FOR POT ROASTING, BUT A LOIN OF PORK WORKS SUPERBLY WELL, TOO. THIS IS A RICH AND FLAVORSOME DISH THAT IS IDEAL FOR ENTERTAINING. SERVE IT WITH BOILED, BAKED, OR ROAST POTATOES AND FRESHLY COOKED PEAS.

**SERVES 4**

**PREPARATION**
**20 MINUTES**
**COOKING**
**1½ HOURS**

**INGREDIENTS**
- 1 TBSP SUNFLOWER OIL
- 4 TBSP BUTTER
- 2 LB 4 OZ/1 KG BONED AND ROLLED PORK LOIN JOINT
- 4 SHALLOTS, CHOPPED
- 6 JUNIPER BERRIES
- 2 FRESH THYME SPRIGS, PLUS EXTRA TO GARNISH
- ⅔ CUP HARD CIDER
- ⅔ CUP CHICKEN STOCK OR WATER
- 8 CELERY STALKS, CHOPPED
- 2 TBSP ALL-PURPOSE FLOUR
- ⅔ CUP HEAVY CREAM
- SALT AND PEPPER

**1** Heat the oil with half the butter in a large, heavy-bottom saucepan or ovenproof casserole. Add the pork and cook over medium heat, turning frequently, for 5–10 minutes, or until browned. Transfer to a plate.

**2** Add the shallots to the pan and cook, stirring frequently, for 5 minutes, or until softened. Add the juniper berries and thyme sprigs and return the pork to the pan, with any juices that have collected on the plate. Pour in the cider and stock, season to taste with salt and pepper, then cover and simmer for 30 minutes. Turn the pork over and add the celery. Re-cover the pan and cook for an additional 40 minutes.

**3** Meanwhile, make a beurre manié by mashing the remaining butter with the flour in a small bowl. Transfer the pork and celery to a platter with a slotted spoon and keep warm. Remove and discard the juniper berries and thyme. Whisk the beurre manié, a little at a time, into the simmering cooking liquid. Cook, stirring constantly, for 2 minutes, then stir in the cream and bring to a boil.

**4** Slice the pork and spoon a little of the sauce over it. Garnish with the thyme sprigs and serve immediately. Hand around the remaining sauce separately.

## VARIATION

SUBSTITUTE 2 THINLY SLICED FENNEL BULBS FOR THE CHOPPED CELERY IF YOU WOULD PREFER AN ANISE FLAVOR IN THIS DISH.

# CITRUS PORK CHOPS

THE ADDITION OF JUNIPER AND FENNEL TO THE PORK CHOPS GIVES AN UNUSUAL AND DELICATE FLAVOR TO THIS DISH. WHEN COMBINED WITH THE SWEET, CITRUS TASTE OF ORANGE, THE RESULT IS AN UNFORGETTABLE, MOUTHWATERING EXPERIENCE THAT WILL LEAVE YOU YEARNING FOR MORE.

**SERVES 4**

**PREPARATION**
**20 MINUTES, PLUS**
**2 HOURS' MARINATING**
**COOKING**
**10–15 MINUTES**

**INGREDIENTS**
- ½ FENNEL BULB
- 1 TBSP JUNIPER BERRIES, LIGHTLY CRUSHED
- ABOUT 2 TBSP OLIVE OIL
- FINELY GRATED ZEST AND JUICE OF 1 ORANGE
- 4 PORK CHOPS, ABOUT 5½ OZ/150 G EACH

**1** Using a sharp knife, finely chop the fennel bulb, discarding the fronds and green parts.

**2** Grind the juniper berries in a mortar and pestle. Mix the crushed juniper berries with the fennel flesh, olive oil, and orange zest.

**3** Using a sharp knife, score a few cuts all over each pork chop.

**4** Place the pork chops in a roasting pan or an ovenproof dish. Spoon the fennel and juniper mixture over the pork chops.

**5** Carefully pour the orange juice over the top of each pork chop, cover, and marinate in the refrigerator for 2 hours.

**6** Preheat the broiler to medium. Cook the pork chops under the hot broiler for 10–15 minutes, depending on the thickness of the meat, turning occasionally, until the meat is tender and cooked through.

**7** Transfer the pork chops to serving plates and serve.

## COOK'S TIP
JUNIPER BERRIES ARE USUALLY ASSOCIATED WITH GIN, BUT ARE OFTEN ADDED TO MEAT DISHES IN ITALY FOR THEIR DELICATE CITRUS FLAVOR. THEY CAN BE BOUGHT DRIED FROM HEALTH FOOD STORES.

# GLAZED HAM STEAKS

HAM STEAKS, WHICH ARE ALSO KNOWN AS GAMMON STEAKS, MAKE A TASTY DISH FOR A LUNCH OR LIGHT SUPPER. THESE STEAKS ARE DELICIOUSLY SWEET GLAZED WITH SUGAR AND MUSTARD. SIMPLY ADD A BAKED POTATO AND LIGHTLY COOKED GREEN BEANS AND YOU HAVE A PERFECT MEAL.

**SERVES 4**

**PREPARATION
5 MINUTES
COOKING
10 MINUTES**

**INGREDIENTS**
- 4 HAM STEAKS
- 4 TBSP BROWN SUGAR
- 2 TSP MUSTARD POWDER
- 4 TBSP BUTTER
- 8 SLICES PINEAPPLE

**1** Preheat a grill pan over medium heat. Place the ham steaks on it and cook for 5 minutes, turning once. If you have room for only 2 steaks at a time, cook them completely and keep them warm while cooking the second pair.

**2** Combine the brown sugar and mustard in a small bowl.

**3** Melt the butter in a large skillet. Add the pineapple and cook for 2 minutes to heat through, turning once. Sprinkle with the sugar and mustard mixture and continue cooking over low heat until the sugar has melted and the pineapple is well glazed. Turn the pineapple once more, so that both sides are coated with sauce. Place the ham steaks on individual plates and arrange 2 pineapple slices either next to them or overlapping on top. Spoon over some of the sweet pan juices and serve.

# BRAISED VEAL IN RED WINE

THIS IS A CLASSIC CASSEROLE OF MEAT BRAISED IN WINE WITH GARLIC, TOMATOES, AND A LIBERAL AMOUNT OF HERBS. YOU CAN USE STEWING VEAL OR BEEF IN THIS RECIPE, AND THIS DISH GOES PARTICULARLY WELL WITH (LONG-GRAIN) RICE.

**SERVES 6**

**PREPARATION**
**25 MINUTES**
**COOKING**
**2 HOURS 20 MINUTES–**
**2 HOURS 25 MINUTES**

**INGREDIENTS**
- ¼ CUP ALL-PURPOSE FLOUR
- 2 LB/900 G STEWING VEAL OR BEEF, CUBED
- 4 TBSP OLIVE OIL
- 12 OZ/350 G PEARL ONIONS
- 2 GARLIC CLOVES, FINELY CHOPPED
- 12 OZ/350 G CARROTS, SLICED
- 1¼ CUPS DRY RED WINE
- ⅔ CUP BEEF OR CHICKEN STOCK
- 14 OZ/400 G CANNED CHOPPED TOMATOES WITH HERBS
- PARED ZEST OF 1 LEMON
- 1 BAY LEAF
- 1 TBSP CHOPPED FRESH FLAT-LEAF PARSLEY
- 1 TBSP CHOPPED FRESH BASIL
- 1 TSP CHOPPED FRESH THYME
- SALT AND PEPPER
- FRESHLY COOKED RICE, TO SERVE

**1** Preheat the oven to 350°F/180°C. Place the flour and some pepper in a plastic bag, add the meat, and shake well to coat each piece. Heat the oil in a large ovenproof casserole. Add the meat and cook, in batches, for 5–10 minutes, stirring constantly, until browned on all sides. Remove with a slotted spoon and set aside.

**2** Add the pearl onions, garlic, and carrots to the casserole and cook for 5 minutes, until beginning to soften. Return the meat to the casserole.

**3** Pour in the wine, stirring in any glazed bits from the bottom, then add the stock, the tomatoes with their juice, lemon rind, bay leaf, parsley, basil, thyme, zest, and salt and pepper. Bring to a boil, then cover the casserole.

**4** Cook in the preheated oven for 2 hours, or until the meat is tender. Serve hot with freshly cooked rice.

## COOK'S TIP

THIS IS A PERFECT CASSEROLE FOR COOKING IN ADVANCE AND THEN REHEATING. ONCE COOKED, LET IT COOL AND THEN STORE IT IN THE REFRIGERATOR. REHEAT IT BY BRINGING IT TO A BOIL, THEN SIMMERING FOR 15 MINUTES.

# OSSO BUCO WITH ORANGE & LEMON

POPULAR THROUGHOUT ALL OF ITALY, YOU'LL ALSO FIND SLOW-COOKED VEAL SHINS IN MANY RESTAURANTS ALONG THE MEDITERRANEAN. THE ORANGE AND LEMON ZEST, ALONG WITH FRESH BASIL, GIVES THE DISH A REAL SOUTHERN ITALIAN FLAVOR.

**SERVES 6**

**PREPARATION
25 MINUTES
COOKING
1¾ HOURS**

## INGREDIENTS
- 1–2 TBSP ALL-PURPOSE FLOUR
- 6 MEATY SLICES OSSO BUCO (VEAL SHINS)
- 2 LB 4 OZ/1 KG FRESH TOMATOES, PEELED, SEEDED, AND DICED, OR 1 LB 12 OZ/800 G CANNED CHOPPED TOMATOES
- 1–2 TBSP OLIVE OIL
- 9 OZ/250 G ONIONS, VERY FINELY CHOPPED
- 9 OZ/250 G CARROTS, FINELY DICED
- 1 CUP DRY WHITE WINE
- 1 CUP VEAL STOCK
- 6 LARGE BASIL LEAVES, TORN
- 1 LARGE GARLIC CLOVE, VERY FINELY CHOPPED
- FINELY GRATED ZEST OF 1 LARGE LEMON
- FINELY GRATED ZEST OF 1 ORANGE
- 2 TBSP FINELY CHOPPED FRESH FLAT-LEAF PARSLEY
- SALT AND PEPPER
- CRUSTY BREAD, TO SERVE

**1** Place the flour in a plastic bag and season with salt and pepper. Add the osso buco, a couple of pieces at a time, and shake until well coated. Remove and shake off the excess flour. Continue until all the pieces are coated.

**2** If using canned tomatoes, pass them through a strainer and let them drain.

**3** Heat 1 tablespoon of the oil in a large ovenproof casserole. Add the osso buco and cook for 10 minutes on each side, until well browned. Remove from the casserole.

**4** Add 1–2 teaspoons of oil to the casserole if necessary. Add the onions and cook for 5 minutes, stirring, until softened. Stir in the carrots and continue cooking until they become soft.

**5** Add the tomatoes, wine, stock, and basil and return the osso buco to the casserole. Bring to a boil, then reduce the heat, cover, and simmer for 1 hour. Check that the meat is tender with the tip of a knife. If not, continue cooking for 10 minutes and test again.

**6** When the meat is tender, sprinkle with the garlic and with the lemon and orange zest, re-cover, and then cook for an additional 10 minutes.

**7** Adjust the seasoning if necessary. Sprinkle with the parsley and serve with crusty bread.

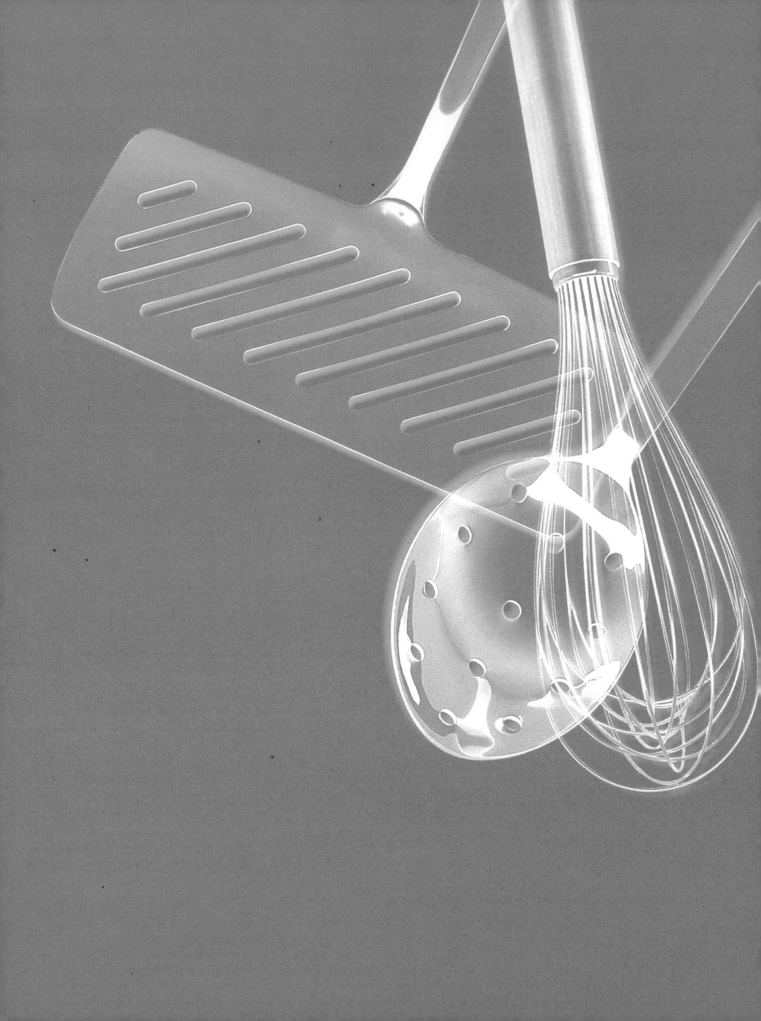

# CHAPTER 4

# POULTRY AND GAME

POULTRY IS DELICIOUS, ECONOMICAL, AND VERY VERSATILE. A ROAST CHICKEN, FOR EXAMPLE, MAKES A MARVELOUS TABLE CENTERPIECE AND, WHEN YOU HAVE EATEN YOUR FILL, THERE ARE ALL KINDS OF INSPIRING DISHES YOU CAN MAKE USING THE LEFTOVERS. GAME IS ALSO DELICIOUS, AND MAKES IMPRESSIVE FARE FOR A DINNER PARTY.

# TRADITIONAL ROAST CHICKEN

ROAST CHICKEN IS A POPULAR DISH IN BRITAIN. IN THIS VERSION, A DELICIOUS MIXTURE OF GARLIC, WALNUTS, AND PARSLEY IS STUFFED UNDERNEATH THE SKIN TO CREATE A MARVELOUS FLAVOR AND TEXTURE OVER THE SURFACE OF THE BIRD. SERVE IT WITH ROAST POTATOES AND VEGETABLES.

**SERVES 4**

**PREPARATION**
**20 MINUTES, PLUS 10 MINUTES' RESTING**
**COOKING**
**1 HOUR 50 MINUTES**

**INGREDIENTS**
- 2 TBSP BUTTER, SOFTENED
- 1 GARLIC CLOVE, FINELY CHOPPED
- 3 TBSP FINELY CHOPPED TOASTED WALNUTS
- 1 TBSP CHOPPED FRESH PARSLEY
- 1 OVEN-READY CHICKEN, WEIGHING 4 LB/1.8 KG
- 1 LIME, CUT INTO QUARTERS
- 2 TBSP VEGETABLE OIL
- 1 TBSP CORNSTARCH
- 2 TBSP WATER
- SALT AND PEPPER
- ROAST POTATOES, TO SERVE

**1** Preheat the oven to 375°F/190°C. Mix 1 tablespoon of the butter with the garlic, walnuts, and parsley in a small bowl. Season well with salt and pepper. Loosen the skin from the breast of the chicken without breaking it. Spread the butter mixture evenly between the skin and breast meat. Place the lime quarters inside the body cavity.

**2** Pour the oil into a roasting pan. Transfer the chicken to the pan and dot the skin with the remaining butter. Roast for 1¾ hours, basting occasionally, until the chicken is tender and the juices run clear when a skewer is inserted into the thickest part of the meat. Lift out the chicken and place on a serving platter to rest for 10 minutes.

**3** Blend the cornstarch with the water, then stir into the juices in the pan. Transfer to the stove. Stir over low heat until thickened. Add more water if necessary. Spoon the thickened juices over the chicken and serve with roast potatoes.

# CHICKEN FRICASSÉE

WHILE IT IS TYPICALLY COOKED IN CREAM, THE TERM "FRICASSÉE" SIMPLY MEANS COOKING THE MEAT—OR SOMETIMES FISH—IN A WHITE SAUCE, WITHOUT BROWNING IT. SERVE THIS CREAM-FREE VERSION WITH PLAIN BOILED RICE OR NEW POTATOES FOR A DELICIOUS, FILLING SUPPER.

**SERVES 4**

**PREPARATION**
**20 MINUTES**
**COOKING**
**35–40 MINUTES**

**INGREDIENTS**
- 1 TBSP ALL-PURPOSE FLOUR
- 4 SKINLESS, BONELESS CHICKEN BREASTS, ABOUT 5 OZ/140 G EACH, TRIMMED OF ALL VISIBLE FAT AND CUT INTO ¾-INCH/2-CM CUBES
- 1 TBSP SUNFLOWER OIL OR CORN OIL
- 8 PEARL ONIONS
- 2 GARLIC CLOVES, CRUSHED
- 1 CUP CHICKEN STOCK
- 2 CARROTS, DICED
- 2 CELERY STALKS, DICED
- 2 CUPS FROZEN PEAS
- 1 YELLOW BELL PEPPER, SEEDED AND DICED
- 2 CUPS WHITE MUSHROOMS, SLICED
- ½ CUP LOW-FAT PLAIN YOGURT
- 3 TBSP CHOPPED FRESH PARSLEY
- SALT AND WHITE PEPPER

**1** Spread out the flour on a dish and season with salt and pepper. Add the chicken and, using your hands, coat in the flour. Heat the oil in a heavy-bottom saucepan. Add the onions and garlic and cook over low heat, stirring occasionally, for 5 minutes. Add the chicken and cook, stirring, for 10 minutes, or until just beginning to color.

**2** Gradually stir in the stock, then add the carrots, celery, and peas. Bring to a boil, then reduce the heat, cover, and simmer for 5 minutes. Add the bell pepper and mushrooms, cover, and simmer for an additional 10 minutes.

**3** Stir in the yogurt and chopped parsley and season to taste with salt and pepper. Cook for 1–2 minutes, or until heated through, then transfer to 4 large, warmed serving plates and serve immediately.

**VARIATION**
YOU CAN SUBSTITUTE SKIM MILK FOR THE YOGURT AND ADD EXTRA FLAVOR WITH 1 TEASPOON OF LEMON JUICE AND A PINCH OF FRESHLY GRATED NUTMEG IN STEP 3.

# CHICKEN BIRYANI

**SERVES 8**

**PREPARATION**
**25 MINUTES, PLUS**
**3 HOURS' MARINATING**
COOKING
**1½–1¾ HOURS**

THIS RECIPE MAY LOOK COMPLICATED, BUT IS NOT DIFFICULT TO FOLLOW. YOU CAN SUBSTITUTE LAMB FOR THE CHICKEN, BUT IF YOU DO, YOU WILL HAVE TO MARINATE IT OVERNIGHT FIRST. GHEE IS A CLARIFIED BUTTER. IF IT IS UNAVAILABLE, USE ORDINARY BUTTER INSTEAD.

## INGREDIENTS
- 1½ TSP FINELY CHOPPED FRESH GINGER
- 1½ TSP CRUSHED GARLIC
- 1 TBSP GARAM MASALA
- 1 TSP CHILI POWDER
- 2 TSP SALT
- 1¼ CUPS PLAIN YOGURT
- 5 CRUSHED CARDAMOM PODS
- 3 LB 5 OZ/1.5 KG CHICKEN
- ⅔ CUP MILK
- 1 TSP SAFFRON STRANDS
- 6 TBSP GHEE
- 2 ONIONS, SLICED
- 1 LB/450 G BASMATI RICE
- 2 CINNAMON STICKS
- 4 FRESH GREEN CHILES
- 2 TBSP CILANTRO LEAVES
- 4 TBSP LEMON JUICE

**1** Mix the ginger, garlic, garam masala, chili powder, half the salt, the yogurt, and the cardamoms in a bowl. Skin and cut the chicken into 8 pieces, add to the spices, and mix well. Cover and marinate in the refrigerator for 3 hours.

**2** Boil the milk in a small saucepan, pour over the saffron, and set aside.

**3** Heat the ghee in a saucepan. Add the onions and cook until golden. Transfer half of the onions and ghee to a bowl and set aside.

**4** Place the rice and cinnamon sticks in a saucepan of water. Bring the rice to a boil and remove from the heat when half-cooked. Drain and place in a bowl. Mix with the remaining salt.

**5** Chop the chiles and set aside. Add the chicken mixture to the pan containing the onions. Add half each of the chopped green chiles, lemon juice, cilantro, and saffron milk. Add the rice, then the rest of the ingredients, including the reserved onions and ghee. Cover tightly. Cook over low heat for 1 hour. Check that the meat is cooked through; if it is not cooked, return to the heat, and cook for an additional 15 minutes. Mix well before serving.

## COOK'S TIP
TO ENHANCE THE FLAVOR OF THE RICE, ADD 4 BLACK PEPPERCORNS AND 1 TEASPOON OF BLACK CUMIN SEEDS WITH THE CINNAMON IN STEP 4.

# THAI RED CHICKEN CURRY

**SERVES 2–4**

**PREPARATION
30 MINUTES
COOKING
40 MINUTES**

THAI CURRY PASTE IS A PASTE OF AROMATIC HERBS, SPICES, AND VEGETABLES THAT IS A POPULAR FLAVORING IN THAI CUISINE. IT COMES IN DIFFERENT VARIETIES. RED CURRY PASTE TENDS TO VARY IN SPICINESS, WHILE GREEN CURRY PASTE IS THE HOTTEST, AND YELLOW IS THE MILDEST.

## INGREDIENTS
- 6 GARLIC CLOVES, CHOPPED
- 2 FRESH RED CHILES, CHOPPED
- 2 TBSP CHOPPED FRESH LEMONGRASS
- 1 TSP FINELY GRATED LIME ZEST
- 1 TBSP CHOPPED FRESH KAFFIR LIME LEAVES
- 1 TBSP THAI RED CURRY PASTE
- 1 TBSP CORIANDER SEEDS, TOASTED AND CRUSHED
- 1 TBSP CHILI OIL
- 4 SKINLESS, BONELESS CHICKEN BREASTS, SLICED
- 1¼ CUPS COCONUT MILK
- 1¼ CUPS CHICKEN STOCK
- 1 TBSP SOY SAUCE
- ⅓ CUP SHELLED UNSALTED PEANUTS, TOASTED AND GROUND
- 3 SCALLIONS, DIAGONALLY SLICED
- 1 RED BELL PEPPER, SEEDED AND SLICED
- 3 THAI EGGPLANTS, SLICED
- 2 TBSP CHOPPED FRESH THAI BASIL OR FRESH CILANTRO
- 1–2 TBSP CHOPPED FRESH CILANTRO, TO GARNISH
- FRESHLY COOKED JASMINE RICE, TO SERVE

**1** Place the garlic, chiles, lemongrass, lime zest, lime leaves, curry paste, and coriander seeds in a food processor and process until the mixture is smooth.

**2** Heat the oil in a preheated wok or large skillet over high heat. Add the chicken and garlic mixture and stir-fry for 5 minutes. Add the coconut milk, stock, and soy sauce and bring to a boil. Reduce the heat and cook, stirring, for an additional 3 minutes. Stir in the ground peanuts and simmer for 20 minutes.

**3** Add the scallions, bell pepper, and eggplants and simmer, stirring occasionally, for an additional 10 minutes. Remove from the heat, stir in the basil, and garnish with cilantro. Serve immediately with freshly cooked jasmine rice.

# COQ AU VIN

THIS IS A DELICIOUS CHICKEN CASSEROLE, COOKED IN RED WINE WITH PEARL ONIONS AND MUSHROOMS. LIKE ALL CASSEROLES, THIS BENEFITS FROM BEING MADE THE DAY BEFORE. COOL IT QUICKLY AND THEN REHEAT IT WHEN NEEDED.

**SERVES 8**

**PREPARATION**
**40 MINUTES**
**COOKING**
**2 HOURS**

## INGREDIENTS
- 2 TBSP ALL-PURPOSE FLOUR
- 4 LB/1.8 KG FRESH CHICKEN, CUT INTO 8 PIECES (ASK YOUR BUTCHER TO DO THIS OR USE 8 CHICKEN JOINTS)
- 2 TBSP OLIVE OIL
- 2 TBSP BUTTER
- 8 OZ/225 G LARDONS OR FATTY BACON, CUT INTO STRIPS
- 1 LB/450 G PEARL ONIONS, PEELED
- 3 CUPS RED WINE
- 2 GARLIC CLOVES, PEELED AND CRUSHED
- 1 BOUQUET GARNI
- 4¾ CUPS WHITE MUSHROOMS
- SALT AND PEPPER

**1** Preheat the oven to 350°F/180°C. Season the flour and put it into a large plastic bag. Add the chicken and shake well to coat it evenly. Heat the oil and butter in the casserole dish. Cook the chicken over high heat for 5–6 minutes, until browned. You will need to do this in two batches. Lift it out of the casserole and keep warm. Cook the bacon in the casserole for 3–4 minutes, until crisp and well colored. Lift it out and keep it warm.

**2** Cook the onions over high heat for 4–5 minutes, until they begin to brown. Pour in the wine and stir well to remove any sediment from the bottom of the casserole dish.

**3** Return the bacon and chicken to the casserole dish and add the garlic and bouquet garni. Bring to a boil, cover, then cook in the center of the preheated oven for 1¼ hours.

**4** Add the mushrooms and cook for an additional 15 minutes. Discard the bouquet garni and use a slotted spoon to lift out the chicken pieces, bacon, onion, and mushrooms. Put them in a serving dish and keep them warm.

**5** Return the casserole and its juices to low heat and check for seasoning. Boil rapidly until the sauce is thick and glossy. Pour the sauce over the dish and serve at once.

# ROAST POUSSINS

IN THIS RECIPE, POUSSINS—BABY CHICKENS—ARE STUFFED WITH LEMONGRASS, LIME LEAVES, AND GINGER, COATED WITH A SPICY MARINADE, THEN ROASTED UNTIL GOLDEN. THE RESULT IS A DISH OF SUCCULENT GOLDEN CHICKEN, PAIRED WITH AN EXCITING FUSION OF ASIAN FLAVORS.

**SERVES 4**

**PREPARATION**
**15 MINUTES**
**COOKING**
**45–55 MINUTES**

**INGREDIENTS**
- 4 SMALL POUSSINS, WEIGHING ABOUT 12 OZ–1 LB 2 OZ/ 350–500 G EACH
- 4 BLADES LEMONGRASS
- 4 FRESH KAFFIR LIME LEAVES
- 4 SLICES FRESH GINGER
- ABOUT 6 TBSP COCONUT MILK, FOR BRUSHING
- A MIXTURE OF FRESHLY COOKED WILD RICE AND BASMATI RICE, TO SERVE

**FOR THE MARINADE**
- 4 GARLIC CLOVES, PEELED
- 2 FRESH CILANTRO ROOTS
- 1 TBSP LIGHT SOY SAUCE
- SALT AND PEPPER

**TO GARNISH**
- FRESH CILANTRO LEAVES
- LIME WEDGES

**1** Preheat the oven to 375°F/190°C. Carefully wash the poussins and pat dry on paper towels.

**2** Place all the ingredients for the marinade in a blender and puree until smooth. Alternatively, grind to a paste with a pestle and mortar.

**3** Rub the marinade mixture into the skin of the poussins, using the back of a spoon to spread it evenly over the skins.

**4** Place a blade of lemongrass, a lime leaf, and a piece of ginger in the cavity of each poussin.

**5** Place the poussins in a roasting pan and brush lightly with the coconut milk. Roast in the preheated oven for 30 minutes.

**6** Remove from the oven, brush again with coconut milk, then return to the oven and cook for an additional 15–25 minutes, or until golden and cooked through, depending upon the size of the poussin. The poussins are cooked if the juices run clear when a skewer is inserted into the thickest part of the meat.

**7** Serve the poussins with the pan juices poured over. Garnish with fresh cilantro leaves and lime wedges and serve with rice.

# DUCK BREASTS WITH CHILI & LIME

**SERVES 4**

**PREPARATION**
**15 MINUTES, PLUS**
**3–8 HOURS' MARINATING**
**COOKING**
**10 MINUTES**

THESE DUCK BREASTS ARE MARVELOUSLY COMPLEMENTED BY THE LIME MARINADE AND PLUM JELLY. THE ACIDITY OF THE LIME CUTS THROUGH THE RICHNESS OF THE DUCK BEAUTIFULLY. DUCK IS A VERY FATTY MEAT, SO DRAIN OFF AS MUCH EXCESS FAT AS YOU CAN DURING COOKING.

**INGREDIENTS**
- 4 BONELESS DUCK BREASTS
- 1 TSP VEGETABLE OIL
- ½ CUP CHICKEN STOCK
- 2 TBSP PLUM JELLY
- SALT AND PEPPER

**FOR THE MARINADE**
- 2 GARLIC CLOVES, CRUSHED
- 4 TSP BROWN SUGAR
- 3 TBSP LIME JUICE
- 1 TBSP SOY SAUCE
- 1 TSP CHILI SAUCE

**TO SERVE**
- MIXED SALAD GREENS
- FRESHLY COOKED RICE

**1** To make the marinade, mix together the garlic, sugar, lime juice, and the soy and chili sauces.

**2** Using a small sharp knife, cut deep slashes in the skin of the duck breasts to make a diamond pattern. Place the duck breasts in a wide, nonmetallic dish.

**3** Spoon the marinade over the duck breasts, turning well to coat them evenly in the mixture. Cover the dish with plastic wrap and then let it marinate in the refrigerator for at least 3 hours, or overnight.

**4** Drain the duck, reserving the marinade. Heat a large, heavy-bottom skillet until very hot and brush with the oil. Add the duck breasts, skin-side down, and cook for 4–5 minutes, until the skin is browned and crisp. Pour off the excess fat.

**5** Turn the duck breasts and cook on the other side for 2–3 minutes to brown. Add the reserved marinade, stock, and jelly, and simmer for 2 minutes. Adjust the seasoning to taste and serve hot, with the juices spooned over the meat, and the salad greens and freshly cooked rice.

# PEKING DUCK

NO COOKBOOK WOULD BE COMPLETE WITHOUT THIS FAMOUS DISH. IN THIS VERSION, DELICIOUS CRISPY DUCK IS SERVED WITH CRÊPES AND A TANGY SAUCE FOR A REALLY SPECIAL MEAL. IT IS AN EXCELLENT CHOICE FOR A DINNER PARTY.

**SERVES 4**

**PREPARATION**
30 MINUTES, PLUS
8 HOURS' STANDING
**COOKING**
1 HOUR 25 MINUTES–
1½ HOURS

**INGREDIENTS**
- 4 LB/1.8 KG DUCK
- 7½ CUPS BOILING WATER
- 4 TBSP HONEY
- 2 TSP DARK SOY SAUCE
- CARROT STRIPS, TO GARNISH

**FOR THE SAUCE**
- 2 TBSP SESAME OIL
- ½ CUP PEKING SAUCE
- SCANT ⅔ CUP SUPERFINE SUGAR
- ½ CUP WATER

**TO SERVE**
- CHINESE CRÊPES
- THIN CUCUMBER STICKS
- SHREDDED SCALLIONS

**COOK'S TIP**
TRY GARNISHING THIS DISH WITH SCALLION CURLS. CUT THE STALKS INTO 2-INCH/5-CM LENGTHS, MAKE SLITS DOWN THE LENGTHS AT NARROW INTERVALS TO ALMOST HALFWAY, THEN TURN AND DO THE SAME AT THE OTHER END. LEAVE IN A BOWL OF ICE WATER TO CURL.

**1** Place the duck on a rack set over a roasting pan and pour 5 cups of the boiling water over it. Remove the duck and rack and discard the water. Pat dry with paper towels, replace the duck and rack, and set aside for several hours.

**2** Mix the honey, 2½ cups of boiling water, and soy sauce together. Brush the mixture as a glaze over the skin and inside the duck. Set aside the remaining glaze. Set aside for 1 hour, until the glaze has dried.

**3** Coat the duck with another layer of glaze. Let it dry and repeat until all of the glaze is used.

**4** Preheat the oven to 375°F/190°C. To make the sauce, heat the oil in a saucepan. Add the Peking sauce, sugar, and water. Simmer for 2–3 minutes, until thickened. Cool and chill until required.

**5** Cook the duck in the preheated oven for 30 minutes. Turn the duck over and cook for 20 minutes. Turn the duck again and cook for 20–30 minutes, or until the meat is cooked through and the skin is crisp.

**6** Remove the duck from the oven and let it stand for 10 minutes. Meanwhile, heat the Chinese crêpes in a bamboo steamer for 5–7 minutes. Cut the skin and duck meat into strips and divide among individual serving plates. Garnish with carrot strips and serve with the crêpes, thin cucumber sticks, shredded scallions, and sauce.

# ROAST DUCK WITH APPLE

**SERVES 4**

**PREPARATION**
**20 MINUTES**
**COOKING**
**1 HOUR**

THIS DISH MAKES AN EXCELLENT SUPPER AND IS FULL OF INTERESTING FLAVORS. THE RICHNESS OF THE DUCK MEAT IN THIS RECIPE CONTRASTS WELL WITH THE APPLES, LEMON, BAY LEAVES, AND APRICOT SAUCE. IF DUCKLING PORTIONS ARE UNAVAILABLE, USE A WHOLE BIRD CUT INTO JOINTS.

**INGREDIENTS**
- 4 DUCKLING PORTIONS, ABOUT 12 OZ/350 G EACH
- 4 TBSP DARK SOY SAUCE
- 2 TBSP BROWN SUGAR
- 2 RED-SKINNED APPLES
- 2 GREEN-SKINNED APPLES
- JUICE OF 1 LEMON
- 2 TBSP HONEY
- A FEW BAY LEAVES
- SALT AND PEPPER
- ASSORTED FRESHLY COOKED VEGETABLES, TO SERVE

**FOR THE APRICOT SAUCE**
- 14 OZ/400 G CANNED APRICOTS IN FRUIT JUICE
- 4 TBSP SWEET SHERRY

**1** Preheat the oven to 375°F/190°C. Wash the duck and trim away any excess fat. Place on a wire rack over a roasting pan and prick all over with a fork or a clean, sharp needle.

**2** Brush the duck with the soy sauce. Sprinkle over the sugar and season with pepper. Cook in the preheated oven, basting occasionally, for 50–60 minutes, or until the meat is cooked through and the juices run clear when a skewer is inserted into the thickest part of the meat.

**3** Meanwhile, core the apples and cut each into 6 wedges, then place in a small bowl and mix with the lemon juice and honey. Transfer to a small roasting pan, add a few bay leaves, and season to taste with salt and pepper. Cook alongside the duck, basting occasionally, for 20–25 minutes, until tender. Discard the bay leaves.

**4** To make the sauce, place the apricots in a blender or food processor with the can juices and the sherry. Process until smooth. Alternatively, mash the apricots with a fork until smooth and mix with the juice and sherry.

**5** Just before serving, heat the apricot sauce in a small pan. Remove the skin from the duck and pat the flesh with paper towels to absorb any fat. Serve the duck with the apple wedges, apricot sauce, and freshly cooked vegetables.

## VARIATION
FRUIT COMPLEMENTS DUCK PERFECTLY. USE CANNED PINEAPPLE IN NATURAL JUICE FOR A DELICIOUS ALTERNATIVE.

# ROAST TURKEY WITH BREAD SAUCE

ROAST TURKEY MAKES AN EXCELLENT TABLE CENTERPIECE FOR CHRISTMAS OR THANKSGIVING. IN THIS RECIPE, CHESTNUTS, SAUSAGE, AND SAGE COMBINE TO MAKE A MARVELOUS STUFFING FOR THE BIRD, WHICH IS COMPLEMENTED BEAUTIFULLY BY A DELICIOUSLY SMOOTH BREAD SAUCE.

**SERVES 8**

**PREPARATION**
**30 MINUTES, PLUS**
**10 MINUTES' RESTING**
**COOKING**
**3¾ HOURS**

**INGREDIENTS**
- 11 LB/5 KG TURKEY
- 4 TBSP BUTTER
- 5 TBSP RED WINE
- 1¾ CUPS CHICKEN STOCK, BOUGHT FRESH OR MADE WITH A BOUILLON CUBE
- 1 TBSP CORNSTARCH
- 1 TSP FRENCH MUSTARD
- 1 TSP SHERRY VINEGAR
- 2 TSP WATER
- ROAST NEW POTATOES, TO SERVE

**FOR THE STUFFING**
- 8 OZ/225 G BULK PORK SAUSAGE
- 8 OZ/225 G UNSWEETENED CHESTNUT PUREE
- ¾ CUP WALNUTS, CHOPPED
- ⅔ CUP PLUMPED DRIED APRICOTS, CHOPPED
- 2 TBSP CHOPPED FRESH PARSLEY
- 2 TBSP CHOPPED FRESH SAGE
- 2 TBSP SNIPPED FRESH CHIVES
- 4–5 TBSP HEAVY CREAM
- SALT AND PEPPER

**FOR THE BREAD SAUCE**
- 1 ONION, PEELED
- 4 CLOVES
- 2½ CUPS MILK
- 2 CUPS FRESH WHITE BREAD CRUMBS
- 4 TBSP BUTTER

**1** Preheat the oven to 425°F/220°C. To make the stuffing, combine the sausage meat and chestnut puree in a bowl, then stir in the walnuts, apricots, and herbs. Stir in enough cream to make a firm, but not dry, mixture. Season to taste with salt and pepper.

**2** Spoon the stuffing into the neck cavity of the turkey and close the flap of skin with a skewer. Place the bird in a large roasting pan and rub all over with 3 tablespoons of the butter. Roast for 1 hour, then reduce the oven temperature to 350°F/180°C and roast for an additional 2½ hours. You may need to pour off the fat from the roasting pan occasionally.

**3** Meanwhile, make the bread sauce. Stud the onion with the cloves, then place in a saucepan with the milk, bread crumbs, and butter. Bring just to boiling point over low heat, then remove from the heat and let it stand in a warm place to infuse. Just before serving, remove the onion and reheat the sauce gently, beating well with a wooden spoon. Season to taste with salt and pepper.

**4** Check that the turkey is cooked by inserting a skewer or the tip of a sharp knife into the thigh; if the juices run clear, it is ready. Transfer the bird to a carving board, cover it loosely with foil, then let it rest.

**5** To make the gravy, skim off the fat from the roasting pan then place the pan on the top of the stove over medium heat. Add the red wine and stir with a wooden spoon, scraping up all the sediment from the bottom of the pan. Stir in the stock. Mix the cornstarch, mustard, vinegar, and the water together in a small bowl, then stir into the wine and stock mixture. Bring to a boil, stirring constantly, until thickened and smooth. Stir in the remaining butter.

**6** Carve the turkey and serve with the warm bread sauce and all the trimmings—including stuffing, roast potatoes, and gravy.

# ROAST PHEASANT WITH RED WINE & HERBS

ROAST PHEASANT IS A DELICIOUS TREAT, AND MAKES A SPLENDID DISH FOR DINNER PARTIES AND ENTERTAINING. IN THIS RECIPE, YOU WILL NEED TO USE YOUNG PHEASANTS, BECAUSE THEIR TENDER FLESH IS JUICY ENOUGH FOR ROASTING AND WILL NOT DRY OUT. OLDER BIRDS ARE NOT SUITABLE.

**SERVES 4**

**PREPARATION**
**20 MINUTES, PLUS**
**15 MINUTES' RESTING**
**COOKING**
**1 HOUR**

**INGREDIENTS**
- SCANT ½ CUP BUTTER, SLIGHTLY SOFTENED
- 1 TBSP CHOPPED FRESH THYME
- 1 TBSP CHOPPED FRESH PARSLEY
- 2 OVEN-READY YOUNG PHEASANTS
- 4 TBSP VEGETABLE OIL
- ½ CUP RED WINE
- SALT AND PEPPER

**TO SERVE**
- ROAST PARSNIPS
- SAUTÉED POTATOES

**1** Preheat the oven to 375°F/190°C. Place the butter in a small bowl and mix in the chopped herbs. Lift the skins off the pheasants, being careful not to tear them, and push the herb butter under the skins. Season to taste with salt and pepper.

**2** Pour the oil into a roasting pan, add the pheasants, and cook in the preheated oven for 45 minutes, basting occasionally. Remove from the oven, pour over the red wine, then return to the oven and cook for an additional 15 minutes, or until cooked through. Check that each bird is cooked by inserting a knife between the legs and body. If the juices run clear, they are cooked.

**3** Remove the pheasants from the oven, cover with foil, and let them stand for 15 minutes. Divide between individual serving plates, and serve with roast parsnips and sautéed potatoes.

# QUAILS WITH GRAPES

THIS IS A VERY POPULAR GAME DISH IN SPAIN, AND APPEARS ON MANY RESTAURANT MENUS. THE CLOVES AND BRANDY GIVE A MARVELOUS AROMATIC FLAVOR TO THE BIRDS AND GRAPES, AND THE WEDGES OF POTATO PANCAKE PROVIDE A LOVELY CONTRAST IN TEXTURE AND FLAVOR.

**SERVES 4**

**PREPARATION**
**30 MINUTES, PLUS**
**30 MINUTES' COOLING**
**COOKING**
**1 HOUR**

**INGREDIENTS**
- 4 TBSP OLIVE OIL
- 8 QUAILS, CLEANED
- 10 OZ/280 G GREEN SEEDLESS GRAPES
- 1 CUP GRAPE JUICE
- 2 CLOVES
- ABOUT ⅔ CUP WATER
- 2 TBSP SPANISH BRANDY
- SALT AND PEPPER

**FOR THE POTATO PANCAKE**
- 1 LB 5 OZ/600 G UNPEELED POTATOES
- 2½ TBSP UNSALTED BUTTER OR PORK FAT
- 1½ TBSP OLIVE OIL

**VARIATION**
INSTEAD OF SERVING THESE QUAILS WITH POTATO PANCAKES, TRY SERVING THEM WITH RICE COOKED IN VEGETABLE STOCK AND SAFFRON.

**1** Preheat the oven to 450°F/230°C. To make the pancake, parboil the potatoes for 10 minutes. Drain and cool completely, then peel, coarsely grate, and season with salt and pepper to taste. Set aside until required.

**2** Heat the 4 tablespoons of oil in a heavy-bottom skillet or ovenproof casserole large enough to hold the quails in a single layer over medium heat. Add the quails and cook on all sides until they are golden brown.

**3** Add the grapes, grape juice, cloves, enough water to come halfway up the side of the quails, and salt and pepper to taste. Cover and simmer for 20 minutes. Transfer the quails and all the juices to a roasting pan, or casserole, and sprinkle with brandy. Roast, uncovered, in the preheated oven for 10 minutes.

**4** Meanwhile, to make the potato pancake, melt the butter or pork fat with the oil in a 12-inch/30-cm nonstick skillet over high heat. When the fat is hot, add the grated potato and spread into an even layer. Reduce the heat and simmer for 10 minutes. Place a plate over the skillet and, wearing oven mitts,

invert them so the potato pancake drops onto the plate. Slide the potato back into the skillet and continue cooking for 10 minutes, or until cooked through and crisp. Slide it out of the skillet and cut into 4 wedges. Keep the pancake warm until the quail is ready.

**5** Place a potato pancake wedge and 2 quails on each individual serving plate. Taste the grape sauce and adjust the seasoning if necessary. Spoon the sauce over the quails and serve

# CHARGRILLED VENISON STEAKS

**SERVES 4**

**PREPARATION**
**15 MINUTES, PLUS
8 HOURS' MARINATING**
**COOKING**
**12–24 MINUTES**

**INGREDIENTS**
- 4 VENISON STEAKS
- ⅔ CUP RED WINE
- 2 TBSP SUNFLOWER OIL
- 1 TBSP RED WINE VINEGAR
- 1 ONION, CHOPPED
- FRESH PARSLEY SPRIGS
- 2 FRESH THYME SPRIGS
- 1 BAY LEAF
- 1 TSP SUPERFINE SUGAR
- ½ TSP MILD MUSTARD
- SALT AND PEPPER
- FRESH THYME SPRIGS, TO GARNISH
- BAKED POTATOES, TO SERVE

VENISON HAS A GOOD STRONG FLAVOR, WHICH MAKES IT AN IDEAL MEAT TO BARBECUE OR BROIL. IN THIS RECIPE, THE VENISON STEAKS ARE FIRST MARINATED IN A DELICIOUS COMBINATION OF WINE, OIL, SUGAR, AND HERBS, AND THEN COOKED TO RELEASE ALL THEIR DELICIOUS FLAVOR.

**1** Place the venison steaks in a shallow, nonmetallic dish.

**2** Combine the wine, oil, wine vinegar, onion, fresh parsley, thyme, bay leaf, sugar, mustard, and salt and pepper to taste in a screw-top jar and shake vigorously until well combined. Alternatively, using a fork, whisk the ingredients together in a bowl.

**3** Pour the marinade mixture over the venison, cover, and marinate in the refrigerator overnight. Turn the steaks over in the mixture occasionally so that the meat is well coated.

**4** Preheat the barbecue to high. Lift out the venison and cook over hot coals, searing the meat over the hottest part of the barbecue for 2 minutes on each side. Alternatively, cook under a hot broiler.

**5** Move the meat to an area with slightly less intense heat, or turn down the broiler to medium, and cook for an additional 4–10 minutes on each side, according to taste. Test by inserting the tip of a knife into the meat—the juices will range from red when the meat is still rare to clear as the meat becomes well cooked.

**6** Transfer the steaks to serving plates, garnish with fresh thyme sprigs, and serve immediately with baked potatoes.

## COOK'S TIP

FARMED VENISON IS AVAILABLE ALL YEAR ROUND. LOOK OUT FOR IT IN THE MEAT SECTION OF THE SUPERMARKET OR ORDER IT FROM AN INDEPENDENT BUTCHER. MARINATING OVERNIGHT TENDERIZES THE MEAT.

# CHAPTER 5

# VEGETABLES AND SALADS

VEGETABLES AND SALADS ARE VERY GOOD FOR YOU AND EXTREMELY VERSATILE. YOU CAN COOK VEGETABLES IN COUNTLESS WAYS, FROM BOILING, STEAMING, AND PAN-FRYING, TO BAKING, ROASTING, AND STEWING. MANY OF THEM CAN BE EATEN RAW, TOO. YOU CAN ALSO PRESENT THEM IN A MULTITUDE OF WAYS, FROM MASHED OR PUREED TO JULIENNED.

### Brassicas

These vegetables are excellent boiled, steamed, or stir-fried. Take care not to overcook them, however—brassicas are best when tender but still slightly crisp to the bite.

### Cabbages

These come in many shapes and colors, ranging from white and green to red. Look for cabbage that is crisp and fresh. You can wash and eat it raw in salads and coleslaw, or cook it in a variety of ways, such as boiling, steaming, or stir-frying.

### Broccoli

This popular vegetable is available all year round and is very nutritious. It can be boiled, steamed, stir-fried, sautéed, or baked.

### Napa cabbage

These crinkly, cream-colored leaves with green tips are available all year round. They can be used raw in salads, or sautéed, steamed, braised, or baked. They are also popular in stir-fries.

### Brussels sprouts

These look like tiny cabbages and are, in fact, related to the cabbage family. They are available fresh during the fall and winter, or frozen all year round. They are very good boiled or steamed, or shredded and added to stir-fries. However, due to their sulfur content, they have a strong flavor that some people dislike.

### Cauliflower

Like cabbage, cauliflower comes in different colors: white, green, and red, although the white variety is the most popular. You can eat it raw, or cook it by boiling, steaming, stir-frying, sautéeing, or baking.

### Bok choy

This is available all year round. It looks a little like celery and has crunchy white stalks and dark green leaves. It is related to Napa cabbage botanically, and is often confused with it. However, it does have similar uses and can be used raw in salads, or stir-fried, sautéed, steamed, braised, or baked.

Broccoli

Cabbage leaf

Brussels sprouts

Cauliflower

Napa cabbage

## The onion family

These members of the onion family contain sulfuric compounds that give them their unmistakable aroma and flavor. Their taste varies from mild to pungent.

### Leeks

These have a very mild onion flavor and range in size from small baby leeks to large. They can be boiled, steamed, sautéed, stir-fried, or baked, and can be substituted for onions in most recipes.

### Garlic

This versatile bulb was popular with the ancient Egyptians for its medicinal qualities and has many uses in modern cooking. It has an unmistakable taste, due to its sulfur content, and adds delicious flavor to many different recipes. It can be boiled, steamed, sautéed, stir-fried, baked, and roasted. When garlic is cooked with wine, it gives off a marvelous flavor and the combination is excellent in soups and sauces. It can also be used to liven up dressings.

### Onions

These are available all year round in a variety of colors, from yellow and white to red. They also range in size from tiny pearl onions, and medium-size onions, to the large Spanish onions, and vary in flavor from mildly pungent to very strong. Once peeled and trimmed, they can be eaten raw in salads or as a garnish, or cooked in a wide variety of dishes, from stir-fries to bakes. You can also pickle onions.

### Shallots

These are small onions that resemble large garlic cloves when they are peeled. Use shallots when you need a milder onion flavor. They are particularly good in stir-fries and bakes, and in kabobs.

### Scallions

These very small onions are available all year round but their peak season is during the spring and summer. They can be used raw in salads or sliced to make an attractive garnish, or they can be boiled, steamed, sautéed, or baked. Scallions are also excellent in stir-fries and soups.

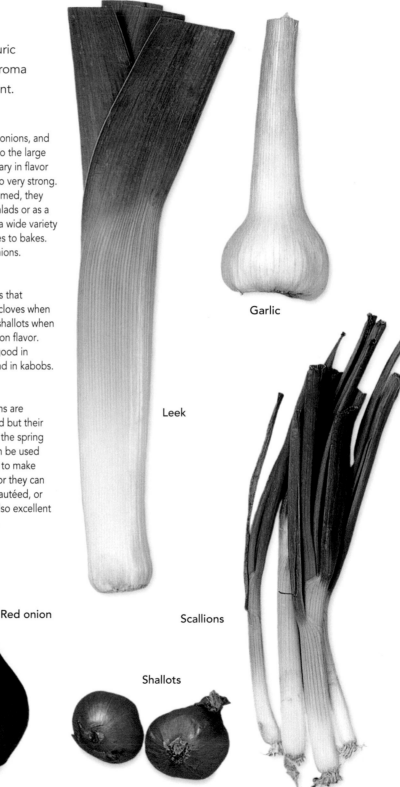

Garlic

Leek

Scallions

Shallots

Yellow onion

Red onion

## Vegetable fruits

The tastes of the vegetables in this category vary from the mild, creamy flavor of avocados, to the fiery heat of chiles. They are popular in a wide range of international dishes.

### Eggplants

These come in different sizes and colors, but the most popular is the large, deep-purple variety. Eggplants must always be cooked, and unless you are using them in a moist recipe with plenty of liquid, you should degorge them to remove any bitter juices first. Simply cut the eggplant into slices about ½ inch/1 cm thick, spread them out in a large, shallow dish, and sprinkle over plenty of salt. Let the slices stand for 30 minutes, then transfer to a colander and rinse off the salt with plenty of cold running water. Pat dry with paper towels, then use in your chosen recipe.

### Avocados

These are green or purplish-black vegetable fruits that are shaped like pears but have a soft, buttery interior. Look for avocados that are just beginning to yield to the touch when pressed, and have no bruises. You can use them halved as an appetizer, sliced in salads, or mashed in dips. Avocados discolor quickly when cut, so use them straight away after cutting, or brush them with lemon juice to prevent discoloration.

### Chiles

These fiery vegetable fruits usually come in red or green, and in many different sizes and shapes, from ¼ inch/5 mm to 12 inches/30 cm in length. Generally, the smaller the chile, the hotter the flavor; the small ones can be so fiery that they can burn the skin. Always wear protective gloves when handling chiles, and keep them away from your eyes. Chiles add a spicy kick to many recipes and are particularly good in sauces and stir-fries, and in dishes such as chili con carne. Seed chiles before use in order to reduce their fiery heat.

### Bell peppers

When bell peppers are young they are green, then as they ripen and get sweeter they turn red. You can also get yellow, orange, purple, and brown bell peppers, or bell peppers in different shapes, such as the long pointed red Mediterranean peppers. Once sliced and seeded, they can be used raw in salads or as crudités, or you can cook them in a variety of dishes. Roasting or broiling brings out their sweet flavor. They can also be sautéed, stir-fried, steamed, braised, and baked.

### Tomatoes

These are available all year round and come in many different sizes and shapes, from tiny cherry tomatoes to large beefsteak tomatoes. Make sure your tomatoes are firm when you buy them. Tomatoes left on the vine are particularly flavorful. In order to preserve their flavor, store them on the vine until you intend to use them. You can eat tomatoes raw in salads, or cook them. They make good sauces, soups, and pizza toppings, and are delicious sautéed, stir-fried, broiled, and baked.

Peas                    Snow peas

Green beans

## Pod vegetables

Pod vegetables have a delicious flavor, and some varieties, such as sugar snap peas, are tender enough to have an edible pod, so you can eat them whole. They are very good stir-fried.

### Pods

These are young vegetables that have edible pods, such as sugar snap peas, snow peas, green beans, and string beans. They have a delicious sweet flavor and can be steamed, boiled, sautéed, or stir-fried.

### Shelled peas and beans

These are seeds that are allowed to grow in the pod; they are served shelled. They include garden peas, petit pois (smaller peas), and fava beans, which are green and slightly kidney-shaped. All of them can be boiled or steamed.

## Other vegetables

Mushrooms and corn are delicious in salads, risottos, and stir-fries, but try experimenting with more exotic varieties of vegetables, too, such as Asian vegetables and seaweeds.

### Exotic vegetables

There is a great variety of exotic vegetables available nowadays, and they come from all over the world. Some of the most popular include kombu, which is a dried form of kelp that is used in Japanese cooking; daikon, a long white root that is used in Asian cooking; and wakame, an edible seaweed popular in Asia.

### Corn

The most popular type of corn these days is yellow corn. The husks and silks need to be removed before cooking, then you can simply cook the corn whole on the cob, or remove the kernels and cook them on their own. Corn comes into season in the summer months, but you can also buy it frozen or canned all year round.

It is delicious boiled on the cob, or the kernels can be cooked and used in soups, salads, and bakes. You can also buy baby corn, which can be boiled, steamed, or stir-fried.

### Mushrooms

Both cultivated or wild mushrooms are available all year round. The former include the common white, cremini, and large, flat portobello mushrooms. Wild mushrooms vary enormously in size, shape, and color, and include shiitake, porcini, and pieds de moutons. They are available fresh or dried. Mushrooms can absorb a lot of water, so it is better to wipe them with a clean, damp cloth instead of washing them. They can be sautéed, stir-fried, deep-fried in batter, broiled, or baked.

## Squashes

Squashes are becoming increasingly popular these days, and we are becoming more creative with them. Small varieties can be particularly flavorful—for example, try mini-zucchini.

### Zucchini

This member of the squash family is shaped like a cucumber and comes in various shades of green, sometimes with yellow stripes. It also comes in a variety of sizes, from 4 inches/10 cm to 2 feet/60 cm long (the largest are known as marrows). The smaller varieties tend to have the most flavor. Zucchini are available all year round, and are very versatile. They can be steamed, broiled, stir-fried, charbroiled, sautéed, deep-fried, baked, and roasted, or you can eat them raw in salads. Zucchini flowers, if you can get them, are marvelous stuffed and cooked, or battered and fried.

### Cucumbers

Although best known as a salad vegetable, the cucumber is, in fact, a member of the squash family. It can be cut into crudités, with or without its skin, and served raw with dips, or lightly sautéed or stir-fried.

### Pumpkins

These large squashes are available in the fall and winter. The large variety is popular at Halloween, when it is carved out and made into a mask or lantern. The smaller, orange variety has a sweeter flavor and is more suitable for cooking. Pumpkin pie is a particular favorite. You can also use pumpkin in soups and casseroles.

### Other squashes

Butternut, acorn, and spaghetti squashes are classed as winter squashes. They are large and have thick skins and firm flesh. Once seeded, they can be roasted, baked, or steamed. Summer squashes, such as patty pans, are smaller and can be cooked fairly quickly by sautéeing, steaming, or baking.

Corn

White mushrooms

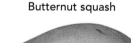
Butternut squash

# LEEK & POTATO SOUP

**SERVES 4**

**PREPARATION**
**15–20 MINUTES, PLUS**
**10 MINUTES' COOLING**
**COOKING**
**35 MINUTES**

LEEKS AND POTATOES MAKE A MARVELOUS COMBINATION, ESPECIALLY WHEN TEAMED WITH HERBS AND CREAM. IN THIS DISH, A DELICIOUS SMOKY FLAVOR HAS BEEN INTRODUCED WITH THE ADDITION OF THE SMOKED CHEESE. IT MAKES A SATISFYING, WARMING SOUP FOR ANY OCCASION.

**INGREDIENTS**
- 2 TBSP BUTTER
- 2 GARLIC CLOVES, CHOPPED
- 3 LARGE LEEKS
- 1 LB/450 G POTATOES
- 1 TBSP CHOPPED FRESH PARSLEY, PLUS EXTRA TO GARNISH
- 1 TBSP CHOPPED FRESH OREGANO
- 1 BAY LEAF
- 3½ CUPS VEGETABLE STOCK
- SCANT 1 CUP SOUR CREAM
- HEAPING ¾ CUP SMOKED FIRM CHEESE, GRATED
- SALT AND PEPPER
- FRESH CHIVES, TO GARNISH
- THICK SLICES OF FRESH CRUSTY BREAD, TO SERVE

**1** Melt the butter in a large saucepan over medium heat. Add the garlic and cook, stirring, for 1 minute. Add the leeks and cook, stirring, for an additional 2 minutes. Add the potatoes, herbs, and stock, and season to taste with salt and pepper. Bring to a boil, then reduce the heat, cover the pan, and simmer for 25 minutes. Remove from the heat, cool for 10 minutes, then remove and discard the bay leaf.

**2** Transfer half of the soup to a food processor and process until smooth (you may need to do this in batches). Return to the pan with the rest of the soup, stir in the sour cream, and reheat gently. Season to taste with salt and pepper.

**3** Remove from the heat and stir in the cheese. Ladle into serving bowls and garnish with chives and chopped fresh parsley. Serve with slices of fresh crusty bread.

## VARIATION

A SMOKED FIRM CHEESE, SUCH AS SMOKED CHEDDAR, WILL GIVE A DELICIOUS FLAVOR TO THIS SOUP, BUT IF YOU PREFER YOU CAN REPLACE IT WITH AN UNSMOKED FIRM CHEESE, SUCH AS REGULAR CHEDDAR. YOU CAN ALSO USE CRÈME FRAÎCHE OR DRAINED PLAIN YOGURT INSTEAD OF THE CREAM.

# ONION SOUP

**SERVES 4**

**PREPARATION
20 MINUTES
COOKING
1 HOUR 10 MINUTES–
1 HOUR 15 MINUTES**

MORE LIKE A THICK ONION STEW THAN A SOUP, THIS TRADITIONAL RECIPE, WHICH INCLUDES A SLUG OF BRANDY, RECALLS THE DAYS WHEN THE LES HALLES DISTRICT OF PARIS WAS HOME TO THE CITY'S MEAT, SEAFOOD, AND FRUIT AND VEGETABLE MARKETS, AND KNOWN AS THE "BELLY OF PARIS."

**INGREDIENTS**
- 6 TBSP BUTTER
- 2 TBSP OLIVE OIL
- 1 LB 10 OZ/750 G ONIONS, THINLY SLICED
- 1 TSP SUGAR
- ½ TSP SALT
- 1½ TBSP ALL-PURPOSE FLOUR
- 2½ CUPS HOT BEEF STOCK
- 4 TBSP BRANDY
- HEAPING 1 CUP GRUYÈRE CHEESE, OR HALF GRUYÈRE AND HALF PARMESAN CHEESE, GRATED
- SALT AND PEPPER

**FOR THE CROÛTES**
- 8 SLICES FRENCH BREAD, ABOUT ½ INCH/1 CM THICK
- 1 GARLIC CLOVE, HALVED

**1** Melt the butter with the oil in a large, heavy-bottom pan with a tight-fitting lid, or an ovenproof casserole, over medium-high heat. Stir in the onions, sugar, and salt, then reduce the heat to low. Cover the surface with a piece of wet wax paper or the lid and cook for 20–30 minutes, stirring occasionally, until the onions are a rich, dark golden brown. Uncover and then stir constantly when they begin to darken, because they can burn easily.

**2** Sprinkle the flour over the onions and continue cooking, stirring for 2 minutes. Stir in the hot stock and simmer, partially covered, for an additional 15 minutes, skimming the surface if necessary.

**3** To make the croûtes, preheat the broiler to high and the oven to 400°F/200°C. Arrange the bread slices on the broiler rack and toast for 1–2 minutes, or until golden and crisp. Flip the slices over and repeat on the other side. Rub the top of each bread slice while it is still hot with the garlic halves, then set aside until required.

**4** Stir the brandy into the soup and season to taste with salt and pepper. At this point, the soup can be left for up to a day, but reheat it before proceeding.

**5** Divide the toasted bread between 4 heatproof soup bowls. Ladle over the soup, then top each with one-quarter of the cheese. Place the bowls in the oven for 20 minutes, or until the cheese is golden and bubbling. Let the soup stand for a couple of minutes before serving.

## COOK'S TIP
THE TOASTED CROÛTES ARE A GOOD WAY TO USE UP DAY-OLD FRENCH BREAD. BE CAREFUL, HOWEVER, YOU DON'T CUT THE BREAD TOO THICK, OR IT WILL ABSORB ALL THE LIQUID.

# CLASSIC ROAST POTATOES

**SERVES 4**

**PREPARATION**
**10 MINUTES**
**COOKING**
**1½ HOURS**

THERE IS NOTHING LIKE LOVINGLY COOKED ROAST POTATOES, GOLDEN AND CRISP ON THE OUTSIDE, AND BEAUTIFULLY FLUFFY ON THE INSIDE. THESE POTATOES HAVE A LITTLE PAPRIKA FOR ADDED SPICE AND COLOR. SIMPLY PILE THEM INTO A BOWL AND WATCH THEM DISAPPEAR.

**INGREDIENTS**
- 2 LB/900 G MEDIUM–LARGE STARCHY POTATOES, PEELED
- ½ TSP SALT
- PAPRIKA
- HEAPING ⅓ CUP VEGETABLE OIL
- PEPPER

**1** Preheat the oven to 400°F/200°C. Using a sharp knife, cut the potatoes in half, or into quarters if very large, then arrange in a roasting pan. Sprinkle over the salt, then season to taste with paprika and pepper.

**2** Pour the oil over the potatoes, then turn them in the oil until well coated. Transfer to the preheated oven and roast, basting occasionally, for 1½ hours, or until golden brown and tender. Remove from the oven and serve immediately.

## VARIATION

FOR SOMETHING DIFFERENT, TRY ADDING 1 CRUSHED GARLIC CLOVE AND 1 TABLESPOON OF LEMON JUICE TO THE OIL BEFORE POURING OVER THE POTATOES. THEY WILL ADD A DELICIOUSLY DIFFERENT FLAVOR AND THE AROMA WILL BE IRRESISTIBLE.

# ROASTED GARLIC MASHED POTATOES

HERE ARE MASHED POTATOES WITH A DIFFERENCE. TANTALIZE EVERY MEMBER OF YOUR HOUSEHOLD WITH THESE DELICIOUS POTATOES MASHED WITH JUICY BULBS OF ROASTED GARLIC AND GARNISHED WITH SPRIGS OF FRAGRANT, FRESH PARSLEY. AN UNFORGETTABLE COMBINATION.

**SERVES 4**

**PREPARATION
20 MINUTES
COOKING
1 HOUR**

**INGREDIENTS**
- 2 WHOLE BULBS OF GARLIC
- 1 TBSP OLIVE OIL
- 2 LB/900 G STARCHY POTATOES, PEELED
- ½ CUP MILK
- 4 TBSP BUTTER
- SALT AND PEPPER
- FRESH PARSLEY SPRIGS, TO GARNISH

**1** Preheat the oven to 350°F/180°C. Separate the garlic cloves, place on a large piece of foil, and drizzle with the oil. Wrap the garlic loosely in the foil and roast in the preheated oven for 1 hour, or until very tender. Cool slightly.

**2** Twenty minutes before the end of the cooking time, cut the potatoes into chunks, then cook in salted boiling water for 15 minutes, or until tender.

**3** Meanwhile, squeeze the cooled garlic cloves out of their skins and push through a strainer into a pan. Add the milk, butter, and salt and pepper to taste. Heat gently, until the butter has melted.

**4** Drain the cooked potatoes, then mash in the pan until smooth. Pour in the garlic mixture and heat gently, stirring, until the ingredients are combined. Serve hot garnished with fresh parsley sprigs.

# SCALLOPED POTATOES

COOKING THE HUMBLE POTATO IN THIS CLASSIC WAY ELEVATES IT TO GOURMET HEIGHTS. THIS DELICIOUS, CREAMY DISH MAKES AN EXCELLENT ACCOMPANIMENT FOR A VEGETABLE BAKE—THEY CAN BE COOKED IN THE OVEN AT THE SAME TIME AND SERVED TOGETHER.

**SERVES 4**

**PREPARATION
20 MINUTES
COOKING
1–1½ HOURS**

## INGREDIENTS

- 2 TBSP BUTTER, DICED, PLUS EXTRA FOR GREASING
- 2 LB/900 G WAXY POTATOES, PEELED AND VERY THINLY SLICED
- 1 LARGE ONION, FINELY CHOPPED
- 2 CUPS EMMENTAL OR GRUYÈRE CHEESE, GRATED
- ⅔ CUP LIGHT CREAM
- SALT AND PEPPER

**1** Preheat the oven to 375°F/190°C. Grease an ovenproof casserole with butter. Make a layer of potato slices in the bottom, dot with a little butter, sprinkle with onion and cheese, and season to taste with salt and pepper. Pour in 2 tablespoons of the cream. Continue making layers in this way, ending with a layer of cheese. Pour over any remaining cream.

**2** Cover and bake in the preheated oven for 1–1½ hours, or until the potatoes are tender.

**3** Preheat the broiler to medium. Remove the lid and place the casserole under the hot broiler for 5 minutes, or until the top of the bake is golden brown and bubbling. Serve immediately.

## VARIATION

FOR ANNA POTATOES, POUR 1 CUP OF MELTED BUTTER BETWEEN 2 LB/900 G OF SEASONED, LAYERED POTATO SLICES. BAKE AT 425°F/220°C FOR 1 HOUR.

# STUFFED BAKED POTATOES

THESE MARVELOUS BAKED POTATOES MAKE AN EXCELLENT LUNCH OR SUPPER DISH. THEY ARE SUITABLE FOR VEGETARIANS IF YOU OMIT THE HAM AND USE A CHEESE MADE WITH NONANIMAL RENNET. THEY ARE EASY TO PREPARE AND THE IDEAL SOLUTION FOR COOKS ON A TIGHT BUDGET.

**SERVES 4**

**PREPARATION
15 MINUTES
COOKING
1¼ HOURS**

**INGREDIENTS**
- 2 LB/900 G BAKING POTATOES, WASHED
- 2 TBSP VEGETABLE OIL
- 1 TSP COARSE SEA SALT
- ½ CUP BUTTER
- 1 SMALL ONION, CHOPPED
- 1 CUP GRATED CHEDDAR CHEESE OR CRUMBLED BLUE CHEESE
- SALT AND PEPPER
- FRESH CHIVES, TO GARNISH

**OPTIONAL INGREDIENTS**
- 4 TBSP COOKED HAM OR BACON, DICED
- 4 TBSP CORN KERNELS
- 4 TBSP COOKED MUSHROOMS, ZUCCHINI, OR BELL PEPPERS

**1** Preheat the oven to 375°F/190°C. Prick the potatoes with a fork, brush with oil, sprinkle with the salt, and bake on a baking tray for 1 hour, or until the skins are crispy and the insides are soft when pierced with a fork.

**2** Melt 1 tablespoon of butter in a small skillet. Add the onion and cook gently for 4–5 minutes, or until softened and golden. Set aside.

**3** Remove the potatoes from the oven and cut in half lengthwise. Scoop the insides into a large mixing bowl and keep the shells. Increase the oven temperature to 400°F/200°C.

**4** Coarsely mash the potato and mix in the onion and remaining butter. Add salt and pepper and 1 or more of the optional ingredients, if using. Spoon the mixture back into the empty shells. Top with cheese.

**5** Return the potatoes to the oven for 10 minutes, or until the cheese melts and begins to brown. Garnish with chives to serve.

# ROAST SUMMER VEGETABLES

THIS APPETIZING AND COLORFUL MIXTURE OF MEDITERRANEAN VEGETABLES MAKES A SENSATIONAL SUMMER LUNCH FOR VEGETARIANS AND MEAT EATERS ALIKE. ROASTING BRINGS OUT THE FULL FLAVOR AND SWEETNESS OF THE BELL PEPPERS, EGGPLANTS, ZUCCHINI, AND ONIONS.

**SERVES 4**

**PREPARATION**
**15 MINUTES**
**COOKING**
**20–25 MINUTES**

**INGREDIENTS**
- 2 TBSP OLIVE OIL
- 1 FENNEL BULB
- 2 RED ONIONS
- 2 BEEFSTEAK TOMATOES
- 1 EGGPLANT
- 2 ZUCCHINI
- 1 YELLOW BELL PEPPER
- 1 RED BELL PEPPER
- 1 ORANGE BELL PEPPER
- 4 GARLIC CLOVES
- 4 FRESH ROSEMARY SPRIGS
- PEPPER
- CRUSTY BREAD, TO SERVE (OPTIONAL)

**1** Preheat the oven to 400°F/200°C. Brush a large ovenproof dish with a little of the oil. Prepare the vegetables. Cut the fennel, red onions, and tomatoes into wedges. Slice the eggplant and zucchini thickly, then seed all the bell peppers and cut into chunks. Arrange the vegetables in the dish and tuck the garlic cloves and rosemary sprigs among them. Drizzle with the remaining oil and season to taste with pepper.

**2** Roast the vegetables in the preheated oven for 10 minutes. Remove the dish from the oven and turn the vegetables over with a slotted spoon. Return to the oven and roast for an additional 10–15 minutes, until tender and beginning to turn golden brown.

**3** Serve the vegetables straight from the dish, or transfer to a warmed serving plate. Serve with crusty bread, if using.

## VARIATION
YOU CAN SUBSTITUTE A HERB-FLAVORED OIL, SUCH AS TARRAGON OR GARLIC AND ROSEMARY, FOR THE PLAIN OLIVE OIL, IF DESIRED.

# CRISP NOODLE & VEGETABLE STIR-FRY

THE CHINESE CAREFULLY SELECT VEGETABLES TO ACHIEVE A HARMONIOUS BALANCE OF CONTRASTING COLORS AND TEXTURES. ONCE YOU HAVE CHOPPED THE VEGETABLES, THIS DISH IS QUICK AND EASY TO PUT TOGETHER, AND MAKES AN ATTRACTIVE AND NUTRITIOUS MEAL.

**SERVES 4**

**PREPARATION**
**15 MINUTES**
**COOKING**
**15–20 MINUTES**

## INGREDIENTS
- PEANUT OR VEGETABLE OIL, FOR DEEP-FRYING
- 4 OZ/115 G RICE VERMICELLI, BROKEN INTO 3-INCH/7.5-CM LENGTHS
- 4 OZ/115 G GREEN BEANS, CUT INTO SHORT LENGTHS
- 2 CARROTS, CUT INTO THIN STICKS
- 2 ZUCCHINI, CUT INTO THIN STICKS
- 1 CUP SHIITAKE MUSHROOMS, SLICED
- 1-INCH/2.5-CM PIECE FRESH GINGER, SHREDDED
- ½ SMALL HEAD NAPA CABBAGE, SHREDDED
- 4 SCALLLIONS, SHREDDED
- ½ CUP BEAN SPROUTS
- 2 TBSP DARK SOY SAUCE
- 2 TBSP CHINESE RICE WINE
- LARGE PINCH OF SUGAR
- 2 TBSP COARSELY CHOPPED FRESH CILANTRO

**1** Half fill a wok or deep, heavy-bottom skillet with oil. Heat to 350–375°F/180–190°C, or until a cube of bread browns in 30 seconds.

**2** Add the noodles, in batches, and cook for 1½–2 minutes, or until crisp and puffed up. Remove and drain on paper towels. Pour off all but 2 tablespoons of oil from the wok.

**3** Heat the remaining oil over high heat. Add the green beans and stir-fry for 2 minutes.

**4** Add the carrot and zucchini sticks, sliced mushrooms, and ginger and stir-fry for an additional 2 minutes.

**5** Add the shredded Napa cabbage, scallions, and bean sprouts and stir-fry for an additional minute.

**6** Add the soy sauce, rice wine, and sugar and cook, stirring constantly, for 1 minute.

**7** Add the noodles and chopped cilantro and toss well. Serve immediately.

## COOK'S TIP
THIS DISH ALSO LOOKS ATTRACTIVE IF YOU SERVE THE NOODLES IN A SMALL NEST ON TOP OF THE STIR-FRIED VEGETABLES, INSTEAD OF TOSSING THEM WITH THE VEGETABLES IN STEP 7.

# GRATIN OF MIXED VEGETABLES

THIS MIXED VEGETABLE GRATIN IS VERY EASY TO PREPARE AND MAKES AN ECONOMICAL SUPPER DISH FOR A GROUP OF PEOPLE. ONCE YOU HAVE IT ASSEMBLED IN THE DISH, IT NEEDS LITTLE ATTENTION. SIMPLY PUT IT IN THE OVEN AND BRING IT OUT WHEN IT IS READY TO SERVE.

**SERVES 6**

**PREPARATION**
**15 MINUTES**
**COOKING**
**1¼ HOURS**

**INGREDIENTS**
- 2 PARSNIPS, SLICED
- 2 TBSP OLIVE OIL
- 1 EGGPLANT, DICED
- 1 GARLIC CLOVE, FINELY CHOPPED
- 2 TSP CHOPPED FRESH THYME
- ½ TBSP BUTTER
- 2 SHALLOTS, CHOPPED
- 4 CANNED ARTICHOKE HEARTS, DRAINED
- 4 CANNED CELERY HEARTS, SLICED
- ½ CUP EMMENTAL CHEESE, GRATED
- ½ CUP FRESHLY GRATED ROMANO CHEESE
- SALT

**1** Preheat the oven to 350°F/180°C. Steam the parsnips over a saucepan of simmering water for 4 minutes, or until just tender. Drain, then let them cool.

**2** Heat the oil in a heavy-bottom skillet. Add the diced eggplant and cook, stirring frequently, for 5 minutes. Add the chopped garlic and thyme, season to taste with salt, and cook for 3 minutes. Transfer the eggplant mixture to a large dish with a slotted spoon. Place the butter in the skillet. When it has melted, add the shallots and a pinch of salt, and cook over very low heat, stirring occasionally, for 7–10 minutes.

**3** Mix the shallots and eggplant mixture together. Cut each artichoke heart into 8 pieces and add to the mixture with the parsnips, celery hearts, Emmental, and half the romano cheese. Mix well, then sprinkle over the remaining romano cheese. Bake in the preheated oven for 45 minutes. Serve immediately.

## VARIATION
YOU CAN ADAPT THIS GRATIN TO WHATEVER INGREDIENTS YOU HAVE AT HAND. TRY DIFFERENT COMBINATIONS OF VEGETABLES, SUCH AS CARROTS INSTEAD OF PARSNIPS, AND VARY THE HERBS—FOR EXAMPLE, USE PARSLEY INSTEAD OF THYME.

# STUFFED RED BELL PEPPERS WITH BASIL

**SERVES 4**

**PREPARATION
15–20 MINUTES
COOKING
1¼–1½ HOURS**

STUFFED BELL PEPPERS ARE POPULAR WITH VEGETARIANS AND MEAT-EATERS ALIKE. THEY ARE EASY TO PREPARE AND NUTRITIOUS: THE WALNUTS AND CHEESE ALONE ARE A RICH SOURCE OF PROTEIN. THIS DISH IS ALSO RICH IN IRON AND VITAMIN C. SERVE THESE BELL PEPPERS FOR LUNCH OR SUPPER.

## INGREDIENTS

- ¾ CUP LONG-GRAIN WHITE OR BROWN RICE
- 4 LARGE RED BELL PEPPERS
- 2 TBSP OLIVE OIL
- 1 GARLIC CLOVE, CHOPPED
- 4 SHALLOTS, CHOPPED
- 1 CELERY STALK, CHOPPED
- 3 TBSP CHOPPED TOASTED WALNUTS
- 2 TOMATOES, PEELED AND CHOPPED
- 1 TBSP LEMON JUICE
- ⅓ CUP RAISINS
- 4 TBSP FRESHLY GRATED CHEDDAR CHEESE
- 2 TBSP CHOPPED FRESH BASIL
- SALT AND PEPPER
- FRESH BASIL SPRIGS, TO GARNISH
- LEMON WEDGES, TO SERVE

**1** Preheat the oven to 350°F/180°C. Cook the rice in a saucepan of lightly salted boiling water for 20 minutes if using white rice, or 35 minutes if using brown. Drain, rinse under cold running water, then drain again.

**2** Using a sharp knife, cut the tops off the bell peppers and set aside. Remove the seeds and white cores, then blanch the bell peppers and reserved tops in boiling water for 2 minutes. Remove from the heat and drain well.

**3** Heat half the oil in a large skillet. Add the garlic and shallots and cook, stirring, for 3 minutes. Add the celery, walnuts, tomatoes, lemon juice, and raisins and cook for an additional 5 minutes. Remove from the heat and stir in the cheese, chopped basil, and seasoning.

**4** Stuff the bell peppers with the rice mixture and arrange them in a baking dish. Place the tops on the bell peppers, drizzle over the remaining oil, loosely cover with foil, and bake in the preheated oven for 45 minutes. Remove from the oven. Garnish with basil sprigs and serve with lemon wedges.

# BRAISED RED CABBAGE

BRAISED RED CABBAGE MAKES A COLORFUL ACCOMPANIMENT TO A VARIETY OF HOT AND COLD DISHES. TRY SERVING IT WITH TARTS AND QUICHES, AND FRESHLY BAKED PIES. THIS CABBAGE HAS A LOVELY FLAVOR, WITH HINTS OF AROMATIC CLOVES AND THE SWEETNESS OF RAISINS.

**SERVES 6**

**PREPARATION**
**15 MINUTES**
**COOKING**
**55 MINUTES**

**INGREDIENTS**
- 2 TBSP SUNFLOWER OIL
- 2 ONIONS, THINLY SLICED
- 2 APPLES, PEELED, CORED, AND THINLY SLICED
- 2 LB/900 G RED CABBAGE, CORED AND SHREDDED
- 4 TBSP RED WINE VINEGAR
- 2 TBSP SUGAR
- ¼ TSP GROUND CLOVES
- ⅓ CUP RAISINS
- ½ CUP RED WINE
- 2 TBSP RED CURRANT JELLY
- SALT AND PEPPER

**1** Heat the oil in a large saucepan. Add the onions and cook, stirring occasionally, for 10 minutes, or until softened and golden. Stir in the apple slices and cook for 3 minutes.

**2** Add the cabbage, vinegar, sugar, cloves, raisins, and red wine, and season to taste with salt and pepper. Bring to a boil, stirring occasionally. Reduce the heat, cover, and cook, stirring occasionally, for 40 minutes, or until the cabbage is tender and most of the liquid has been absorbed.

**3** Stir in the red currant jelly, transfer the cabbage to a warmed dish, and serve.

## VARIATION
YOU CAN VARY THE FLAVOR AND TEXTURE OF THIS DISH BY SUBSTITUTING 2 TABLESPOONS HONEY FOR THE SUGAR, AND REPLACING HALF OF THE RAISINS WITH GOLDEN RAISINS.

# BAKED EGGPLANTS

THIS DELICIOUS RECIPE IS FROM PARMA, AND CONTAINS LAYERS OF SLICED EGGPLANTS BAKED WITH TOMATO SAUCE AND MOZZARELLA CHEESE. YOU MAY NEED TO REDUCE THE TOMATO SAUCE A LITTLE BY BOILING IT DOWN BEFORE USING, SO THAT THE END RESULT IS NOT TOO RUNNY.

**SERVES 4**

**PREPARATION**
**20 MINUTES**
**COOKING**
**1¼ HOURS**

**INGREDIENTS**
- 4 EGGPLANTS, TRIMMED
- 3 TBSP OLIVE OIL, PLUS EXTRA FOR OILING
- 10½ OZ/300 G MOZZARELLA CHEESE, THINLY SLICED
- 4 SLICES PROSCIUTTO, SHREDDED
- 1 TBSP CHOPPED FRESH MARJORAM
- ¼ CUP PARMESAN CHEESE, GRATED
- FRESH SAGE SPRIGS, TO GARNISH

**FOR THE TOMATO SAUCE**
- 4 TBSP OLIVE OIL
- 1 LARGE ONION, SLICED
- 4 GARLIC CLOVES, CRUSHED
- 14 OZ/400 G CANNED CHOPPED TOMATOES
- 1 LB/450 G FRESH TOMATOES, PEELED AND CHOPPED
- 4 TBSP CHOPPED FRESH PARSLEY
- 2½ CUPS HOT VEGETABLE STOCK
- 1 TBSP SUGAR
- 2 TBSP LEMON JUICE
- ⅔ CUP DRY WHITE WINE
- SALT AND PEPPER

**FOR THE BÉCHAMEL SAUCE**
- 2 TBSP BUTTER
- SCANT ¼ CUP ALL-PURPOSE FLOUR
- 1 TSP MUSTARD POWDER
- 1¼ CUPS MILK
- FRESHLY GRATED NUTMEG

**1** Preheat the oven to 375°F/190°C. To make the tomato sauce, heat the oil in a large skillet. Add the onion and garlic and cook until just beginning to soften. Add the canned and fresh tomatoes, parsley, stock, sugar, and lemon juice. Cover and simmer for 15 minutes. Stir in the wine and season to taste with salt and pepper.

**2** Slice the eggplants thinly lengthwise. Bring a large saucepan of water to a boil and cook the eggplant slices for 5 minutes. Drain on paper towels and pat dry.

**3** Pour half of the fresh tomato sauce into a large, oiled ovenproof dish. Cover with half of the cooked eggplants and drizzle with a little oil. Cover with half of the mozzarella, prosciutto, and marjoram. Season to taste with salt and pepper. Repeat the layers until the tomato sauce is used up.

**4** To make the béchamel sauce, heat the butter in a large saucepan. When it has melted, add the flour and mustard powder. Stir until smooth and cook over low heat for 2 minutes. Slowly beat in the milk. Simmer gently for 2 minutes. Remove from the heat and season with a large pinch of nutmeg, and salt and pepper to taste.

**5** Pour the sauce over the eggplant mixture, then sprinkle over the Parmesan cheese. Bake in the preheated oven for 35–40 minutes, until golden on top. Garnish with sage sprigs and serve.

# CAESAR SALAD

THIS SALAD WAS THE INVENTION OF A CHEF AT CAESAR'S, A RESTAURANT IN TIJUANA, MEXICO. IT HAS RIGHTLY EARNED AN INTERNATIONAL REPUTATION. CAESAR SALAD MAKES AN EXCELLENT LUNCH AS WELL AS AN ACCOMPANIMENT, AND IS FULL OF NUTRIENTS, ESPECIALLY PROTEIN.

**SERVES 4**

**PREPARATION**
**25 MINUTES**
**COOKING**
**15–20 MINUTES**

## INGREDIENTS
- 4 THICK SLICES DAY-OLD BREAD
- 1 LARGE ROMAINE LETTUCE OR 2 BOSTON LETTUCES
- SALT AND PEPPER
- PARMESAN SHAVINGS, TO GARNISH

### FOR THE DRESSING
- 3 GARLIC CLOVES, CRUSHED
- 1½ TSP DIJON MUSTARD
- 1 TSP WORCESTERSHIRE SAUCE
- 8 CANNED ANCHOVIES IN OIL
- 1 EGG YOLK
- 1 TBSP LEMON JUICE
- ¾ CUP OLIVE OIL
- 4 TBSP FRESHLY GRATED PARMESAN CHEESE

**1** Preheat the oven to 350°F/180°C. To make the dressing, place 2 garlic cloves, the mustard, Worcestershire sauce, anchovies, egg yolk, lemon juice, and seasoning in a food processor or blender and process for 30 seconds until foaming. With the machine still running, add ⅔ cup of olive oil, drop by drop, until the mixture begins to thicken. Continue adding the oil in a steady stream until all the oil has been incorporated. Transfer to a bowl. Add a little hot water if the dressing is too thick. Stir in the grated Parmesan cheese. Season to taste with salt and pepper and chill until required.

**2** To make the croutons, cut the bread into ½ inch/1 cm cubes. Toss with the remaining oil and garlic in a bowl. Spread out on a baking sheet in a single layer. Bake in the preheated oven for 15–20 minutes, stirring occasionally, until browned and crisp. Remove from the oven and let them cool.

**3** Separate the lettuce into individual leaves and wash and spin dry in a salad spinner or pat dry on paper towels. (Excess moisture will dilute the dressing.) Transfer to a plastic bag and place in the refrigerator.

**4** To assemble the salad, tear the lettuce into pieces and place in a large serving bowl. Add the dressing and toss well. Top with the halved anchovies, croutons, and Parmesan shavings. Serve immediately.

# ROAST CHICKEN SALAD WITH ORANGE DRESSING

THIS COLORFUL SALAD MAKES A DELICIOUS SUMMER LUNCH, AND IS AN EXCELLENT WAY OF USING UP ANY LEFTOVER ROAST CHICKEN. IT IS ALSO MOUTHWATERING FARE FOR A PICNIC. THE SUCCULENT ROAST CHICKEN AND SWEET TANG OF ORANGE MAKE A LOVELY COMBINATION.

**SERVES 4**

**PREPARATION
20 MINUTES
COOKING
NONE**

## INGREDIENTS
- 5½ CUPS YOUNG SPINACH LEAVES
- HANDFUL OF FRESH PARSLEY LEAVES
- ½ CUCUMBER, THINLY SLICED
- ¾ CUP WALNUTS, TOASTED AND CHOPPED
- 12 OZ/350 G BONELESS LEAN ROAST CHICKEN, THINLY SLICED
- 2 RED APPLES
- 1 TBSP LEMON JUICE

## FOR THE ORANGE DRESSING
- 2 TBSP EXTRA VIRGIN OLIVE OIL
- JUICE OF 1 ORANGE
- FINELY GRATED ZEST OF ½ ORANGE
- 1 TBSP SOUR CREAM
- FRESH FLAT-LEAF PARSLEY SPRIGS, TO GARNISH
- ORANGE WEDGES, TO SERVE

**1** Wash and drain the spinach and parsley leaves, if necessary, then arrange on a large serving platter. Top with the cucumber and walnuts. Arrange the chicken slices on top of the leaves.

**2** Core the apples, then cut them in half. Cut each half into slices and brush with the lemon juice to prevent discoloration. Arrange the apple slices over the salad.

**3** Place all the dressing ingredients in a screw-top jar, screw on the lid tightly, and shake well until thoroughly combined. Drizzle the dressing over the salad, garnish with parsley sprigs, and serve immediately with orange wedges.

## VARIATION
THIS CHICKEN SALAD WOULD ALSO WORK WELL WITH PEARS INSTEAD OF APPLES. SLICE AND BRUSH THEM WITH LEMON JUICE IN THE SAME WAY TO PREVENT DISCOLORATION.

# GREEK SALAD

WALK INTO ANY TAVERNA OR CAFÉ IN GREECE OR SOUTHERN CYPRUS AND YOU WILL SEE THIS SALAD, OR A VARIATION OF IT, ON THE MENU. IT MAKES A DELICIOUS ACCOMPANIMENT TO OTHER GREEK DISHES, OR A SATISFYING LUNCH IN ITS OWN RIGHT IF SERVED WITH FRESH PITAS.

**SERVES 4**

**PREPARATION**
**15 MINUTES**
**COOKING**
**NONE**

**INGREDIENTS**
- 4 TOMATOES, CUT INTO WEDGES
- 1 ONION, SLICED
- ½ CUCUMBER, SLICED
- 1⅓ CUPS KALAMATA OLIVES, PITTED
- 8 OZ/225 G FETA CHEESE, CUBED (DRAINED WEIGHT)
- 2 TBSP FRESH CILANTRO LEAVES
- FRESH FLAT-LEAF PARSLEY, TO GARNISH
- FRESH PITAS, TO SERVE

FOR THE DRESSING
- 5 TBSP EXTRA VIRGIN OLIVE OIL
- 2 TBSP WHITE WINE VINEGAR
- 1 TBSP LEMON JUICE
- ½ TSP SUGAR
- 1 TBSP CHOPPED FRESH CILANTRO
- SALT AND PEPPER

**1** To make the dressing, place the oil, vinegar, lemon juice, sugar, and cilantro in a large bowl. Season with salt and pepper and mix together well.

**2** Add the tomatoes, onion, cucumber, olives, feta cheese, and cilantro. Toss all the ingredients together, then divide between individual serving bowls. Garnish with fresh parsley and serve with fresh pitas.

## COOK'S TIP
FOR AN AUTHENTIC GREEK SALAD YOU NEED TO USE KALAMATA OLIVES, BUT IF THEY ARE UNAVAILABLE, THEN THE SAME QUANTITY OF PITTED GREEN OR BLACK OLIVES WILL WORK WELL IN THIS RECIPE.

# SPICY TOMATO SALAD

TOMATO SALAD MAKES A COLORFUL ACCOMPANIMENT TO MANY DISHES. THIS VERSION HAS A DELICIOUS SPICY FLAVOR AND MAKES AN EXCELLENT SALAD FOR A PICNIC OR BUFFET. IT IS ALSO SUITABLE FOR VEGANS AND WILL SUIT ANYONE ON A MEAT-FREE OR DAIRY-FREE DIET.

**SERVES 4**

PREPARATION
**10 MINUTES, PLUS
10 MINUTES' COOLING**
COOKING
**NONE**

## INGREDIENTS
- 4 LARGE RIPE TOMATOES
- 1 SMALL FRESH RED CHILE
- 1 GARLIC CLOVE
- ⅔ CUP FRESH BASIL
- 4 TBSP EXTRA VIRGIN OLIVE OIL
- 1 TBSP LEMON JUICE
- 2 TBSP BALSAMIC VINEGAR
- SALT AND PEPPER
- FRESH BASIL SPRIGS, TO GARNISH
- FRESH CRUSTY BREAD, TO SERVE

**1** Bring a kettle or saucepan of water to a boil. Place the tomatoes in a heatproof bowl, then pour over enough boiling water to cover them. Let them soak for 2–4 minutes, then lift out of the water and cool slightly.

**2** When the tomatoes are cool enough to handle, gently pierce the skins with the tip of a knife. The skins should now be easy to remove. Discard the skins, then chop the tomatoes and place them in a large salad bowl.

**3** Seed and finely chop the chile, then chop the garlic. Rinse and finely chop the basil, then add it to the tomatoes in the bowl with the chile and the garlic.

**4** Mix the oil, lemon juice, and balsamic vinegar together in a separate bowl, then season to taste with salt and pepper. Pour the mixture over the salad and toss together well. Garnish with basil sprigs and serve immediately with fresh crusty bread.

## COOK'S TIP

IF POSSIBLE, CHOOSE RIPE TOMATOES THAT ARE STILL ON THE VINE. THEIR FLAVOR IS UNMISTAKABLE, AND WILL REALLY ENHANCE THE TASTE OF THE SALAD. IF YOU CAN'T FIND TOMATOES ON THE VINE, THEN ANY TOMATOES WILL WORK, BUT TRY TO FIND SOME THAT HAVE A GOOD FLAVOR.

# CHAPTER 6

# HERBS AND SPICES

HERBS AND SPICES HAVE A VERY WIDE RANGE OF
MARVELOUS FLAVORS, AND THE MEREST PINCH OF
A WELL-CHOSEN HERB OR SPICE CAN ELEVATE THE
TASTE OF A DISH TO AN ALTOGETHER NEW AND
INSPIRING LEVEL. TAKE YOUR INSPIRATION FROM
THE RECIPES FEATURED HERE, OR EXPERIMENT
WITH YOUR OWN COMBINATIONS FOR NEW AND
EXCITING RESULTS.

# PEA & MINT SOUP

THE SWEETNESS OF GARDEN PEAS AND THE FRESH TASTE OF MINT PAIR TOGETHER MARVELOUSLY IN THIS DISH, AND THE SHALLOTS AND LEEKS ADD AN APPEALING DEPTH. THIS SOUP IS IDEAL FOR VEGETARIANS BUT ENJOYABLE FOR ALL. IT MAKES A DELICOUS APPETIZER OR LIGHT LUNCH.

**SERVES 4**

PREPARATION
**15 MINUTES, PLUS
10 MINUTES' COOLING**
COOKING
**40 MINUTES**

**INGREDIENTS**
- 1 TBSP BUTTER
- 3 SHALLOTS, CHOPPED
- 2 LEEKS, TRIMMED AND FINELY CHOPPED
- 1 POTATO, PEELED AND CHOPPED
- 1 LB/450 G FROZEN PEAS
- 2 TBSP CHOPPED FRESH MINT
- 3½ CUPS VEGETABLE STOCK
- SALT AND PEPPER
- FRESH MINT SPRIGS, TO GARNISH
- SLICES OF FRESH WHOLE-WHEAT BREAD, TO SERVE

**1** Melt the butter in a large saucepan over medium heat. Add the shallots and cook, stirring, for 2 minutes. Add the leeks and cook, stirring, for an additional 2 minutes. Add the potato, peas, chopped mint, and stock, and season with salt and pepper. Bring to a boil, then reduce the heat, cover the pan, and simmer for 30 minutes. Remove the pan from the heat and cool for 10 minutes.

**2** Transfer the soup to a food processor and process until smooth (you may need to do this in batches).

**3** Return to the saucepan, season to taste with salt and pepper, and reheat gently. Remove from the heat and pour into serving bowls. Garnish with fresh mint sprigs and serve with slices of fresh whole-wheat bread.

**COOK'S TIP**
THIS WOULD BE A VERY EASY FIRST COURSE FOR A DINNER PARTY BECAUSE YOU CAN MAKE THIS SOUP BEFOREHAND AND SIMPLY REHEAT IT WHEN YOU ARE READY TO SERVE.

# BASIL & PINE NUT PESTO

**SERVES 4**

**PREPARATION**
**15 MINUTES**
**COOKING**
**5–10 MINUTES**

PESTO IS DELICIOUS STIRRED INTO PASTA, SOUPS, AND SALAD DRESSINGS. IT IS AVAILABLE IN MOST SUPERMARKETS, BUT MAKING YOUR OWN GIVES A CONCENTRATED FLAVOR. YOU CAN MAKE THIS PESTO A DAY AHEAD AND KEEP IT IN THE REFRIGERATOR UNTIL YOU ARE READY TO COOK THE PASTA.

**INGREDIENTS**
- ABOUT 40 FRESH BASIL LEAVES
- 3 GARLIC CLOVES, CRUSHED
- 2 TBSP PINE NUTS
- SCANT ½ CUP PARMESAN CHEESE, FINELY GRATED
- 2–3 TBSP EXTRA VIRGIN OLIVE OIL
- 1 LB 8 OZ/675 G FRESH PASTA OR 12 OZ/350 G DRIED PASTA
- SALT AND PEPPER

**1** Rinse the basil leaves and pat them dry with paper towels.

**2** Place the basil leaves, garlic, pine nuts, and grated Parmesan cheese in a food processor and process for 30 seconds, or until smooth. Alternatively, pound all of the ingredients by hand, using a mortar and pestle.

**3** If you are using a food processor, keep the motor running and slowly add the olive oil. Alternatively, add the oil drop by drop while stirring briskly. Season to taste with salt and pepper.

**4** Bring a large, heavy-bottom saucepan of water to a boil. Add the pasta, return to a boil, and cook for 3–4 minutes for fresh pasta or 8–10 minutes for dried, until tender but still firm to the bite. Drain the pasta thoroughly, then transfer to a serving plate and serve with the pesto. Toss to mix well and serve hot.

## COOK'S TIP
ONLY BUY PINE NUTS IN SMALL QUANTITIES BECAUSE THEIR HIGH OIL CONTENT MEANS THEY QUICKLY TURN RANCID. PINE NUTS ARE AVAILABLE IN MOST LARGE SUPERMARKETS OR HEALTH FOOD STORES.

# TARRAGON CHICKEN

THIS IS A CLASSIC FRENCH RECIPE AND IS SUCH A STYLISH, YET UNDERSTATED DISH THAT IT WOULD BE AN EXCELLENT CHOICE FOR A MAIN COURSE AT AN INFORMAL DINNER PARTY. TARRAGON HAS A POWERFUL FLAVOR, SO USE IT SPARINGLY OR IT WILL DOMINATE THE OTHER FLAVORS.

**SERVES 4**

**PREPARATION
5 MINUTES
COOKING
22–25 MINUTES**

**INGREDIENTS**
- 4 SKINLESS, BONELESS CHICKEN BREASTS, ABOUT 6 OZ/175 G EACH
- ½ CUP DRY WHITE WINE
- 1–1¼ CUPS CHICKEN STOCK
- 1 GARLIC CLOVE, FINELY CHOPPED
- 1 TBSP DRIED TARRAGON
- ¾ CUP HEAVY CREAM
- 1 TBSP CHOPPED FRESH TARRAGON
- SALT AND PEPPER
- FRESH TARRAGON SPRIGS, TO GARNISH

**1** Season the chicken with salt and pepper and place in a single layer in a large, heavy-bottom skillet. Pour in the wine and enough chicken stock just to cover and add the garlic and dried tarragon. Bring to a boil, reduce the heat, and cook gently for an additional 10 minutes, or until the chicken is tender and cooked through.

**2** Remove the chicken with a slotted spoon or tongs, cover, and keep warm. Strain the poaching liquid into a clean skillet and skim off any fat from the surface. Bring to a boil and cook for 12–15 minutes, or until reduced by about two-thirds.

**3** Stir in the cream, return to a boil, and cook until reduced by about half. Stir in the fresh tarragon. Slice the chicken breasts and arrange on warmed plates. Spoon over the sauce, garnish with tarragon sprigs, and serve immediately.

## COOK'S TIP
TONGS ARE THE EASIEST WAY TO REMOVE THE CHICKEN BREASTS FROM THE SKILLET. MAKE SURE THAT THE CHICKEN IS COMPLETELY COOKED THROUGH BEFORE SERVING.

# OMELETS WITH FINES HERBES

**SERVES 2**

**PREPARATION**
**10 MINUTES**
**COOKING**
**4 MINUTES**

**INGREDIENTS**
- 6 EGGS
- 4 TBSP CHOPPED FRESH PARSLEY
- 4 TBSP CHOPPED FRESH TARRAGON
- 4 TBSP CHOPPED FRESH CHERVIL
- 2 TBSP SNIPPED FRESH CHIVES
- 2 TBSP BUTTER
- SALT AND PEPPER
- MIXED SALAD GREENS, TO SERVE

FINES HERBES ARE SIMPLY A MIXTURE OF VERY FINELY CHOPPED FRESH HERBS, AND THE CLASSIC COMBINATION IS PARSLEY, TARRAGON, CHERVIL, AND CHIVES. THESE SUBTLY FLAVORED OMELETS PAIR WELL WITH A TOMATO SALAD OR MIXED SALAD GREENS FOR A LIGHT, SUMMERY LUNCH.

**1** Beat the eggs with the parsley, tarragon, chervil, and chives. Season to taste with salt and pepper.

**2** Melt half the butter in an omelet pan or small, heavy-bottom skillet. Add half the egg mixture and stir with a fork. As the egg sets, draw it toward the center, and tilt the omelet pan so that the uncooked egg runs underneath. Cook until the underside of the omelet is golden and set, but the top is still moist.

**3** Remove the omelet pan from the heat and slide the omelet on to a plate, flipping the pan gently so that the omelet folds. Keep the omelet warm. Melt the remaining butter and cook a second omelet in the same way. Serve immediately with mixed salad greens.

**COOK'S TIP**
IF YOU CANNOT FIND ANY OF THE FOUR HERBS NORMALLY USED TO MAKE "FINES HERBES," USE MARJORAM, OREGANO, OR DILL INSTEAD.

# SALMON COOKED WITH DILL

**SERVES 4**

**PREPARATION**
**5 MINUTES**
**COOKING**
**20–30 MINUTES**

SALMON IS ALWAYS POPULAR AT PARTIES, AND THE COMBINATION OF THE HERBS AND FENNEL, AND THE SMOKY BARBECUE TASTE, GIVES THIS DISH A MOUTHWATERING FLAVOR THAT YOUR GUESTS WILL FIND DIFFICULT TO RESIST. SERVE IT WITH CRUSTY BREAD FOR A SATISFYING MEAL.

**INGREDIENTS**
- ½ LARGE BUNCH DRIED THYME
- 5 FRESH ROSEMARY BRANCHES, 6–8 INCHES/ 15–20 CM LONG
- 8 BAY LEAVES
- 2 LB 4 OZ/1 KG SALMON FILLET
- 1 BULB FENNEL, CUT INTO 8 PIECES
- 2 TBSP LEMON JUICE
- 2 TBSP OLIVE OIL

**TO SERVE**
- CRUSTY BREAD
- GREEN SALAD

**1** Preheat the barbecue. Make a base on the hot barbecue with the dried thyme, rosemary branches, and bay leaves, overlapping them so that they cover a slightly bigger area than the salmon.

**2** Carefully place the salmon on top of the herbs, then arrange the fennel around the edge of the fish.

**3** Combine the lemon juice and oil and brush the salmon with it. Cover the salmon loosely with a piece of foil, to keep it moist.

**4** Cook for about 20–30 minutes, basting frequently with the lemon juice mixture.

**5** Remove the salmon from the barbecue, cut it into slices, and serve with the fennel, slices of crusty bread, and a green salad.

## VARIATION

USE WHATEVER COMBINATION OF HERBS YOU MAY HAVE AT HAND—BUT AVOID THE STRONGER TASTING HERBS, SUCH AS SAGE AND MARJORAM, WHICH ARE UNSUITABLE FOR FISH.

# TAGINE OF LAMB

THIS IS A TYPICAL MOROCCAN MIXTURE OF MEAT, VEGETABLES, AND APRICOTS, FLAVORED WITH PLENTY OF FRESH HERBS AND SPICES. IT IS DELICIOUS—AND AUTHENTIC—IF SERVED WITH COUSCOUS, WHICH CAN BE COOKED IN A STEAMER SET OVER THE STEW FOR 6–7 MINUTES.

**SERVES 4**

**PREPARATION**
**15 MINUTES**
**COOKING**
**1 HOUR 40 MINUTES**

## INGREDIENTS

- 1 TBSP SUNFLOWER OIL OR CORN OIL
- 1 ONION, CHOPPED
- 12 OZ/350 G BONELESS LAMB, TRIMMED OF ALL VISIBLE FAT AND CUT INTO 1-INCH/2.5-CM CUBES
- 1 GARLIC CLOVE, FINELY CHOPPED
- 2½ CUPS VEGETABLE STOCK
- GRATED ZEST AND JUICE OF 1 ORANGE
- 1 TSP CLEAR HONEY
- 1 CINNAMON STICK
- ½-INCH/1-CM PIECE FRESH GINGER, FINELY CHOPPED
- 1 EGGPLANT
- 4 TOMATOES, PEELED AND CHOPPED
- ⅔ CUP PLUMPED DRIED APRICOTS
- 2 TBSP CHOPPED FRESH CILANTRO
- SALT AND PEPPER
- FRESHLY COOKED COUSCOUS, TO SERVE

**1** Heat the oil in a large, heavy-bottom skillet or ovenproof casserole over medium heat. Add the onion and lamb cubes and cook, stirring frequently, for 5 minutes, or until the meat is lightly browned all over. Add the garlic, stock, orange zest and juice, honey, cinnamon stick, and ginger. Bring to a boil, then reduce the heat, cover, and simmer for 45 minutes.

**2** Using a sharp knife, halve the eggplant lengthwise and slice thinly. Add to the skillet with the chopped tomatoes and apricots. Cover and cook for an additional 45 minutes, or until the lamb is tender.

**3** Stir in the cilantro and season to taste with salt and pepper. Serve immediately, straight from the skillet, with freshly cooked couscous.

## VARIATION

IF YOU DON'T MIND DEPARTING FROM THE TRADITIONAL, YOU CAN PAIR THIS TAGINE WITH OTHER GRAINS INSTEAD OF THE COUSCOUS, SUCH AS FRESHLY COOKED BASMATI RICE OR BULGUR WHEAT.

# CHAPTER 7

# RICE, PASTA, BEANS, AND GRAINS

THE SLOW-RELEASING CARBOHYDRATES IN PASTA, BEANS, AND GRAINS MAKE THEM A GOOD SOURCE OF ENERGY. THEY ARE ALSO VERY VERSATILE AND CAN BE USED IN A WIDE VARIETY OF DISHES. SIMPLY ADD A TASTY SAUCE AND YOU HAVE A VERY SATISFYING MEAL.

# INTRODUCTION

CARBOHYDRATES, SUCH AS PASTA, NOODLES, AND GRAINS, PROVIDE A GOOD, INEXPENSIVE SOURCE OF ENERGY, ESPECIALLY THE WHOLE-WHEAT/WHOLE-GRAIN VARIETIES, AND ARE A VALUABLE SOURCE OF DIETARY FIBER. COMBINE THEM WITH PROTEIN-RICH LEGUMES, AND YOU HAVE A DELICIOUS MEAL THAT IS NUTRITIOUS, SATISFYING, AND HEALTHY.

### Buying and storing pasta

You can buy fresh and dried pasta in a wide variety of colors, shapes, and sizes. It is usually made with durum wheat or whole-wheat flour. Fresh pasta usually keeps for up to 2 days in the refrigerator, and dried pasta for up to 2 years in the pantry, but always use them by their expiration date.

### Buying and storing noodles

In addition to Italian pasta, there are also different types of Asian noodles. Asian noodles should be stored in a cool, dry place, and used by their expiration date.

### How to cook pasta

Cooking pasta is quick and easy. Bring a large saucepan of lightly salted water to a boil, add the pasta, and return to a boil, stirring at intervals to prevent it from sticking together. Reduce the heat slightly and cook until it is tender but still firm to the bite; this is known as "al dente." Remove from the heat, drain, and serve tossed with olive oil or accompanied by your chosen sauce or recipe.

Fine egg noodles

Medium egg noodles

Thick egg noodles

**PASTA NAMES**

**Anelli** Very small rings

**Cannelloni** Large, hollow tubes

**Conchiglie** Ridged shells

**Farfalle** Bows

**Fettucine** Long, narrow ribbons

**Fusilli** Spirals

**Lasagna** Large, flat rectangular sheets

**Linguine** Long, narrow ribbons with flattened edges

**Lumaconi** Snail shapes

**Macaroni** Long or short narrow tubes, often curved

**Penne** Hollow quills

**Ravioli** Square cushions

**Spaghetti** Long, narrow strings

**Tagliatelle** Long ribbons, a little wider than fettucine

**Vermicelli** Long, very fine, hairlike strings

#### Cellophane noodles
These threadlike noodles are also known as Chinese vermicelli and are made from the starch of mung beans. Dried cellophane noodles should be soaked briefly before use, although this isn't necessary in dishes that contain a lot of liquid, such as soups.

#### Egg noodles
These are very popular in Asian cooking, especially in Chinese stir-fries. Check cooking

instructions on the package—some need to be soaked in hot water for about 4–5 minutes, while others can be put straight into the wok.

#### Ramen noodles
These noodles are deep-fried and sold packaged, often accompanied by prepared broth mix.

#### Rice noodles
These delicate, fine, white noodles are very easy to prepare. Simply soak them in hot water for

4–5 minutes. They are very good added to soups and stir-fries, and when deep-fried they become deliciously crunchy.

#### Soba noodles
These thin noodles are made from wheat flour and buckwheat. They are popular in Japanese cooking.

#### Udon noodles
These thick Japanese noodles are like spaghetti, except that they can be square as well as round.

They are made from cornstarch or wheat flour, and are available fresh or dried.

## Making your own fresh pasta

You can buy good-quality fresh pasta nowadays, but if you prefer to make your own, the process is simple. You might also like to invest in a pasta machine in order to create perfect pasta shapes of your choice.

## Home-made pasta

Serves 6

2 cups all-purpose flour, plus extra for dusting

1 tsp salt

2 eggs, lightly beaten

3 tbsp tomato paste (optional— use if you want a red, tomato-flavored pasta)

Lightly dust a clean counter with flour. Sift the flour and salt into a mound on the counter.

**1** Make a well in the center of the flour, add the beaten eggs, and tomato paste if using, and mix to a stiff dough. If necessary, stir in a few tablespoons of water.

**2** Knead the dough vigorously for about 8 minutes, then wrap it in plastic wrap and let it rest for 30 minutes, or for up to 2 days if not required straight away. Roll out the dough to the desired thickness, then use a sharp knife to cut it into pieces of the required shape and size.

**3** Alternatively, use a pasta machine to cut the dough. The pasta is now ready to be cooked.

1

2

3

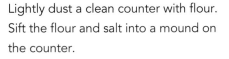

Conchigliette

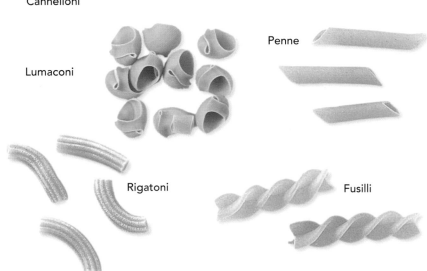

Cannelloni

Lumaconi

Penne

Rigatoni

Fusilli

### Buying and storing beans

Beans, lentils, and peas are all very useful items to keep in your pantry. You can buy these protein-rich foods dried, or ready to use in cans if you are short of time. When buying dried beans, store them in airtight containers in a cool, dry place and use by the expiration date, or, if there is no date on the package, within 1 year for best results. Do not mix old and new beans because they will take different lengths of time to cook. Once cooked, refrigerate leftover beans and use within 3 days, or freeze them in an airtight container and use within 6 months.

### Preparing and cooking beans

Most beans need soaking for at least 8 hours, then boiling rapidly for 10 minutes, followed by additional cooking for at least 45 minutes, or until they are tender. The main exceptions are soybeans, which need 12 hours soaking and 4 hours to cook, and chickpeas, which need 8 hours to soak and 2 hours to cook. Cannellini beans need soaking overnight and 1½ hours to cook. Lentils and split peas usually need no soaking and can be cooked in 25–30 minutes.

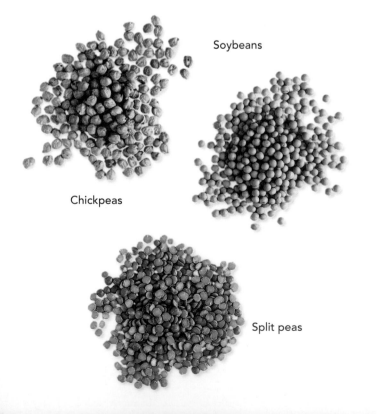

Soybeans

Chickpeas

Split peas

Black-eyed peas

#### Chickpeas

These round and cream-colored beans have a nutty flavor, and are excellent in soups, salads, dips, and stews, as well as pasta or grain dishes. Chickpeas can also be roasted for snacks, and are used in falafel, a Middle Eastern dish in which the mashed beans are formed into balls and deep-fried. Soak chickpeas for at least 8 hours before use. After soaking, drain and rinse them, then cover with fresh water and bring to a boil. Reduce the heat and let the beans simmer for 2 hours, until they are thoroughly cooked.

#### Soybeans

The most common color of soybeans is pale yellow. These beans are good in soups and other savory dishes, such as curries. Remember that they need to be soaked for at least 12 hours. After soaking, drain and rinse them, then cover with fresh water and bring to a boil. Boil them for the first hour of cooking, then let them simmer for another 3 hours, until they are thoroughly cooked.

#### Adzuki beans

These small red beans are good in soups and salads.

#### Split peas

These small peas are disk-shaped like lentils, but they are split along a natural seam. Split peas are yellow or green. They can be cooked and pureed, and used in soups, bakes, and other savory dishes.

#### Lentils

These are small, disk-shaped legumes. Use red or orange lentils pureed and in soups and sauces; green or brown lentils are best in salads, sauces, stews, and other savory dishes.

#### Red kidney beans

These red kidney-shaped beans can be added to soups, salads, and stews, and other savory dishes, such as chili con carne.

#### Cannellini beans

These white beans, such as navy beans and great Northern beans, can be used in a wide variety of savory dishes, including soups, salads, stews, and casseroles.

#### Lima beans

These white kidney-shaped beans are excellent in soups and salads.

#### Flageolet beans

These small green beans are excellent in salads and also make a delicious accompaniment to meat dishes.

#### Borlotti beans

These oval beans vary in color from pale pink to maroon-streaked skin. Use them in soups, dips, and other savory dishes.

#### Black-eyed peas

These beans are small and beige and have a circular black "eye." Use them in sauces, stir-fries, and soups.

Long-grain rice

Pudding rice

## Buying and storing rice

There are many different varieties of rice available. Store rice in airtight containers for up to 3 years in a cool, dry place, or use by the expiration date if sooner.

### Short-grain rice
This rice has short, fat grains that are more starchy and moist than medium- and long-grain rice. Varieties of short-grain rice include arborio and carnaroli rice, which are used in risottos.

### Medium-grain rice
These grains are a little shorter than long-grain rice. They are more moist and, therefore, tend to clump together when cooked. Medium-grain rice is used in savory dishes.

### Long-grain rice
Both white and brown long-grain rice are excellent for savory dishes because the grains stay dry and separate when cooked.

### Basmati rice
This Himalayan long-grain rice has a nutty flavor and is excellent in savory dishes. It is available in white or brown and the grains stay dry and separate when cooked.

### Jasmine rice
This tender rice has a delicate, fragrant, aromatic flavor. It is popular in both Vietnamese and Thai cooking.

### Arborio rice
This starchy, short-grain creamy rice is ideal in risottos.

### Carnaroli rice
This short-grain rice has often been called "the king of Italian rice." It has a high starch content and makes a lovely creamy risotto.

### Pudding rice
This rice has a high starch content and becomes very sticky and creamy when cooked. It is popular in desserts, especially rice pudding.

### Instant rice
These rice grains are polished and partly boiled so that they are quick to cook. They stay fluffy and separate when cooked, but have less flavor than white or brown rice.

### Red rice
This rice is grown in the Camargue region of France and in China. It has a pale red color and a nutty flavor that is similar to brown rice.

### Wild rice
This grain is in fact a marsh grass, not a rice. The grains are long and black, with a nutty flavor. It is often mixed with brown long-grain rice for reasons of economy.

## How to cook long-grain and basmati rice

To cook rice for four people, put 1½ cups rice into a strainer and rinse under cold running water. Transfer to a large saucepan and pour in 2½ cups cold water. Add a large pinch of salt, then bring to a boil. Reduce the heat, stir briefly, then cover the pan and simmer gently until the rice is tender and all the liquid has been absorbed (but do not let the rice burn). As a rough guide, white rice will need 15 minutes, and brown rice will need 25–30 minutes. Remove from the heat and let it stand for 5 minutes with the lid on. Fluff the grains with a fork and serve.

## Other grains

It is always worthwhile experimenting with other types of grain. Try using them in salads, soups, and stews, or piling them on a platter and topping them with tasty cooked vegetables.

### Barley
The polished variety of barley, known as pearl barley, is the kind most widely available. You can also buy pot barley, which is unpolished, from specialty stores and health-food stores. Barley is excellent in soups, casseroles, and stews.

### Millet
This protein-rich grain is a staple in Africa and Asia, and is boiled in a similar way to rice.

### Couscous
This is not a true grain, but pieces of semolina. Steam it in accordance with the instructions on the package. It makes an excellent bed of grains on which to pile meats and vegetables.

### Cornmeal
This yellow grain is made from cornmeal and features widely in Italian cooking. Follow the cooking instructions on the package because methods and cooking times vary. To serve cold, once the mixture pulls away from the pan, pour it onto a baking sheet, let it cool, then cut it into squares and serve. To serve hot, at the same stage stir in a generous tablespoon of butter, then remove from the heat and stir vigorously until the cornmeal stays firm.

### Bulgur wheat
This comprises wheat kernels that have been precooked. It is a golden-brown grain with a nutty flavor. Since it has already been cooked, you simply need to soak it in plenty of cold water for 20–30 minutes, then strain it in a strainer, pressing out as much water as possible. This grain is excellent in salads, especially the Middle Eastern dish known as tabbouleh. It is also good in pilaus.

# SPAGHETTI BOLOGNESE

THE CLASSIC MEAT SAUCE IN THIS RECIPE IS MOST OFTEN PARTNERED WITH SPAGHETTI, AS SHOWN HERE. HOWEVER, IT ALSO GOES WELL WITH LASAGNA, CANNELLONI, OR ANY OTHER BAKED PASTA DISHES. YOU CAN ALSO SERVE IT WITH A BAKED POTATO FOR A TASTY LUNCH OR SUPPER.

**SERVES 4**

**PREPARATION**
**15 MINUTES**
**COOKING**
**1 HOUR 10 MINUTES**

**INGREDIENTS**
- 3 TBSP OLIVE OIL
- 2 GARLIC CLOVES, CRUSHED
- 1 LARGE ONION, FINELY CHOPPED
- 1 CARROT, DICED
- 1 CUP FRESH LEAN GROUND BEEF OR CHICKEN
- 3 OZ/85 G CHICKEN LIVERS, FINELY CHOPPED
- 3½ OZ/100 G LEAN PROSCIUTTO, DICED
- ⅔ CUP MARSALA WINE
- 10 OZ/280 G CANNED CHOPPED PLUM TOMATOES
- 1 TBSP CHOPPED FRESH BASIL LEAVES
- 2 TBSP TOMATO PASTE
- 1 LB/450 G DRIED SPAGHETTI
- SALT AND PEPPER

**1** Heat 2 tablespoons of the oil in a large saucepan. Add the garlic, onion, and carrot, and cook for 6 minutes.

**2** Add the ground meat, chicken livers, and prosciutto to the pan and cook over medium heat for 12 minutes, or until well browned.

**3** Stir in the Marsala, tomatoes, basil, and tomato paste and cook for 4 minutes. Season to taste with salt and pepper. Cover and simmer for 30 minutes.

**4** Remove the lid from the pan, stir, and simmer for an additional 15 minutes.

**5** Meanwhile, bring a large pan of lightly salted water to a boil. Add the spaghetti and the remaining oil, return to a boil, and cook for 12 minutes, or until tender but still firm to the bite. Drain and transfer to a serving dish. Pour the sauce over the pasta, toss, and serve hot.

## VARIATION

CHICKEN LIVERS ARE CONSIDERED AN ESSENTIAL INGREDIENT IN A CLASSIC BOLOGNESE SAUCE, ADDING RICHNESS. HOWEVER, YOU CAN SUBSTITUTE THEM WITH THE SAME QUANTITY OF GROUND BEEF OR CHICKEN, IF YOU PREFER.

# VEGETABLE LASAGNE

THIS COLORFUL AND TASTY LASAGNE HAS LAYERS OF DICED AND SLICED VEGETABLES IN TOMATO SAUCE, ALL TOPPED WITH A RICH CHEESE SAUCE. IN THIS RECIPE, VERDI (GREEN) SHEETS OF PASTA HAVE BEEN USED, BUT IF YOU PREFER YOU COULD USE NO-PRECOOK WHITE PASTA SHEETS INSTEAD.

**SERVES 4**

**PREPARATION**
**20 MINUTES, PLUS**
**20 MINUTES' STANDING**
**COOKING**
**55 MINUTES**

## INGREDIENTS
- 1 EGGPLANT, SLICED
- 3 TBSP OLIVE OIL
- 2 GARLIC CLOVES, CRUSHED
- 1 RED ONION, HALVED AND SLICED
- 3 MIXED BELL PEPPERS, SEEDED AND DICED
- 8 OZ/225 G MIXED MUSHROOMS, SLICED
- 2 CELERY STALKS, SLICED
- 1 ZUCCHINI, DICED
- ½ TSP CHILI POWDER
- ½ TSP GROUND CUMIN
- 2 TOMATOES, CHOPPED
- 1¼ CUPS STRAINED CANNED TOMATOES
- 2 TBSP CHOPPED FRESH BASIL
- 8 NO-PRECOOK LASAGNE VERDI SHEETS
- SALT AND PEPPER

FOR THE CHEESE SAUCE
- 2 TBSP BUTTER OR MARGARINE
- 1 TBSP ALL-PURPOSE FLOUR
- ½ CUP VEGETABLE STOCK
- 1¼ CUPS MILK
- SCANT ¾ CUP GRATED CHEDDAR CHEESE
- 1 TSP DIJON MUSTARD
- 1 TBSP CHOPPED FRESH BASIL
- 1 EGG, BEATEN

**1** Place the eggplant slices in a colander, sprinkle with salt, and let them stand for 20 minutes. Rinse under cold water, drain, and set aside.

**2** Preheat the oven to 350°F/180°C. Heat the oil in a saucepan. Add the garlic and onion and sauté for 1–2 minutes. Add the bell peppers, mushrooms, celery, and zucchini, then cook, stirring constantly, for 3–4 minutes.

**3** Stir in the spices and cook for 1 minute. Mix in the tomatoes, strained canned tomatoes, and basil, then season to taste with salt and pepper.

**4** To make the sauce, melt the butter in a saucepan. Stir in the flour and cook for 1 minute. Remove from the heat, stir in the stock and milk, return to the heat, and add half the cheese and the mustard. Boil, stirring, until thickened. Stir in the basil. Remove from the heat and stir in the egg.

**5** Place half the lasagne in an ovenproof dish. Top with half the vegetables, half the tomato sauce, then half the eggplants. Repeat and then spoon the cheese sauce on top. Sprinkle with the remaining cheese and bake for 40 minutes, or until golden brown and bubbling.

## COOK'S TIP

WHEN DICING BELL PEPPERS, CUT THEM IN HALF AND PLACE THEM ON A CUTTING BOARD, SHINY SIDE DOWNWARD, TO PREVENT THE KNIFE FROM SLIPPING

# GNOCCHI WITH QUICK TOMATO SAUCE

THE WORD "GNOCCHI" IS ITALIAN FOR "DUMPLINGS," AND IS USED TO DESCRIBE SMALL BALLS OR CONCAVE OVAL DISKS MADE FROM A DOUGH OF POTATOES AND/OR FLOUR. THEY ARE USUALLY BOILED OR BAKED, AND SERVED WITH A SAUCE OR JUST SOME PARMESAN CHEESE. USE STARCHY POTATOES FOR THIS DISH.

**SERVES 4**

**PREPARATION**
**25 MINUTES**
**COOKING**
**35–40 MINUTES**

## INGREDIENTS
- 2 LB/900 G POTATOES
- 3 TBSP OLIVE OIL
- 1⅔–2 CUPS ALL-PURPOSE FLOUR
- 1 TSP SALT
- 1 TSP BAKING POWDER
- 1 EGG, BEATEN
- 1 LARGE ONION, CHOPPED
- 2 GARLIC CLOVES, CHOPPED
- ½ VEGETABLE BOUILLON CUBE
- 14 OZ/400 G CANNED CHOPPED TOMATOES
- 2 TBSP SHREDDED FRESH BASIL
- SALT AND PEPPER
- FRESHLY GRATED PARMESAN CHEESE, TO SERVE

**1** Peel the potatoes and cut into chunks. Cook in lightly salted boiling water for 15 minutes, or until tender. Drain well, then push through a strainer into a large bowl. Mix in 1 tablespoon of the oil.

**2** Stir the flour, 1 teaspoon of salt, and the baking powder together. Add half to the potatoes, with the egg, and mix together. Gradually knead in the remaining flour to form a smooth, slightly sticky dough.

**3** For the tomato sauce, heat the remaining oil in a saucepan. Add the onion and garlic and cook for 3–4 minutes. Dissolve the stock cube in scant ½ cup of boiling water, then add to the saucepan with the tomatoes. Cook, uncovered, for 10 minutes. Season with salt and pepper to taste.

**4** Shape the dough on a floured counter into 1-inch/2.5-cm thick rolls, then cut into ¾-inch/2-cm pieces. Using the tines of a fork, roll each piece toward you to curl in the sides and mark the top.

**5** Bring a large saucepan of water to a boil, then reduce to a simmer. Add about 30 gnocchi and cook for 1–2 minutes, until they float to the surface. Repeat until all the gnocchi are cooked.

**6** Stir the basil into the tomato sauce and pour over the gnocchi. Toss to coat and season with pepper to taste. Sprinkle with grated Parmesan and serve.

## VARIATION
ENHANCE THE COLOR AND FLAVOR OF THIS DISH BY REPLACING HALF OF THE STOCK WITH RED WINE AND ADDING 1 TABLESPOON OF TOMATO PASTE WITH THE TOMATOES IN STEP 3.

# GOLDEN CORNMEAL, ITALIAN-STYLE

CORNMEAL, ALSO CALLED POLENTA, IS A STAPLE FOOD OF NORTHERN ITALY. ONCE COOKED, IT CAN BE EATEN HOT OR COLD. THIS RECIPE MAKES A DELICIOUS APPETIZER OR TASTY ACCOMPANIMENT TO A MAIN MEAL. IT ALSO MAKES A SATISFYING BREAKFAST.

**SERVES 4**

**PREPARATION
20 MINUTES, PLUS
2½ HOURS' COOLING AND
STANDING
COOKING
1 HOUR**

**INGREDIENTS**
- 6⅓ CUPS WATER
- 1½ TSP SALT
- SCANT 2 CUPS CORNMEAL
- VEGETABLE OIL, FOR COOKING AND OILING
- 2 BEATEN EGGS (OPTIONAL)
- 2¼ CUPS FRESH FINE WHITE BREAD CRUMBS (OPTIONAL)

**FOR THE TOMATO SAUCE**
- 2 TBSP OLIVE OIL
- 1 SMALL ONION, CHOPPED
- 1 GARLIC CLOVE, CHOPPED
- 14 OZ/400 G CANNED CHOPPED TOMATOES
- 2 TBSP CHOPPED FRESH PARSLEY
- 1 TSP DRIED OREGANO
- 2 BAY LEAVES
- 2 TBSP TOMATO PASTE
- 1 TSP SUGAR
- SALT AND PEPPER

**1** Bring the water and salt to a boil in a large saucepan and gradually sprinkle in the cornmeal, stirring constantly to prevent lumps from forming. Simmer gently, stirring frequently, for 30 minutes, or until the cornmeal becomes very thick and begins to draw away from the sides of the pan.

**2** Oil an 11 x 7-inch/28 x 18-cm shallow pan, then spoon in the cornmeal. Spread out evenly, using a wet wooden spoon or spatula. Let the cornmeal cool, then let it stand for 2 hours at room temperature, if possible.

**3** Cut the cornmeal into 30–36 squares. Heat the oil in a skillet. Add the pieces and cook until golden brown all over, turning several times, for about 5 minutes. Alternatively, dip each piece of cornmeal in beaten egg and coat in bread crumbs before cooking in the hot oil. Keep warm.

**4** To make the tomato sauce, heat the oil in a saucepan over medium heat. Add the onion and sauté for 2 minutes until translucent. Add the garlic and sauté for 1 minute. Stir in the chopped tomatoes, herbs, tomato paste, sugar, and salt and pepper to taste. Bring to a

boil, then simmer, uncovered, for about 20 minutes, or until the sauce has reduced by half. Discard the bay leaves.

**5** Serve the cornmeal pieces with the hot tomato sauce.

# CHINESE STIR-FRIED RICE

THIS IS A DELICIOUS ADAPTATION OF A POPULAR CHINESE RECIPE. THE STRIPS OF BACON ARE A MOUTHWATERING ADDITION AND GIVE AN IRRESISTIBLE FLAVOR TO THE RICE. TO MAKE THIS DISH WORK REALLY WELL, MAKE SURE YOU USE COLD, DRY RICE WITH GRAINS THAT ARE WELL SEPARATED.

**SERVES 4**

**PREPARATION**
**15 MINUTES, PLUS**
**20 MINUTES' COOLING**
**COOKING**
**25–30 MINUTES**

**INGREDIENTS**
- 3 CUPS WATER
- ½ TSP SALT
- 1½ CUPS LONG-GRAIN RICE
- 2 EGGS
- 4 TSP COLD WATER
- 3 TBSP SUNFLOWER OIL
- 4 SCALLIONS, SLICED DIAGONALLY
- 1 RED, GREEN, OR YELLOW BELL PEPPER, CORED, SEEDED, AND THINLY SLICED
- 3–4 LEAN BACON SLICES, RINDED AND CUT INTO STRIPS
- 1⅓ CUPS FRESH BEAN SPROUTS
- 1⅛ CUPS FROZEN PEAS, THAWED
- 2 TBSP SOY SAUCE (OPTIONAL)
- SALT AND PEPPER

**1** Pour the water into the wok with the salt and bring to a boil. Rinse the rice in a strainer under cold running water until the water runs clear, drain thoroughly, and add to the boiling water. Stir well, then cover the wok tightly with the lid and let it simmer gently for 12–13 minutes. (Do not remove the lid during cooking or the steam will escape and the rice will not be cooked.)

**2** Remove the lid, give the rice a good stir, and spread out on a large plate or baking sheet to cool and dry.

**3** Meanwhile, beat each egg separately with salt and pepper and 2 teaspoons of cold water. Heat 1 tablespoon of oil in a preheated wok, pour in the first egg, swirl it around, and let it cook undisturbed until set. Transfer to a cutting board and cook the second egg. Cut the omelets into thin slices.

**4** Add the remaining oil to the wok and when really hot add the scallions and bell pepper and stir-fry for 1–2 minutes. Add the bacon and continue to stir-fry for an additional 2 minutes. Add the bean sprouts and peas and toss together thoroughly. Stir in the soy sauce, if using.

**5** Add the rice, and salt and pepper to taste, and stir-fry for 1 minute, then add the strips of omelet and continue to stir-fry for 2 minutes, or until the rice is piping hot. Serve immediately.

# RISOTTO MILANESE

**SERVES 4**

**PREPARATION**
**10 MINUTES**
**COOKING**
**30 MINUTES**

RISOTTO IS A DELICIOUS ITALIAN DISH AND VERY EASY TO MAKE, BUT IT DOES REQUIRE CONSTANT ATTENTION AND STIRRING WHILE COOKING. MAKE SURE YOU USE A STARCHY, SHORT-GRAIN RICE, SUCH AS ARBORIO OR CARNAROLI, BECAUSE THIS WILL GIVE A LOVELY CREAMY CONSISTENCY.

**INGREDIENTS**
- 4 CUPS CHICKEN STOCK
- 4 CUPS WHITE WINE
- 1 TSP SAFFRON STRANDS
- 1 TBSP OLIVE OIL
- 3 TBSP BUTTER
- 1 SMALL ONION, FINELY CHOPPED
- 1 LB/400 G ARBORIO RICE
- ½ CUP FRESHLY GRATED PARMESAN CHEESE, PLUS PARMESAN SHAVINGS TO GARNISH
- SALT AND PEPPER

**1** Bring the stock and white wine to a boil, then reduce the heat and simmer. Infuse the saffron strands in the stock and continue to simmer while preparing the risotto.

**2** Heat the oil with 2 tablespoons of butter in a deep pan over medium heat until the butter has melted. Stir in the onion and cook gently until soft and beginning to turn golden but not brown.

**3** Add the rice and mix to coat in oil and butter. Cook, stirring, for 2–3 minutes, or until the grains are translucent.

**4** Gradually add the stock and saffron mixture, a ladleful at a time. Stir constantly, adding more liquid as the rice absorbs it. Increase the heat slightly so that the liquid bubbles. Cook for 20 minutes, or until all the liquid is absorbed.

**5** Remove the risotto from the heat. Add the remaining butter, mix well, then stir in the Parmesan cheese. Season to taste with salt and pepper and serve immediately.

## VARIATION
YOU CAN USE THIS DELIGHTFUL RISOTTO AS A MARVELOUS BASIS FOR ADDITIONAL INGREDIENTS. FOR EXAMPLE, TRY ADDING 2 TABLESPOONS OF CANNED CORN KERNELS OR CHOPPED COOKED CARROT ABOUT 5 MINUTES BEFORE THE END OF THE COOKING TIME, OR SCATTER OVER A HANDFUL OF LIGHTLY TOASTED CASHEWS.

# BROWN RICE VEGETABLE PILAF

**SERVES 4**

**PREPARATION
30 MINUTES
COOKING
15 MINUTES**

PILAFS ARE POPULAR AROUND THE EASTERN MEDITERRANEAN AND IN ASIA. THE COOKING METHOD INVOLVES SAUTÉEING THE RICE IN HOT BUTTER OR OIL, THEN POURING IN THE STOCK AND SIMMERING. PILAF INGREDIENTS VARY—THEY CAN CONTAIN VEGETABLES, MEATS, POULTRY, OR FISH.

**INGREDIENTS**
- 4 TBSP VEGETABLE OIL
- 1 RED ONION, FINELY CHOPPED
- 2 TENDER CELERY STALKS, LEAVES INCLUDED, QUARTERED LENGTHWISE AND DICED
- 2 CARROTS, COARSELY GRATED
- 1 FRESH GREEN CHILE, SEEDED AND FINELY CHOPPED
- 3 SCALLIONS, GREEN PARTS INCLUDED, FINELY CHOPPED
- GENEROUS ¼ CUP WHOLE ALMONDS, SLICED LENGTHWISE
- 1¾ CUPS COOKED BROWN BASMATI RICE
- ¾ CUP COOKED SPLIT RED LENTILS
- ¼ CUP CHICKEN STOCK OR VEGETABLE STOCK
- 5 TBSP FRESH ORANGE JUICE
- SALT AND PEPPER
- FRESH CELERY LEAVES, TO GARNISH

**1** Heat 2 tablespoons of the oil in a high-sided skillet with a lid over medium heat. Add the onion. Cook for 5 minutes, or until softened.

**2** Add the celery, carrots, chile, scallions, and almonds. Stir-fry for 2 minutes, or until the vegetables are tender but still firm and brightly colored. Transfer to a bowl and set aside until required.

**3** Add the remaining oil to the skillet. Stir in the rice and lentils. Cook over medium–high heat, stirring, for 1–2 minutes, or until heated through. Reduce the heat. Stir in the stock and orange juice. Season to taste with salt and pepper.

**4** Return the vegetables to the skillet. Toss with the rice for a few minutes until heated through. Transfer to a warmed dish, garnish with celery leaves, and serve.

# VEGETABLE COUSCOUS

COUSCOUS IS A SEMOLINA GRAIN THAT IS WIDELY EATEN IN NORTH AFRICA. IT IS VERY QUICK AND EASY TO COOK, AND MAKES A PLEASANT CHANGE FROM RICE OR PASTA. IT CAN ALSO BE COOKED WITH MILK TO MAKE A PORRIDGE, OR MIXED WITH FRUITS AND SERVED AS A DESSERT.

**SERVES 4**

PREPARATION
**20 MINUTES**
COOKING
**35–40 MINUTES**

## INGREDIENTS
- 2 TBSP VEGETABLE OIL
- 1 LARGE ONION
- 1 CARROT, CHOPPED
- 1 TURNIP, CHOPPED
- 2½ CUPS VEGETABLE STOCK
- SCANT 1 CUP COUSCOUS
- 1 RED BELL PEPPER
- 2 TOMATOES
- 2 ZUCCHINI, CHOPPED
- 4½ OZ/125 G GREEN BEANS, CHOPPED
- GRATED ZEST OF 1 LEMON
- PINCH OF TURMERIC (OPTIONAL)
- 1 TBSP FINELY CHOPPED FRESH CILANTRO
- SALT AND PEPPER

**1** Heat the oil in a large saucepan. Add the onion, carrot, and turnip and sauté for 3–4 minutes. Add the stock, bring to a boil, cover, and simmer for 20 minutes.

**2** Meanwhile, place the couscous in a bowl and moisten with a little boiling water, stirring, until the grains have swollen and separated.

**3** Seed and chop the bell pepper, then add to the pan with the tomatoes, zucchini, bell pepper, and green beans. Stir together.

**4** Stir the lemon zest into the couscous, add the turmeric if using, and mix thoroughly. Place the couscous in a steamer and position it over the saucepan of vegetables. Simmer the vegetables so that the couscous steams for 8–10 minutes.

**5** Pile the couscous onto warmed serving plates. Ladle the vegetables and some of the liquid over the top. Sprinkle over the cilantro and serve immediately, garnished with parsley sprigs.

## VARIATION
YOU CAN REPLACE THE CHOPPED CILANTRO WITH 1 TABLESPOON OF FINELY CHOPPED FRESH FLAT-LEAF PARSLEY, AND GARNISH THE DISH WITH FRESH FLAT-LEAF PARSLEY SPRIGS.

# TABBOULEH

**SERVES 4**

**PREPARATION
15 MINUTES, PLUS
1½ HOURS' MARINATING
AND STANDING
COOKING
NONE**

THIS MIDDLE EASTERN SALAD IS BECOMING INCREASINGLY FASHIONABLE IN OTHER PARTS OF THE WORLD. IT IS A CLASSIC ACCOMPANIMENT TO LAMB, BUT IT ALSO GOES WELL WITH MOST BROILED MEATS. ALTERNATIVELY, SERVE IT WITH HUMMUS AND PITAS FOR A VEGETARIAN LUNCH.

**INGREDIENTS**
- SCANT 1 CUP BULGUR WHEAT
- 3 TBSP EXTRA VIRGIN OLIVE OIL
- 4 TBSP LEMON JUICE
- 4 SCALLIONS
- 1 GREEN BELL PEPPER, SEEDED AND SLICED
- 4 TOMATOES, CHOPPED
- 2 TBSP CHOPPED FRESH PARSLEY
- 2 TBSP CHOPPED FRESH MINT
- 8 BLACK OLIVES, PITTED
- SALT AND PEPPER
- FRESH MINT SPRIGS, TO GARNISH

**1** Place the bulgur wheat in a large bowl and add enough cold water to cover. Let it stand for 30 minutes, or until it has doubled in size. Drain well and press out as much liquid as possible. Spread out the wheat on paper towels to dry.

**2** Place the wheat in a serving bowl. Mix the olive oil and lemon juice together in a pitcher and season to taste with salt and pepper. Pour the lemon mixture over the wheat and marinate for 1 hour.

**3** Using a sharp knife, finely chop the scallions, then add to the salad with the green bell pepper, tomatoes, parsley, and mint and toss lightly to mix. Top the salad with the olives and garnish with fresh mint sprigs, then serve immediately.

## COOK'S TIP
THE BULGUR WHEAT GRAINS HAVE BEEN CRACKED BY BOILING AND SO ARE ALREADY PARTIALLY COOKED, MEANING IT JUST NEEDS TO BE REHYDRATED. DON'T MAKE THIS SALAD TOO FAR IN ADVANCE OR IT MAY BECOME SOGGY.

# CASSOULET

A STICK-TO-THE-RIBS WINTER WARMER, THIS TRADITIONAL GASCONY BEAN FEAST HAS SO MANY VARIATIONS THAT IT IS ALMOST IMPOSSIBLE TO GIVE A DEFINITIVE RECIPE. WHAT IS IMPORTANT, HOWEVER, IS TO USE SMALL, WHITE KIDNEY BEANS THAT HOLD THEIR SHAPE DURING COOKING.

**SERVES 6–8**

**PREPARATION**
**30 MINUTES, PLUS
5–8 HOURS' SOAKING**
**COOKING**
**6½–7 HOURS**

**INGREDIENTS**
- SCANT 2 CUPS DRIED WHITE KIDNEY BEANS, SOAKED FOR AT LEAST 5 HOURS OR ACCORDING TO THE PACKAGE INSTRUCTIONS
- 5 OZ/140 G PLAIN OR SMOKED BELLY OF PORK, RIND REMOVED, CUT INTO THICK PIECES
- 4 LARGE GARLIC CLOVES, CHOPPED
- 1 LARGE BOUQUET GARNI OF 4 FRESH PARSLEY SPRIGS, 6 FRESH THYME SPRIGS, AND 1 BAY LEAF
- LARGE PINCH OF QUATRE ÉPICES
- 8 TOULOUSE SAUSAGES
- 4 PIECES OF GOOSE CONFIT OR DUCK CONFIT, ABOUT 14 OZ/400 G
- 14 OZ/400 G BONELESS SHOULDER OF PORK, CUT INTO 2-INCH/5-CM CHUNKS
- 4-INCH/10-CM LENGTH DAY-OLD FRENCH BREAD, MADE INTO FINE BREAD CRUMBS
- 2 CUPS FINELY CHOPPED FRESH FLAT-LEAF PARSLEY
- CHICKEN OR VEGETABLE STOCK, IF NEEDED
- SALT AND PEPPER

**1** Rinse the beans, then place them in a large, heavy-bottom saucepan with water to cover, over high heat. Bring to a boil, boil rapidly for 10 minutes, then drain. Return the beans to the wiped-out saucepan with 2 inches/5 cm of water to cover and bring to a boil. Reduce the heat to a simmer and skim the surface until the gray foam stops rising.

**2** Add the belly of pork, garlic, bouquet garni, quatre épices, and pepper to taste. Adjust the heat so that bubbles just appear around the edge, then partially cover the pan and let the beans simmer for 1–½ hours, or according to the package instructions, until the beans are just slightly less than tender. The older the beans, the longer they will take to cook. Do not let them boil or the skins will split.

**3** Meanwhile, preheat the broiler to high. Broil the sausages, turning them frequently, just until the casings are browned, then set aside.

**4** Heat 2 tablespoons of fat from the confit in a skillet over medium–high heat. Add the pork shoulder chunks and sauté until brown on each side. Set aside.

**5** Preheat the oven to 300°F/150°C. When the beans are almost tender, place a large strainer over a large bowl and strain the beans, discarding the bouquet garni, but reserving the cooking liquid.

**6** Place half the beans in a large ovenproof casserole. Add the sausages, confit, and pork chunks. Season to taste with salt and pepper, then cover with the remaining beans.

**7** Pour in enough of the reserved cooking liquid to cover all the ingredients, topping up with stock if necessary. Mix the bread crumbs and parsley together, then spread half thickly over the surface.

**8** Bake, uncovered, for 4 hours. After 1 hour, use the back of a spoon to lightly push the bread crumbs into the liquid, repeating this twice more at hourly intervals.

**9** After 4 hours, sprinkle the top with the remaining bread crumbs but do not press into the liquid. Return the casserole to the oven and continue baking for 1 hour, or until the top is golden and crisp. If the liquid appears to evaporate too quickly, pour in a little extra stock at the edges. Serve from the casserole.

# CHILI CON CARNE

THIS TEX-MEX FAVORITE IS OFTEN SERVED WITH RICE, BUT IT IS JUST AS DELICIOUS EATEN WITH A BAKED POTATO, THICK SLICES OF FRESH CRUSTY BREAD, OR TORTILLAS. YOU CAN BUY PREPARED SOFT FLOUR TORTILLAS AND HEAT THEM THROUGH BRIEFLY IN A DRY SKILLET BEFORE SERVING.

**SERVES 4**

**PREPARATION**
**15 MINUTES**
**COOKING**
**30–35 MINUTES**

**INGREDIENTS**
- 2 TBSP SUNFLOWER OIL
- 1 LB 2 OZ/500 G FRESH GROUND BEEF
- 1 GREEN BELL PEPPER
- 1 LARGE ONION, CHOPPED
- 1 GARLIC CLOVE
- 1 TSP CHILI POWDER
- 1 LB 12 OZ/800 G CANNED CHOPPED TOMATOES
- 1 LB 12 OZ/800 G CANNED RED KIDNEY BEANS
- 2 CUPS BEEF STOCK
- SALT
- HANDFUL OF FRESH CILANTRO SPRIGS, PLUS EXTRA TO GARNISH
- 2 TBSP SOUR CREAM, TO SERVE

**1** Heat the oil in a large, heavy-bottom pan or ovenproof casserole. Add the beef and cook over medium heat, stirring frequently, for 5 minutes, or until broken up and browned.

**2** Seed and dice the bell pepper. Reduce the heat, add the onion, garlic, and bell pepper and cook, stirring frequently, for 10 minutes.

**3** Stir in the chili powder, tomatoes with their juices, and kidney beans. Pour in the stock and season to taste with salt. Bring to a boil, reduce the heat, and simmer, stirring frequently, for 15–20 minutes, or until the meat is tender.

**4** Chop the cilantro sprigs, reserving a few for a garnish, and stir into the chili. Adjust the seasoning, if necessary. Either garnish with cilantro sprigs and serve immediately with a splash of sour cream, or cool and store in the refrigerator overnight. Reheating it the next day makes the dish even more flavorsome.

## VARIATION
SUBSTITUTE 1–2 FINELY CHOPPED, SEEDED FRESH CHILES FOR THE CHILI POWDER IN STEP 3. ANAHEIM (MILD) OR JALAPEÑO (HOT) CHILES ARE BOTH CLASSIC TEX-MEX VARIETIES.

# CHINESE NOODLES

THIS DISH IS USUALLY SERVED AS A SNACK OR LIGHT MEAL, BUT IT MAY ALSO BE SERVED AS AN ACCOMPANIMENT TO PLAIN MEAT AND FISH DISHES. STIR-FRYING IS QUICK, EASY, AND INEXPENSIVE. IT IS ALSO A HEALTHY WAY TO COOK BECAUSE IT USES A MINIMUM OF FAT.

**SERVES 2–4**

**PREPARATION
10 MINUTES
COOKING
10–15 MINUTES**

## INGREDIENTS
- 12 OZ/350 G EGG NOODLES
- 3 TBSP VEGETABLE OIL
- 1 LB 8 OZ/675 G LEAN BEEF STEAK, CUT INTO THIN STRIPS
- 4½ OZ/125 G GREEN CABBAGE, SHREDDED
- 2¾ OZ/75 G BAMBOO SHOOTS
- 6 SCALLIONS, SLICED
- 1 OZ/25 G GREEN BEANS, HALVED
- 1 TBSP DARK SOY SAUCE
- 2 TBSP BEEF STOCK
- 1 TBSP DRY SHERRY
- 1 TBSP BROWN SUGAR
- 2 TBSP FRESH CHOPPED PARSLEY, TO GARNISH

**1** Cook the noodles in a pan of boiling water for 2–3 minutes. Drain well, rinse under cold running water, and drain thoroughly again.

**2** Heat 1 tablespoon of the oil in a preheated wok or large skillet, swirling it around until it begins to smoke.

**3** Add the noodles and stir-fry for 1–2 minutes. Drain the noodles and set aside until required.

**4** Heat the remaining oil in the wok. Add the beef and stir-fry for 2–3 minutes. Add the cabbage, bamboo shoots, scallions, and beans to the wok and stir-fry for 1–2 minutes.

**5** Add the soy sauce, stock, dry sherry, and sugar to the wok, stirring to mix well. Stir the noodles into the mixture in the wok, tossing to mix well. Transfer to serving bowls, garnish with chopped parsley, and serve immediately.

## VARIATION
TRY REPLACING THE EGG NOODLES IN THIS RECIPE WITH THE SAME QUANTITY OF RICE NOODLES, AND ADD A FEW CANNED WATER CHESTNUTS TO THE WOK IN STEP 4.

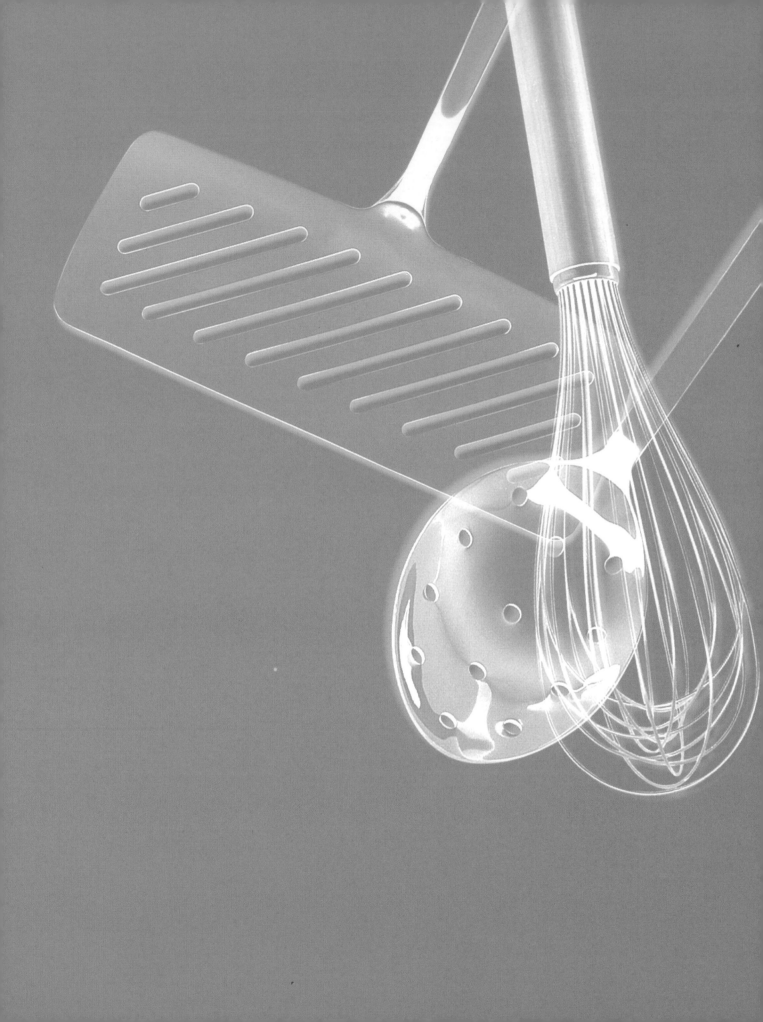

# CHAPTER 8

# FRUIT

FRUIT IS DELICIOUS. IT CAN BE EATEN RAW OUT OF YOUR HAND OR COOKED IN A MULTITUDE OF WAYS, BOTH SAVORY AND SWEET. IN THE FOLLOWING PAGES YOU WILL FIND AN INSPIRING COLLECTION OF RECIPES TO WHET YOUR APPETITE, WHETHER YOU ARE LOOKING FOR A LOWFAT DESSERT FOR A SLIMMER, OR A SUMPTUOUS CREATION FOR ENTERTAINING.

# TROPICAL FRUIT SALAD

A TROPICAL FRUIT SALAD IS DELIGHTFULLY REFRESHING DURING HOT SUMMER DAYS OR SULTRY EVENINGS. THIS ONE CONTAINS A LITTLE PUMPKIN PIE SPICE FOR A TANTALIZING HINT OF AROMATIC SWEETNESS. YOU CAN ALSO SERVE THIS WITH LIGHT SOUR CREAM, IF YOU PREFER.

**SERVES 6**

**PREPARATION**
**20 MINUTES, PLUS**
**1 HOUR'S CHILLING**
**COOKING**
**3 MINUTES**

**INGREDIENTS**
- 6 TBSP SUPERFINE SUGAR
- 1¾ CUPS WATER
- ½ TSP PUMPKIN PIE SPICE
- GRATED ZEST OF ½ LEMON
- 1 PAPAYA
- 1 MANGO
- 1 PINEAPPLE
- 4 ORANGES, PEELED AND CUT INTO SEGMENTS
- ¾ CUP STRAWBERRIES, HULLED AND QUARTERED
- LIGHT OR HEAVY CREAM, TO SERVE (OPTIONAL)

1 Place the sugar, water, pumpkin pie spice, and lemon zest in a saucepan. Bring to a boil, stirring constantly, then continue to boil for 1 minute. Remove from the heat and let it cool to room temperature.

2 Transfer to a pitcher or bowl, cover with plastic wrap, and chill in the refrigerator for at least 1 hour.

3 Peel and halve the papaya and remove the seeds. Cut the flesh into small chunks or slices, and place in a large bowl.

4 Cut the mango twice lengthwise, close to the pit. Remove and discard the pit. Peel and cut the flesh into small chunks or slices, and add to the bowl.

5 Cut off the top and bottom of the pineapple and remove the hard skin. Cut the pineapple in half lengthwise, then into quarters and remove the tough core. Cut the remaining flesh into small pieces and add to the bowl.

6 Add the orange segments and strawberries. Pour over the chilled syrup, cover with plastic wrap, and chill until required. Serve with cream, if desired.

## VARIATION

YOU CAN ADD SOME SLICED BANANA TO THIS FRUIT SALAD JUST BEFORE SERVING, OR SCATTER OVER SOME FINELY GRATED COCONUT.

# TRADITIONAL APPLE PIE

THIS SWEET APPLE PIE HAS A DELICIOUS DOUBLE CRUST. IT IS A SUBSTANTIAL DESSERT AND MAKES AN IMPRESSIVE FINISH TO ANY MEAL. IT CAN BE SERVED EITHER HOT OR COLD, ON ITS OWN, OR WITH CREAM OR CUSTARD. YOU CAN ADJUST THE AMOUNT OF SUGAR ACCORDING TO YOUR TASTE.

**SERVES 6**

**PREPARATION**
**30 MINUTES, PLUS**
**30 MINUTES' CHILLING**
COOKING
**50 MINUTES**

**INGREDIENTS**
- 1 LB 10 OZ–2 LB 4 OZ/750 G– 1 KG COOKING APPLES
- ABOUT ⅔ CUP BROWN OR WHITE SUGAR, PLUS EXTRA FOR SPRINKLING
- ½–1 TSP GROUND CINNAMON
- 1–2 TBSP WATER

FOR THE PIE DOUGH
- HEAPING 2½ CUPS ALL-PURPOSE FLOUR
- PINCH OF SALT
- 6 TBSP BUTTER
- 6 TBSP WHITE VEGETABLE FAT
- ABOUT 6 TBSP COLD WATER
- MILK OR BEATEN EGG, TO GLAZE

**1** To make the pie dough, sift 2½ cups of flour and a pinch of salt into a large bowl. Add the butter and fat and rub it in with your fingertips until the mixture resembles fine bread crumbs. Add enough water to mix to a dough, wrap in plastic wrap, and chill for 30 minutes.

**2** Preheat the oven to 425°F/220°C. Roll out almost two-thirds of the pie dough thinly on a lightly floured counter and use to line an 8–9-inch/20–23-cm deep pie plate or shallow pie pan.

**3** Peel, core, and slice the apples, then mix them with the sugar and cinnamon and pack into the pastry shell; the filling can come up above the rim. If the apples are a dry variety add a little water to moisten.

**4** Roll out the remaining dough to form a lid. Dampen the edges of the pie rim with water and position the lid, pressing the edges firmly together. Trim and crimp the edges.

**5** Use the pie dough trimmings to cut out leaves or other shapes to decorate the top of the pie. Dampen the shapes and attach. Glaze the top of the pie with milk or beaten egg, make 1–2 slits in the top, and put the pie on a baking sheet.

**6** Bake in the oven for 20 minutes, then reduce the oven temperature to 350°F/180°C and cook for 30 minutes, or until the pastry is a light golden brown. Serve hot or cold, sprinkled with sugar.

## COOK'S TIP
TO REDUCE THE FAT CONTENT OF THIS PIE, YOU CAN REPLACE THE BUTTER WITH MARGARINE. YOU CAN ALSO USE PUMPKIN PIE SPICE OR GROUND GINGER INSTEAD OF THE CINNAMON.

# STUFFED BAKED APPLES

BAKED APPLES ARE A TRADITIONAL FAMILY FAVORITE AND ARE USUALLY STUFFED WITH A TASTY COMBINATION OF GOLDEN RAISINS, RAISINS, BROWN SUGAR, AND SWEET SPICES. THIS GINGER-FLAVORED OATY FILLING IS MORE UNUSUAL, AND MAKES A WELCOME CHANGE.

**SERVES 4**

**PREPARATION
10 MINUTES
COOKING
45 MINUTES**

**INGREDIENTS**
- 2 TBSP BLANCHED ALMONDS
- ⅓ CUP PLUMPED DRIED APRICOTS
- 1 PIECE PRESERVED GINGER, DRAINED
- 1 TBSP HONEY
- 1 TBSP SYRUP FROM THE PRESERVED GINGER JAR
- 4 TBSP ROLLED OATS
- 4 LARGE COOKING APPLES

**1** Preheat the oven to 350°F/180°C. Using a sharp knife, chop the almonds very finely. Chop the apricots and preserved ginger very finely. Set aside.

**2** Place the honey and syrup in a saucepan and heat until the honey has melted. Stir in the oats and cook gently over low heat for 2 minutes. Remove the saucepan from the heat and stir in the almonds, apricots, and preserved ginger.

**3** Core the apples, widen the tops slightly, and score around the circumference of each to prevent the skins from bursting during cooking. Place the apples in an ovenproof dish and fill the cavities with the filling. Pour just enough water into the dish to come about one-third of the way up the apples. Bake in the preheated oven for 40 minutes, or until tender. Serve immediately.

**VARIATION**
USE AN EXTRA TABLESPOON OF HONEY INSTEAD OF THE PRESERVED GINGER AND SYRUP, REPLACE THE ALMONDS WITH WALNUTS, AND ADD ½ TEASPOON OF GROUND CINNAMON.

# TARTE AU CITRON

FEW DESSERTS CAN BE MORE APPEALING TO ROUND OFF A MEAL ON A HOT EVENING THAN THIS DELICIOUSLY TANGY TART. IT LOOKS MARVELOUSLY INVITING AND IS ATTRACTIVE TO SERVE, MAKING IT THE IDEAL DESSERT TO TEMPT YOUR DINNER GUESTS OR MEMBERS OF YOUR HOUSEHOLD.

**SERVES 6–8**

**PREPARATION**
**25 MINUTES, PLUS**
**1 HOUR'S CHILLING**
**COOKING**
**35 MINUTES**

**INGREDIENTS**
- GRATED ZEST OF 2–3 LARGE LEMONS
- ⅔ CUP LEMON JUICE
- ½ CUP SUPERFINE SUGAR
- ½ CUP HEAVY CREAM OR SOUR CREAM, PLUS EXTRA TO SERVE
- 3 LARGE EGGS
- 3 LARGE EGG YOLKS
- CONFECTIONERS' SUGAR, FOR DUSTING

**FOR THE PIE DOUGH**
- SCANT 1¼ CUPS ALL-PURPOSE FLOUR, PLUS EXTRA FOR DUSTING
- ½ TSP SALT
- ½ CUP COLD UNSALTED BUTTER, DICED
- 1 EGG YOLK BEATEN WITH 2 TBSP ICE-COLD WATER

**TO SERVE**
- CANDIED CITRUS PEEL
- FRESH WHOLE RASPBERRIES

**1** To make the pie dough, sift the flour and salt into a large bowl. Add the butter and rub it in with your fingertips until the mixture resembles fine bread crumbs. Add the egg yolk and water and stir to mix to a dough.

**2** Gather the dough into a ball, wrap in plastic wrap, and chill for at least 1 hour.

**3** Preheat the oven to 400°F/200°C. Roll the dough out on a lightly floured counter and use to line a 9–10-inch/23–25-cm fluted tart pan with a removable bottom. Prick the bottom all over with a fork and line with parchment paper and baking beans.

**4** Bake in the preheated oven for 15 minutes, until the dough looks set. Remove the paper and beans. Reduce the oven temperature to 375°F/190°C.

**5** Beat the lemon zest, lemon juice, and sugar together until blended. Slowly beat in the cream, then beat in the eggs and yolks, one by one.

**6** Set the pastry shell on a baking tray and pour in the filling. Transfer to the preheated oven and bake for 20 minutes, until the filling is set.

**7** Let the tart cool completely on a wire rack. Dust with confectioners' sugar. Serve with a spoonful of cream, candied citrus peel, and whole raspberries.

**VARIATION**
YOU CAN SERVE THIS DESSERT WITH OTHER FRUITS INSTEAD OF RASPBERRIES, SUCH AS STRAWBERRIES. ALTERNATIVELY, TRY DECORATING IT WITH TWISTS OF ORANGE.

# GOLDEN BAKED APPLE DESSERT

THIS IS A WARM AND SATISFYING DESSERT DURING COLD WEATHER, YET IT IS SURPRISINGLY LOW IN FAT, MAKING IT THE IDEAL CHOICE FOR DIETERS AND THE HEALTH-CONSCIOUS. YOU CAN ADJUST THE AMOUNT OF SUGAR ACCORDING TO YOUR TASTE. TRY SERVING IT WITH LOW-FAT CUSTARD.

**SERVES 4**

**PREPARATION**
**15 MINUTES**
**COOKING**
**30–35 MINUTES**

**INGREDIENTS**
- 1 LB/450 G COOKING APPLES
- 1 TSP GROUND CINNAMON
- 2 TBSP GOLDEN RAISINS
- 4 SLICES WHOLE-WHEAT BREAD
- GENEROUS ½ CUP LOWFAT COTTAGE CHEESE
- 4 TBSP BROWN SUGAR
- GENEROUS 1 CUP LOW-FAT MILK

**1** Preheat the oven to 425°F/220°C. Peel and core the apples and chop the flesh into ½-inch/1-cm pieces. Place in a bowl and toss with the cinnamon and golden raisins.

**2** Remove the crusts and cut the bread into ½-inch/1-cm cubes. Add to the apples with the cottage cheese and 3 tablespoons of the brown sugar and mix together. Stir in the milk.

**3** Turn the mixture into an ovenproof dish and sprinkle with the remaining sugar. Bake in the preheated oven for 30–35 minutes, or until golden brown. Serve hot.

## VARIATION

REPLACE THE CHEESE WITH CREAM CHEESE OR RICOTTA, AND THE GOLDEN RAISINS WITH RAISINS, IF DESIRED.

# TROPICAL FRUIT DESSERT

FRUIT FOOLS ARE ALWAYS POPULAR, AND THIS LIGHTLY TANGY VERSION WILL BE NO EXCEPTION. YOU CAN VARY THIS RECIPE BY USING YOUR FAVORITE COMBINATIONS OF FRUITS IF YOU PREFER. FOR EXAMPLE, TRY USING PAPAYA INSTEAD OF THE MANGO, AND MELON INSTEAD OF THE KIWIS.

**SERVES 4**

**PREPARATION**
**20 MINUTES, PLUS**
**20 MINUTES' CHILLING**
**COOKING**
**NONE**

**INGREDIENTS**
- 1 RIPE MANGO
- 2 KIWIS
- 1 BANANA
- 2 TBSP LIME JUICE
- ½ TSP FINELY GRATED LIME ZEST, PLUS EXTRA TO DECORATE
- 2 EGG WHITES
- SCANT 2 CUPS CANNED LOW-FAT CUSTARD
- ½ TSP VANILLA EXTRACT
- 2 PASSION FRUIT

**1** Peel the mango and slice either side of the smooth, flat central pit. Coarsely chop the flesh and process the fruit in a food processor or blender until smooth. Alternatively, mash with a fork.

**2** Peel the kiwis, chop the flesh into small pieces, and place in a bowl. Peel and chop the banana and add to the bowl. Toss all of the fruit in the lime juice and zest and mix well.

**3** Whisk the egg whites in a grease-free bowl until stiff, then gently fold in the custard and vanilla extract until thoroughly mixed.

**4** Alternately layer the chopped fruit, mango puree, and custard mixture, finishing with a layer of custard in 4 tall glasses. Chill in the refrigerator for 20 minutes.

**5** Halve the passion fruit, scoop out the seeds, and spoon over the fruit fools. Decorate each serving with extra lime zest and serve immediately.

## VARIATION

OTHER TROPICAL FRUITS TO TRY INCLUDE PAPAYA PUREE, WITH CHOPPED PINEAPPLE AND DATES, AND POMEGRANATE SEEDS TO DECORATE. ALTERNATIVELY, MAKE A SUMMER FRUIT FOOL BY USING STRAWBERRY PUREE, TOPPED WITH BLACKBERRIES, AND CHERRIES TO FINISH.

# APPLE STRUDEL WITH WARM CIDER SAUCE

**SERVES 2–4**

**PREPARATION**
**25 MINUTES**
**COOKING**
**15–20 MINUTES**

STRUDELS ARE POPULAR IN GERMANY AND AUSTRIA, AND ARE STUFFED WITH SAVORY OR SWEET FILLINGS. APPLE IS THE MOST FAMOUS SWEET STRUDEL, AND THIS VERSION HAS AN ADDED ADVANTAGE IN THAT IT IS EXTREMELY LOW IN FAT AND SUITABLE FOR PEOPLE ON LOW-FAT DIETS.

**INGREDIENTS**
- 8 CRISP EATING APPLES
- 1 TBSP LEMON JUICE
- ½ CUP GOLDEN RAISINS
- 1 TSP GROUND CINNAMON
- ½ TSP GRATED NUTMEG
- 1 TBSP BROWN SUGAR
- 6 SHEETS FILO DOUGH
- VEGETABLE OIL SPRAY
- CONFECTIONERS' SUGAR, TO SERVE

**FOR THE CIDER SAUCE**
- 1 TBSP CORNSTARCH
- 2 CUPS HARD CIDER

**1** Preheat the oven to 375°F/190°C. Line a baking sheet with nonstick paper. Peel and core the apples and chop them into ½-inch/1-cm cubes. Toss the pieces in a bowl with the lemon juice, golden raisins, cinnamon, nutmeg, and sugar.

**2** Lay out a sheet of filo dough, spray with vegetable oil, and lay a second sheet on top. Repeat with a third sheet. Spread over half the apple mixture and roll up lengthwise, tucking in the ends to enclose the filling. Repeat to make a second strudel. Slide onto the baking

sheet, spray with oil, and bake in the oven for 15–20 minutes.

**3** For the sauce, blend the cornstarch in a pan with a little hard cider until smooth. Add the remaining hard cider and heat gently, stirring constantly, until the mixture boils and thickens. Serve the strudel warm or cold, dredged with confectioners' sugar and accompanied by the sauce.

## COOK'S TIP
WORK WITH ONE SHEET OF FILO DOUGH AT A TIME, AND KEEP THE REST COVERED WITH A CLEAN, DAMP DISH TOWEL TO PREVENT THEM FROM DRYING OUT.

# DATE & APRICOT TART

THIS DRIED FRUIT TART IS RICH IN PROTEIN AND DIETARY FIBER, AND, THEREFORE, MAKES A HEALTHY CHOICE FOR A DESSERT. THERE IS NO NEED TO ADD ANY EXTRA SUGAR TO THIS FILLING BECAUSE THE DRIED FRUIT IS NATURALLY SWEET. THE TART CAN BE SERVED HOT OR COLD.

**SERVES 8**

**PREPARATION**
25 MINUTES, PLUS
30 MINUTES' CHILLING
**COOKING**
45–50 MINUTES

**INGREDIENTS**
- HEAPING 1½ CUPS WHOLE-WHEAT FLOUR, PLUS EXTRA FOR DUSTING
- ½ CUP GROUND MIXED NUTS
- SCANT ½ CUP MARGARINE, CUT INTO SMALL PIECES
- 4 TBSP WATER
- 1⅓ CUPS DRIED APRICOTS, CHOPPED
- 1⅓ CUPS CHOPPED PITTED DATES
- SCANT 2 CUPS APPLE JUICE
- 1 TSP GROUND CINNAMON
- GRATED ZEST OF 1 LEMON
- CUSTARD, TO SERVE (OPTIONAL)

**1** Place the flour and ground nuts in a large bowl. Add the margarine and rub it in with your fingertips until the mixture resembles fine bread crumbs. Stir in the water and mix to a dough. Wrap the dough in plastic wrap and chill in the refrigerator for 30 minutes.

**2** Meanwhile, place the apricots and dates in a saucepan, with the apple juice, cinnamon, and lemon zest. Bring to a boil, cover, and simmer over low heat for 15 minutes, until the fruit softens. Mash to a puree.

**3** Preheat the oven to 400°F/200°C. Set aside a small ball of dough for making lattice strips. Roll out the rest of the dough on a lightly floured counter to form a circle and use to line a 9-inch/23-cm loose-bottom tart pan.

**4** Spread the fruit filling evenly over the bottom of the pastry shell. Roll out the reserved dough and cut into strips ½ inch/1 cm wide. Cut the strips to fit the tart and twist them across the top of the fruit to form a decorative lattice pattern. Moisten the edges of the strips with a little water and seal them firmly around the rim of the tart.

**5** Bake for 25–30 minutes, until golden brown. Cut into slices, and serve with custard if using.

**VARIATION**
FOR A LUXURIOUS TREAT, INSTEAD OF SERVING THIS TART WITH CUSTARD, TRY SERVING IT WITH GENEROUS SPOONFULS OF MASCARPONE CHEESE SPRINKLED WITH A LITTLE CINNAMON.

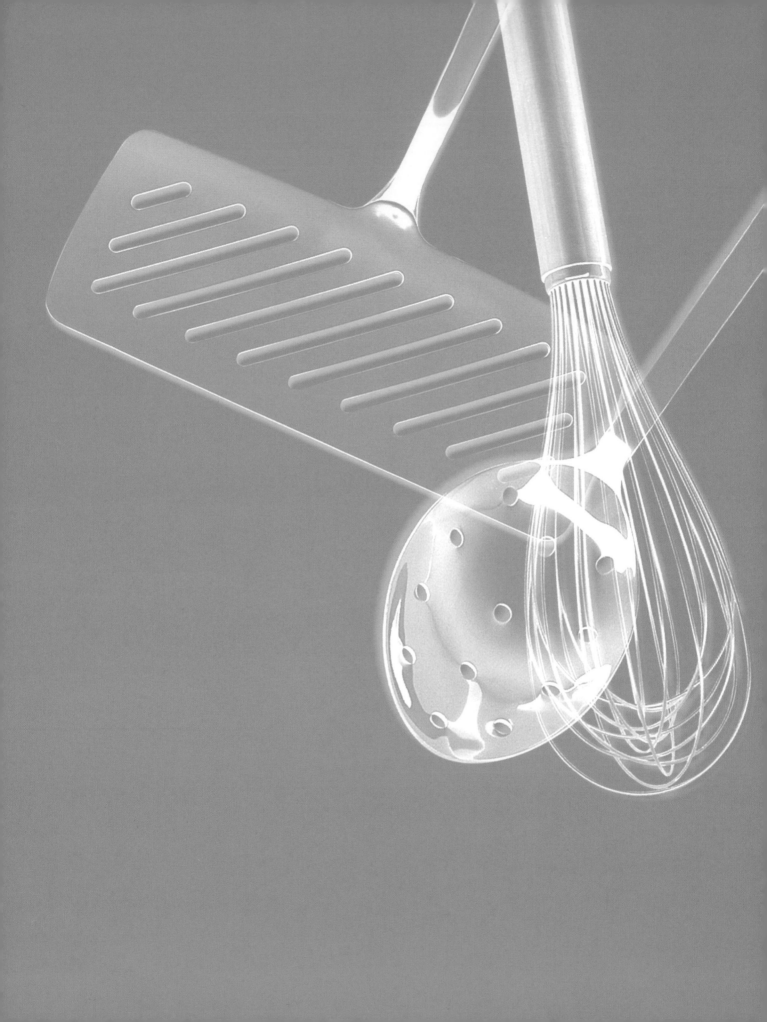

# CHAPTER 9

# BAKING

THERE IS NOTHING LIKE THE SMELL OF FRESHLY HOME-BAKED BREAD AND PASTRIES TO GET EVERY MEMBER OF THE HOUSEHOLD HOVERING AROUND THE KITCHEN. IN THIS CHAPTER YOU WILL ENCOUNTER SOME TRULY INSPIRATIONAL BREAD RECIPES, AND A MARVELOUS SELECTION OF OTHER BAKED TREATS, INCLUDING SAVORY PASTRIES AND SWEET, DELICIOUS MUFFINS.

# INTRODUCTION

THERE IS NOTHING LIKE THE AROMA OF FRESHLY BAKED BREAD, PIE DOUGH, CAKES, AND COOKIES TO STIMULATE THE APPETITE. BAKING THESE ITEMS FOR YOURSELF IS VERY SATISFYING, AND THE MOUTHWATERING AROMAS WILL PROVE TO BE AN IRRESISTIBLE TEMPTATION FOR YOUR FAMILY AND FRIENDS.

### Making bread at home

Making your own bread does not have to be difficult—anyone can make delicious loaves and rolls with the minimum of effort. The key to making perfect bread is to use the right ingredients at the right temperature. Always use white bread flour instead of ordinary flour. Bread flour has a higher gluten content than ordinary flour, which increases the elasticity of the dough. You can use any of the different kinds of yeast, but each has a different method for breadmaking. You will also need to use the correct quantities: ½ oz/15 g fresh yeast or 1 tbsp dried yeast is enough to make 1 lb 10 oz/750 g strong bread flour rise. When you add water, make sure it is tepid, because if it is too hot, it will kill the yeast.

#### Fresh yeast
Crush this compressed cake from of yeast in a pitcher with a little warm water, then cover and let it stand until the surface starts to bubble.

#### Active dry yeast
Sprinkle the dried yeast over a little warm water in a pitcher, then stir in a pinch of sugar. Cover and let it stand until it froths. One package of dry yeast is equivalent to one cake of fresh yeast.

Yeast

Bread

### Key techniques for making dough

Making the perfect dough can be straightforward, but it is important to follow a certain procedure to achieve good results every time.

#### Mixing

To mix the dough, sift the flour and salt into a mixing bowl. Make a well in the center, then add the yeast. Pour in lukewarm water, then gradually pull in the flour from the edges and mix together, adding more lukewarm water as necessary in order to form a soft dough (see step 1, opposite).

#### Kneading

This process is necessary in order to make the dough smooth and increase its elasticity. To knead the dough, push your hand into it, then stretch it away from you. Pick up the farthest end of the dough and pull it back to the top, then turn the dough 45° and repeat the kneading action away from you. Keep turning the dough 45° and repeating the kneading action (see step 2, opposite). Kneading usually takes about 5 minutes. To save time and effort, you could use a free-standing mixer or food processor with a dough hook to mix and knead the dough for you. Kneading will take about 3 minutes this way.

### Rising

After the dough has been kneaded, place it in an oiled bowl, cover it with plastic wrap, and put it in a warm place (see step 3, below). Let it rise to about double its original size.

### Punching down

This is also known as "knocking back." Punch your fist into the risen dough so that it collapses and releases the air. Then turn the dough out onto a floured counter (some of it may need scraping out) and knead for 1 minute, until it has lost its cold feel and has an even temperature.

### Proving

This stage literally means proving that the yeast is still active. To do this, after punching down the dough, you need to divide and shape it as required (see below). Cover as before and let it rise for a second (but shorter) time, until the dough has doubled in size.

### Shaping

To shape the dough correctly for a loaf pan, use your hands to form the dough into an oval, then bring over the two short sides to the center, turn the dough over, and transfer, seam-side down, to a greased loaf pan (see step 4, below). To make rolls, simply use your hands to roll even-size pieces of the dough into balls, and place on a greased baking sheet.

### Baking and storing bread

The dough will keep, covered, in the refrigerator for up to a day before baking. To bake the bread, you will need a hot oven, so make sure you preheat it beforehand. Underbaked bread has a moist, doughlike consistency and flavor, so it is always better to overbake if necessary. To test if the bread is properly baked, remove it from the oven, turn it out of its pan, and use your knuckles to give it a sharp tap on the bottom. If it sounds hollow, the bread is done. It it does not, return it to the oven and bake for another 5 minutes, or until

the bread is properly baked. When it is done, remove from the oven, and let it cool on a wire rack. If you want a soft crust, cover the loaf with a clean dish towel while it is cooling. Freshly baked bread will keep, covered, for 2–3 days at room temperature, but no longer because it has no added preservatives. You can also keep it wrapped in the refrigerator for up to a week, or wrap it in a freezer bag and freeze it for up to a month.

1   2   3   4

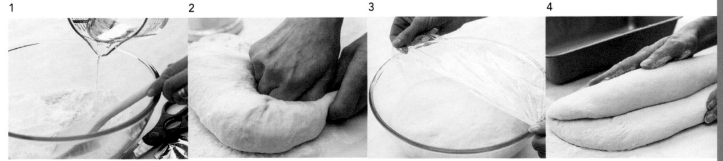

### Making pie dough

Pie dough is very versatile and lends a professional finish to a wide range of savory and sweet dishes. Choose your dough to match the occasion: unsweetened pie dough for savory or sweet pies, and tarts; choux pastry for profiteroles and eclairs; filo dough for pancake rolls or apple strudel; or puff pastry for sausage rolls and a wide range of desserts.

### Pie pastry

This recipe will make enough pie dough to line an 8-inch/20-cm tart pan.

scant 1¼ cups all-purpose flour,
    plus extra for dusting
6 tbsp butter, diced
2–3 tbsp cold water

Sift the all-purpose flour, then use your fingertips to rub in the butter until the mixture resembles fine bread crumbs. Gradually mix in enough water to make a soft dough. Use your hands to shape the dough into a ball. Cover with plastic wrap and refrigerate. When you are ready to use it, turn it out onto a clean counter lightly dusted with flour. Use a rolling pin to roll it out to the desired thickness.

**Variation:** To make a sweet pie dough, stir 1 tablespoon of superfine sugar into the flour after sifting, and replace half the water with 2 beaten egg yolks.

### Choux pastry

This quantity will make about 24 round choux puffs.

heaping ¾ cup water
5¾ tbsp butter
heaping ¾ cup all-purpose flour
½ tsp salt
½ tsp confectioners' sugar
3 eggs

Preheat the oven to 400°F/200°C. Pour the water into a saucepan and add the butter. Gently bring to a boil. Sift the flour and salt into a bowl, then mix in the confectioners' sugar. In a separate bowl, beat the eggs. When the butter is just beginning to boil, remove from the heat and stir in the flour mixture. Continue to stir until smooth, then return to the heat and stir until the mixture begins to pull away from the sides of the pan. Remove from the heat and gradually beat in the eggs until the mixture forms a thick, glossy paste. Put 24 round spoonfuls of the mixture onto greased baking sheets and brush the tops with a little beaten egg. Bake in the preheated oven for 20 minutes, or until golden. Remove from the oven and cool.

**Serving suggestion:** Split the cooled puffs in half horizontally and sandwich with whipped cream. You can also brush melted chocolate over the tops and let it cool, or serve the puffs with a chocolate sauce.

### Making cakes and cookies

For cakes and cookies there are four basic methods of mixing, as follows:

#### Creaming

This is a good method for making light sponge cakes. Simply beat

1    2    3    4

the butter and sugar together until light, then beat in the eggs and fold in the flour. Use softened butter or margarine for this method.

### All-in-one

This method saves time and effort when making light sponge cakes, and can be done manually or in a machine. Put all the ingredients into a bowl and beat well until smooth. Alternatively, put the ingredients into a freestanding mixer or food processor and beat on slow speed for 2–3 minutes, until smooth.

### Rubbing in

This method is ideal for cookies and quick breads. Use your fingertips to rub the butter into the flour until it resembles fine bread crumbs. Mix in the sugar, egg, and other liquid ingredients. Stir in the flour from the sides of the bowl.

### Melting

Use this method for moist cakes and cookies. Melt the butter in a pan along with the sugar and any other dissolvable ingredients. Remove from the heat and cool slightly. Meanwhile, sift the flour into a bowl and make a well in the center. Beat together the eggs and milk and pour into the well, then add the egg mixture. Stir in the flour from the sides of the bowl.

## Basic sponge mixture

This recipe will make enough for two 8-inch/20-cm greased and lined round cake pans.

1 cup unsalted butter, softened, or
   soft margarine suitable for baking
1⅛ cups superfine sugar
4 eggs
1⅝ cups self-rising flour, sifted
2 tsp baking powder
pinch of salt

Preheat the oven to 375°F/190°C. Grease and line the round cake pans. Place the butter in a large bowl, then add the sugar and use a wooden spoon to beat together until the mixture is smooth and light. Gradually beat in the eggs, making sure that the mixture stays smooth throughout. In a separate bowl, sift together the flour, baking powder, and salt, then fold into the egg mixture in a figure-eight movement. Divide the mixture between the round cake pans and bake for about 25 minutes, until golden and risen. Remove from the oven and cool in the pans for about 5 minutes before turning out on a wire rack to cool completely.

**Variation:** To make a chocolate version of this sponge, replace 1 tablespoon of the self-rising flour with 1 tablespoon of unsweetened cocoa.

## Butter shortbread

This recipe makes 8 large pieces of shortbread or 16 smaller pieces.

heaping ½ cup unsalted butter,
   softened, plus extra for greasing
scant 1¼ cups all-purpose flour
scant ⅓ cup rice flour
¼ cup superfine sugar, plus extra
   for sprinkling

Preheat the oven to 325°F/160°C. Grease an 8-inch/20-cm loose-bottom tart pan. Sift the all-purpose and rice flours into a large bowl.

In a separate bowl, cream together the butter and superfine sugar, then stir in the sifted flours. Put the mixture into the prepared tart pan and smooth the surface. Lightly sprinkle over some superfine sugar, then prick all over the surface with a fork. Using a sharp knife, score the surface into 8 wedges (or 16 smaller wedges, if preferred), then bake in the preheated oven for 30 minutes, or until lightly golden.

Remove from the oven and let it cool in the pan for 5 minutes. Slide the shortbread out of the pan, then use a sharp knife to cut along the score marks and divide the shortbread into wedges. Cool on a wire rack, then serve immediately or store in an airtight container for up to a week.

# CRUSTY WHITE BREAD

**MAKES 1 MEDIUM LOAF**

**PREPARATION**
**30 MINUTES, PLUS**
**1½ HOURS' RISING**
**COOKING**
**30 MINUTES**

THERE IS A LOT OF MYSTIQUE THAT SURROUNDS BREADMAKING, BUT IN REALITY ANYONE CAN BAKE THEIR OWN BREAD AT HOME. THIS RECIPE IS EASY TO DO, AND WILL MAKE YOU WANT TO BAKE YOUR OWN BREAD AGAIN AND AGAIN.

**INGREDIENTS**
- 1 EGG
- 1 EGG YOLK
- LUKEWARM WATER, AS REQUIRED
- 1 LB 2 OZ/500 G WHITE BREAD FLOUR, PLUS EXTRA FOR DUSTING
- 1½ TSP SALT
- 2 TSP SUGAR
- 1 TSP ACTIVE DRY YEAST
- 2 TBSP BUTTER, DICED
- SUNFLOWER OIL, FOR GREASING

**1** Place the egg and egg yolk in a pitcher and beat lightly to mix. Add enough lukewarm water to make up to 1¼ cups. Stir well.

**2** Place the flour, salt, sugar, and yeast in a large bowl. Add the butter and rub it in with your fingertips until the mixture resembles bread crumbs. Make a well in the center and add the egg mixture and work to a smooth dough.

**3** Turn the dough out onto a lightly floured counter and knead for 10 minutes, or until the dough is smooth and elastic. Place the dough in an oiled bowl, cover with plastic wrap, and let stand in a warm place to rise for 1 hour, or until it has doubled in size.

**4** Oil a loaf pan. Turn the dough out onto a lightly floured counter and knead for 1 minute, until smooth. Shape the dough the length of the pan and three times the width. Fold the dough into three lengthwise and place it in the pan with the seam underneath. Cover and let stand in a warm place for 30 minutes, until it has risen above the pan.

**5** Preheat the oven to 425°F/220°C. Bake in the oven for 30 minutes, or until firm and golden brown. Test that the loaf is cooked by tapping it on the bottom—it should sound hollow. Transfer to a wire rack to cool completely before serving.

# WHOLE-WHEAT HARVEST BREAD

**MAKES 1 SMALL LOAF**

**PREPARATION
30 MINUTES, PLUS
1½ HOURS' RISING
COOKING
30 MINUTES**

THIS WHOLE-WHEAT LOAF IS FULL OF HEALTHY FIBER AND NATURAL GOODNESS. IT NEEDS VERY LITTLE PREPARATION AND IS VERY EASY TO MAKE. SIMPLY FOLLOW THE INSTRUCTIONS GIVEN HERE, PUT THE DOUGH IN THE OVEN, AND WAIT FOR THE DELICIOUS AROMA TO PERVADE YOUR KITCHEN.

**INGREDIENTS**
- HEAPING 1½ CUPS WHOLE-WHEAT BREAD FLOUR, PLUS EXTRA FOR DUSTING
- 1 TBSP SKIM MILK POWDER
- 1 TSP SALT
- 2 TBSP BROWN SUGAR
- 1 TSP ACTIVE DRY YEAST
- 1½ TBSP SUNFLOWER OIL, PLUS EXTRA FOR GREASING
- ¾ CUP LUKEWARM WATER

**1** Place the flour, milk, salt, sugar, and yeast in a large bowl. Pour in the oil and add the water, then mix well to make a smooth dough.

**2** Turn the dough out onto a lightly floured counter and knead for 10 minutes, or until the dough is smooth. Place the dough in an oiled bowl, cover with plastic wrap, and let stand in a warm place to rise for 1 hour, or until it has doubled in size.

**3** Oil a 2-lb/900-g loaf pan. Turn the dough out onto a lightly floured counter and knead for 1 minute until smooth. Shape the dough the length of the pan and three times the width. Fold the dough into three lengthwise and place it in the pan with the seam underneath. Cover and let stand in a warm place for 30 minutes, until it has risen above the pan.

**4** Preheat the oven to 425°F/220°C. Bake in the oven for 30 minutes, or until firm and golden brown. Test that the loaf is cooked by tapping it on the bottom—it should sound hollow. Transfer to a wire rack to cool completely before serving.

# MIXED SEED BREAD

THIS SEEDED BREAD IS DELICIOUSLY AROMATIC, TASTES MARVELOUS, AND IS RICHER IN CALCIUM AND PROTEIN THAN A PLAIN LOAF. IT IS ALSO RICH IN OMEGA-3 ESSENTIAL FATTY ACIDS, WHICH NUTRITIONISTS SAY CONTRIBUTE TO GOOD HEALTH AND OVERALL WELL-BEING.

**MAKES 1 MEDIUM LOAF**

**PREPARATION**
**30 MINUTES, PLUS**
**1½ HOURS' RISING**
**COOKING**
**30 MINUTES**

**INGREDIENTS**
- HEAPING 2½ CUPS WHITE BREAD FLOUR, PLUS EXTRA FOR DUSTING
- SCANT 1½ CUPS RYE FLOUR
- 1½ TBSP SKIM MILK POWDER
- 1½ TSP SALT
- 1 TBSP BROWN SUGAR
- 1 TSP ACTIVE DRY YEAST
- 1½ TBSP SUNFLOWER OIL, PLUS EXTRA FOR GREASING
- 2 TSP LEMON JUICE
- 1¼ CUPS LUKEWARM WATER
- 1 TSP CARAWAY SEEDS
- ½ TSP POPPY SEEDS
- ½ TSP SESAME SEEDS

**FOR THE TOPPING**
- 1 EGG WHITE
- 1 TBSP WATER
- 1 TBSP SUNFLOWER SEEDS OR PUMPKIN SEEDS

**1** Place the flours, milk powder, salt, sugar, and yeast in a large bowl. Pour in the oil and add the lemon juice and water. Stir in the seeds and mix well to make a smooth dough.

**2** Turn the dough out onto a lightly floured counter and knead for 10 minutes, or until the dough is smooth and elastic. Place the dough in an oiled bowl, cover with plastic wrap, and let stand in a warm place to rise for 1 hour, or until it has doubled in size.

**3** Oil a 2-lb/900-g loaf pan. Turn the dough out onto a lightly floured counter and knead for 1 minute, until smooth. Shape the dough the length of the pan and three times the width. Fold the dough into three lengthwise and place it in the pan with the seam underneath. Cover and let stand in a warm place for 30 minutes, until it has risen above the pan.

**4** Preheat the oven to 425°F/220°C. For the topping, lightly beat the egg white with the water to make a glaze. Just before baking, brush the glaze over the loaf, then gently press the sunflower seeds or pumpkin seeds all over the top.

**5** Bake in the oven for 30 minutes, or until firm and golden brown. Test that the loaf is cooked by tapping it on the bottom—it should sound hollow. Transfer to a wire rack to cool completely before serving.

# OLIVE & SUN-DRIED TOMATO BREAD

**SERVES 4**

**PREPARATION**
**20 MINUTES, PLUS**
**2¼ HOURS' RISING**
**COOKING**
**40 MINUTES**

THIS DELICIOUS BREAD CONJURES UP AROMAS AND FLAVORS OF THE WARM MEDITERRANEAN, WITH PLUMP, JUICY OLIVES AND RIPE, FLAVORFUL TOMATOES DRIED IN THE HOT MIDDAY SUN. THE TASTE IS IRRESISTIBLE—IT WILL LEAVE YOUR HOUSEHOLD AND YOUR GUESTS LONGING FOR MORE.

**INGREDIENTS**
- HEAPING 2¾ CUPS ALL-PURPOSE FLOUR, PLUS EXTRA FOR DUSTING
- 1 TSP SALT
- 1 PACKAGE ACTIVE DRY YEAST
- 1 TSP BROWN SUGAR
- 1 TBSP CHOPPED FRESH THYME
- SCANT 1 CUP WARM WATER (HEATED TO 122°F/50°C)
- 4 TBSP OLIVE OIL, PLUS EXTRA FOR GREASING
- ⅓ CUP BLACK OLIVES
- ⅓ CUP GREEN OLIVES
- SCANT ½ CUP SUN-DRIED TOMATOES IN OIL, DRAINED
- 1 EGG YOLK, BEATEN

**1** Place the flour, salt, and yeast in a bowl and mix together, then stir in the sugar and thyme. Make a well in the center. Slowly stir in enough water and oil to make a dough. Mix in the olives and sun-dried tomatoes. Knead the dough for 5 minutes, then form it into a ball. Brush a bowl with oil, add the dough, and cover with plastic wrap. Let the dough rise in a warm place for about 1½ hours, or until it has doubled in size.

**2** Dust a baking sheet with flour. Knead the dough lightly, then cut into two halves and shape into ovals or circles. Place them on the baking sheet, cover with plastic wrap, and let them rise again in a warm place for 45 minutes, or until they have doubled in size.

**3** Preheat the oven to 400°F/200°C. Make 3 shallow diagonal cuts on the top of each piece of dough. Brush with the egg. Bake for 40 minutes, or until cooked through—they should be golden on top and sound hollow when tapped on the bottom. Transfer to wire racks to cool. Store in an airtight container for up to 3 days.

## VARIATION
FOR A CHANGE OF PACE, AND TO GIVE AN AUTHENTIC GREEK FLAVOR TO THIS BREAD, YOU CAN USE KALAMATA OLIVES INSTEAD OF THE BLACK AND GREEN OLIVES, AND CHOPPED FRESH CILANTRO INSTEAD OF THE THYME.

# BANANA & ORANGE BREAD

**MAKES 1 MEDIUM LOAF**

**PREPARATION
30 MINUTES, PLUS
1½ HOURS' RISING
COOKING
30 MINUTES**

THE SWEETNESS OF THE BANANA AND THE CITRUS TANG OF THE ORANGE MAKE A MARVELOUS COMBINATION IN THIS BREAD. IT IS DELICIOUS SPREAD WITH CREAMY UNSALTED BUTTER, BUT YOU CAN ALSO USE A LOWER-FAT MARGARINE TO KEEP THE FAT CONTENT LOW.

**INGREDIENTS**
- 4½ CUPS WHITE BREAD FLOUR, PLUS AN EXTRA 1–3 TBSP FOR STICKY DOUGH AND FOR DUSTING
- 1 TSP SALT
- 1 TSP BROWN SUGAR
- 1 TSP ACTIVE DRY YEAST
- 3 TBSP BUTTER, DICED
- 2 MEDIUM RIPE BANANAS OR 1 LARGE RIPE BANANA, PEELED AND MASHED
- 3 TBSP CLEAR HONEY
- 4 TBSP ORANGE JUICE
- SCANT 1 CUP LUKEWARM BUTTERMILK OR WATER
- 1½ TBSP SKIM MILK POWDER (IF USING WATER)
- SUNFLOWER OIL, FOR GREASING
- MILK, TO GLAZE (OPTIONAL)

**1** Place the flour, salt, sugar, and yeast in a large bowl. Rub in the butter and add the mashed banana and the honey. Make a well in the center and gradually work in the the orange juice and the buttermilk or water to make a smooth dough. If using water, add the skim milk powder to the mixture.

**2** Turn the dough out onto a lightly floured counter and knead for 5–7 minutes, or until the dough is smooth and elastic. If the dough looks very sticky, add an additional 1–2 tablespoons of white bread flour. (The stickiness depends on the ripeness and size of the bananas.) Place the dough in an oiled bowl, cover with plastic wrap, and let stand it in a warm place to rise for 1 hour, or until it has doubled in size.

**3** Oil a 2-lb/900-g loaf pan. Turn the dough out onto a lightly floured counter and knead for 1 minute, until smooth. Shape the dough the length of the pan and three times the width. Fold the dough into three lengthwise and place it in the pan with the seam underneath. Cover and let stand it in a warm place for 30 minutes, until it has risen above the pan.

**4** Preheat the oven to 425°F/220°C. Just before baking, brush the milk over the loaf to glaze, if using.

**5** Bake in the oven for 30 minutes, or until firm and golden brown. Test that the loaf is cooked by tapping it on the bottom—it should sound hollow. Transfer to a wire rack to cool completely before serving.

# FRESH CROISSANTS

PREPARE THIS RECIPE THE NIGHT BEFORE. MAKE THE DOUGH AND ROLL INTO CROISSANT SHAPES, THEN BRUSH WITH THE GLAZE, COVER WITH PLASTIC WRAP, AND REFRIGERATE OVERNIGHT. THE NEXT MORNING, LET THEM RISE FOR 30–45 MINUTES, THEN PLACE ON A BAKING SHEET AS PER THE RECIPE.

**MAKES 12**

**PREPARATION**
**40 MINUTES, PLUS
2 HOURS' RISING AND
CHILLING**
**COOKING**
**15–20 MINUTES**

**INGREDIENTS**
- 4½ CUPS WHITE BREAD FLOUR, PLUS EXTRA FOR DUSTING
- SCANT ¼ CUP SUPERFINE SUGAR
- 1 TSP SALT
- 2 TSP ACTIVE DRY YEAST
- 1¼ CUPS MILK, HEATED UNTIL JUST WARM TO THE TOUCH
- 1¼ CUPS BUTTER, SOFTENED, PLUS EXTRA FOR GREASING
- 1 EGG, LIGHTLY BEATEN WITH
- 1 TBSP MILK, TO GLAZE
- JELLY, TO SERVE (OPTIONAL)

**1** Stir the flour, sugar, salt, and yeast into a large bowl, make a well in the center, and add the milk. Mix to a soft dough, adding more milk if too dry. Knead on a lightly floured counter for 5–10 minutes, or until smooth and elastic. Transfer to a large, greased bowl, cover, and let it rise in a warm place until doubled in size. Meanwhile, flatten the butter with a rolling pin between 2 sheets of wax paper to form a rectangle ¼-inch/5-mm thick, then let it chill.

**2** Knead the dough for 1 minute. Remove the butter from the refrigerator and let it soften slightly. Roll out the dough to 18 x 6 inches/46 x 15 cm on a well-floured counter. Place the butter in the center, folding up the sides, and squeezing the edges together gently. With the short end of the dough toward you, fold the top third down toward the center, then fold the bottom third up. Rotate 45° clockwise so that the fold is to your left and the top flap toward your right. Roll out to a rectangle and fold again. If the butter feels soft, wrap the dough in plastic wrap, and let it chill. Repeat the rolling process twice more. Cut the dough in half. Roll out one-half into a triangle ¼ inch/5 mm thick (keep the other half refrigerated). Use a cardboard triangular template, with the bottom measuring 7 inches/18 cm and the sides 8 inches/20 cm, to cut out the croissants.

**3** Brush the triangles lightly with the glaze. Roll into croissant shapes, starting at the base and tucking the point underneath to prevent it from unrolling while cooking. Brush again with the glaze. Place on an ungreased baking sheet and let them double in size. Preheat the oven to 400°F/200°C. Bake for 15–20 minutes, until golden brown. Serve with jelly, if using.

# BLINIS

BLINIS COME FROM RUSSIA. TRADITIONALLY, THESE SMALL YEAST CRÊPES ARE MADE WITH BUCKWHEAT FLOUR, WHICH GIVES THEM A TASTY AND UNUSUAL FLAVOR. THIS RECIPE PRESERVES THAT TRADITION. YOU CAN ALSO SERVE THESE CRÊPES WITH CAVIAR.

**MAKES 8**

**PREPARATION**
**20 MINUTES, PLUS**
**1 HOUR'S STANDING**
**COOKING**
**20 MINUTES**

**INGREDIENTS**
• ¾ CUP BUCKWHEAT FLOUR
• ¾ CUP WHITE BREAD FLOUR
• ¼-OZ/7-G PACKAGE ACTIVE DRY YEAST
• 1 TSP SALT
• SCANT 1¾ CUPS TEPID MILK
• 2 EGGS, 1 WHOLE AND 1 SEPARATED
• VEGETABLE OIL, FOR BRUSHING

**TO SERVE**
• SOUR CREAM
• SMOKED SALMON
• CAVIAR

**1** Sift both flours into a large, warmed bowl. Stir in the yeast and salt. Beat in the milk, whole egg, and egg yolk until smooth. Cover the bowl and let it stand in a warm place for 1 hour.

**2** Place the egg white in a spotlessly clean bowl and whisk until soft peaks form. Fold into the batter. Brush a heavy-bottom skillet with oil and set over medium-high heat. When the skillet is hot, pour enough of the batter onto the surface to make a blini about the size of a saucer.

**3** When bubbles rise, turn the blini over with a spatula and cook the other side until light brown. Wrap in a clean dish towel to keep warm while cooking the remainder. Serve the warm blinis with sour cream, smoked salmon, and caviar.

## VARIATION
IF BUCKWHEAT FLOUR IS UNAVAILABLE, USE WHOLE WHEAT BREAD FLOUR INSTEAD.

# LEEK & ONION TARTLETS

THESE FLAVORSOME TARTLETS ARE LIKE MINI QUICHES. THEY ARE RICH IN PROTEIN AND VERY VERSATILE. YOU CAN SERVE THEM WARM OR COLD, AND THEY MAKE AN EXCELLENT CHOICE FOR A LUNCH BOX OR A PICNIC, ACCOMPANIED BY A CRISP SALAD.

**SERVES 6**

**PREPARATION**
**30 MINUTES, PLUS 45 MINUTES' CHILLING AND COOLING**
**COOKING**
**40 MINUTES**

**INGREDIENTS**
- BUTTER, FOR GREASING
- 8 OZ/225 G READY-MADE UNSWEETENED PIE DOUGH
- ALL-PURPOSE FLOUR, FOR DUSTING

FOR THE FILLING
- 2 TBSP UNSALTED BUTTER
- 1 ONION, THINLY SLICED
- 1 LB/450 G LEEKS, THINLY SLICED
- 2 TSP CHOPPED FRESH THYME
- ½ CUP GRUYÈRE CHEESE, GRATED
- 3 EGGS
- 1¼ CUPS HEAVY CREAM
- SALT AND PEPPER

**1** Lightly grease six 4-inch/10-cm tartlet pans with butter. Roll out the dough on a lightly floured counter and stamp out 6 circles with a 5-inch/13-cm cutter. Ease the dough into the pans, prick the bottoms, and chill for 30 minutes.

**2** Preheat the oven to 375°F/190°C. Line the pastry shells with foil and baking beans, then place on a baking sheet and bake for 8 minutes. Remove the foil and beans and bake for an additional 2 minutes. Transfer the pans to a wire rack to cool. Reduce the oven temperature to 350°F/180°C.

**3** Meanwhile, make the filling. Melt the butter in a large, heavy-bottom skillet. Add the onion and cook, stirring constantly, for 5 minutes, or until softened. Add the leeks and thyme and cook, stirring, for 10 minutes, or until softened. Divide the leek mixture between the tartlet shells. Sprinkle with Gruyère cheese.

**4** Lightly beat the eggs with the cream and season to taste with salt and pepper. Place the tartlet pans on a baking sheet and divide the egg mixture between them. Bake in the preheated oven for 15 minutes, or until the filling is set and golden brown. Transfer to a wire rack to cool slightly before removing from the pans and serving.

## VARIATION

FOR A SLIGHTLY MILDER VERSION OF THESE TARTLETS, SUBSTITUTE 1 LB/450 G OF SLICED ZUCCHINI FOR THE LEEKS.

# SPOON BREAD

THE WORD "BREAD" IN THE TITLE OF THIS SOUTHERN CLASSIC IS A MISNOMER, BECAUSE THE TEXTURE IS MORE LIKE A CORNMEAL SOUFFLÉ OR PUDDING. ITS NAME MIGHT BE DERIVED FROM THE NATIVE AMERICAN WORD FOR PORRIDGE, "SUPPAWN," OR SIMPLY MIGHT BE A REFERENCE TO THE SPOON USED TO SERVE IT STRAIGHT FROM THE BAKING DISH.

**SERVES 4–6**

**PREPARATION**
**10 MINUTES, PLUS**
**15 MINUTES' COOLING**
**COOKING**
**40–45 MINUTES**

**INGREDIENTS**
- 2 CUPS YELLOW CORNMEAL
- 1½ TSP SALT
- 2 TBSP BUTTER, PLUS EXTRA FOR GREASING AND TO SERVE (OPTIONAL)
- 2½ CUPS BOILING WATER
- 2 EGGS, SEPARATED
- 1 TSP BAKING SODA
- 1½ CUPS BUTTERMILK

**1** Preheat the oven to 425°F/220°C. Grease a 1½-quart/1.4-liter baking dish, which is also suitable for serving.

**2** Stir the cornmeal and salt together in a heatproof bowl. Add the butter and boiling water and stir until the mixture is smooth, then set it aside to cool slightly.

**3** Stir the egg yolks into the cornmeal mixture. Stir the baking soda into the buttermilk in a pitcher until dissolved, then stir into the cornmeal mixture to make a thin, smooth batter.

**4** Using an electric mixer, beat the egg whites in a separate bowl until stiff peaks form. Beat a large spoonful of the egg whites into the cornmeal batter to lighten, then fold in the remaining egg whites.

**5** Spoon the batter into the prepared dish and bake in the oven for 40–45 minutes, until the top is set and golden brown. Serve straight from the dish while the spoon bread is hot, with plenty of butter to melt over the top of each portion.

# MUSHROOM & SPINACH PACKAGES

**SERVES 4**

**PREPARATION**
**20 MINUTES**
**COOKING**
**30–35 MINUTES**

THESE PUFF-PASTRY PACKAGES HAVE A MOUTHWATERING FILLING OF GARLIC, MUSHROOMS, AND SPINACH. THEY ARE EASY TO MAKE AND DELICIOUS TO EAT, AND MAKE A SUPERB SNACK, LUNCH, OR SUPPER. SERVE THEM HOT, OR LET THEM COOL AND POP THEM INTO LUNCH BOXES FOR A PICNIC.

## INGREDIENTS
- 2 TBSP BUTTER
- 1 RED ONION, HALVED AND SLICED
- 2 GARLIC CLOVES, CRUSHED
- 8 OZ/225 G OPEN-CAP MUSHROOMS, SLICED
- 3½ CUPS BABY SPINACH
- PINCH OF NUTMEG
- 4 TBSP HEAVY CREAM
- 8 OZ/225 G PREPARED PUFF PASTRY
- ALL-PURPOSE FLOUR, FOR DUSTING
- 1 EGG, BEATEN
- 2 TSP POPPY SEEDS
- SALT AND PEPPER

**1** Preheat the oven to 400°F/200°C. Melt the butter in a skillet. Add the onion and garlic and sauté for 3–4 minutes, until the onion has softened.

**2** Add the mushrooms, spinach, and nutmeg and cook for an additional 2–3 minutes. Stir in the cream, mixing well. Season to taste with salt and pepper and remove the skillet from the heat.

**3** Roll the pastry out on a lightly floured counter and cut into four 6-inch/15-cm circles. Spoon one-quarter of the filling onto one half of each circle and fold the pastry over to encase the filling. Press down to seal the edges of the pastry and brush with the beaten egg. Sprinkle with the poppy seeds.

**4** Place the packages onto a dampened baking sheet and cook in the preheated oven for 20 minutes, until risen and golden brown.

**5** Transfer the mushroom and spinach packages to serving plates and serve immediately.

## COOK'S TIP
THE BAKING SHEET IS DAMPENED SO THAT STEAM FORMS WITH THE HEAT OF THE OVEN AND HELPS THE PASTRY TO RISE AND SET.

# LATTICED VEGETABLE TART

**SERVES 4**

**PREPARATION**
**30 MINUTES**
**COOKING**
**40–45 MINUTES**

A JALOUSIE IS A SMALL FRENCH LATTICED CAKE MADE WITH PUFF PASTRY AND AN ALMOND AND JELLY FILLING. THIS JALOUSIE IS A SAVORY VERSION. IT LOOKS IMPRESSIVE, BUT IS REALLY VERY EASY TO MAKE. THE MIXTURE OF VEGETABLES GIVES IT A MARVELOUS COLOR AND FLAVOR.

## INGREDIENTS
- 2 TBSP BUTTER
- 1 LEEK, SHREDDED
- 2 GARLIC CLOVES, CRUSHED
- 1 RED BELL PEPPER
- 1 YELLOW BELL PEPPER
- SCANT 1 CUP MUSHROOMS
- 2¾ OZ/75 G SMALL ASPARAGUS SPEARS
- 3 TBSP ALL-PURPOSE FLOUR
- 6 TBSP VEGETABLE STOCK
- 6 TBSP MILK
- 4 TBSP DRY WHITE WINE
- 1 TBSP CHOPPED FRESH OREGANO
- 1 LB/450 G PREPARED PUFF PASTRY
- 1 EGG, BEATEN, TO GLAZE
- SALT AND PEPPER

**1** Preheat the oven to 400°F/200°C. For the filling, melt the butter in a saucepan. Add the leek and garlic and sauté for 2 minutes. Slice the bell peppers and add to the saucepan with the remaining vegetables. Cook, stirring, for 3–4 minutes.

**2** Add the flour and cook for 1 minute. Remove the saucepan from the heat and stir in the stock, milk, and white wine. Return the pan to the heat and bring to a boil, stirring, until thickened. Stir in the oregano and season to taste.

**3** Roll half of the pastry out on a lightly floured counter to form a rectangle 15 x 6 inches/38 x 15 cm.

**4** Roll out the other half of the pastry to the same shape, but a little larger. Place the smaller rectangle on a baking sheet lined with dampened parchment paper.

**5** Spoon the filling on top of the smaller rectangle, leaving a ½-inch/1-cm clean edge. Cut parallel slits across the larger rectangle to within 1 inch/2.5 cm of each edge.

**6** Brush the edge of the smaller rectangle with egg and place the larger rectangle on top, sealing the edges well.

**7** Brush the whole jalousie with egg and cook in the preheated oven for 30–35 minutes, until risen and golden. Serve immediately.

## VARIATION
YOU CAN REPLACE THE LEEK WITH A SMALL, FINELY SLICED ONION, AND USE A CHOPPED ZUCCHINI INSTEAD OF ONE OF THE BELL PEPPERS.

# POTATO, BEEF & LEEK EMPANADAS

THESE MOUTHWATERING TURNOVERS ARE FILLED WITH POTATOES, SUCCULENT CUBES OF BEEF, CARROTS, AND LEEKS. THEY MAKE A SATISFYING MEAL AT ANY TIME OF DAY. SINCE YOU CAN SERVE THEM COLD AS WELL AS HOT, THEY ARE IDEAL FARE FOR LUNCH BOXES AND PICNICS.

**MAKES 4**

**PREPARATION
35 MINUTES
COOKING
50 MINUTES**

## INGREDIENTS
- 1 TBSP BUTTER, PLUS EXTRA FOR GREASING
- 8 OZ/225 G WAXY POTATOES, DICED
- 1 SMALL CARROT, DICED
- 8 OZ/225 G BEEF STEAK, CUBED
- 1 LEEK, SLICED
- 8 OZ/225 G PREPARED UNSWEETENED PIE DOUGH
- ALL-PURPOSE FLOUR, FOR DUSTING
- 1 EGG, BEATEN
- SALT AND PEPPER
- GREEN SALAD OR ONION GRAVY, TO SERVE

## VARIATION
USE OTHER TYPES OF MEAT, SUCH AS PORK OR CHICKEN, IN THE TURNOVERS AND ADD CHUNKS OF APPLE IN STEP 2, IF PREFERRED.

**1** Preheat the oven to 400°F/200°C. Lightly grease a baking sheet with butter. Mix the potatoes, carrot, beef, and leek together in a large bowl. Season well with salt and pepper.

**2** Divide the pie dough into 4 equal portions. Roll each portion out on a lightly floured counter into an 8-inch/20-cm circle.

**3** Spoon the potato mixture onto one half of each circle, to within ½ inch/1 cm of the edge. Top the potato mixture with the remaining butter, dividing it equally between the circles. Brush the dough edge with a little of the beaten egg.

**4** Fold the dough over to encase the filling and crimp the edges together. Transfer the turnovers to the prepared baking sheet and brush them with the beaten egg.

**5** Cook in the oven for 20 minutes. Reduce the oven temperature to 325°F/160°C and cook the turnovers for an additional 30 minutes until cooked through. Serve the empanadas with a crisp green salad or onion gravy.

# PROFITEROLES

WHO CAN RESIST THE RICH, BUTTERY TASTE OF PROFITEROLES, WITH THEIR SUMPTUOUS CREAMY CENTERS? THESE PROFITEROLES HAVE A LUXURIOUS CHOCOLATE AND BRANDY SAUCE POURED OVER THEM—THE ULTIMATE EXPERIENCE FOR THE HOPELESSLY INFATUATED CHOCOLATE LOVER.

**SERVES 4**

**PREPARATION**
**25 MINUTES, PLUS**
**5 MINUTES' COOLING**
COOKING
**35 MINUTES**

**INGREDIENTS**

FOR THE CHOUX PASTRY
- 5 TBSP BUTTER, PLUS EXTRA FOR GREASING
- SCANT 1 CUP WATER
- ¾ CUP ALL-PURPOSE FLOUR
- 3 EGGS, BEATEN

FOR THE CREAM FILLING
- 1¼ CUPS HEAVY CREAM
- 3 TBSP SUPERFINE SUGAR
- 1 TSP VANILLA EXTRACT

FOR THE CHOCOLATE & BRANDY SAUCE
- 4½ OZ/125 G SEMISWEET CHOCOLATE, BROKEN INTO SMALL PIECES
- 2½ TBSP BUTTER
- 6 TBSP WATER
- 2 TBSP BRANDY

**1** Preheat the oven to 400°F/200°C. Grease a large baking sheet with butter.

**2** To make the dough, place the butter and water in a saucepan and bring to a boil. Meanwhile, sift the flour into a bowl. Turn off the heat and beat in the flour until smooth. Cool for 5 minutes.

**3** Beat in enough of the eggs to give the mixture a soft, dropping consistency. Transfer to a pastry bag with a ½-inch/1-cm plain tip attached. Pipe small balls onto the baking sheet. Bake for 25 minutes.

**4** Remove from the oven. Pierce each ball with a skewer to let the steam escape.

**5** To make the filling, whip the cream, sugar, and vanilla extract together. Cut the balls across the middle, then fill with the cream mixture.

**6** To make the sauce, gently melt the chocolate, butter, and water together in a small saucepan, stirring constantly, until smooth. Stir in the brandy. Pile the profiteroles onto individual serving dishes or into a pyramid on a raised cake stand. Pour over the sauce and serve.

## VARIATION

GIVE AN UNUSUAL TWIST TO THE FLAVOR OF THESE PROFITEROLES BY REPLACING THE VANILLA EXTRACT WITH ALMOND EXTRACT AND USING DARK RUM INSTEAD OF BRANDY.

# MOLASSES TART

THIS IS A TRADITIONAL DESSERT THAT NEVER SEEMS TO GO OUT OF FASHION—IT STILL DELIGHTS PEOPLE TIME AFTER TIME. IT IS ALSO VERY QUICK TO MAKE IF YOU USE PREPARED DOUGH, WHICH YOU CAN BUY FROZEN FROM MOST SUPERMARKETS. SIMPLY THAW IT AND IT IS READY TO USE.

**SERVES 8**

**PREPARATION**
**25 MINUTES, PLUS**
**30 MINUTES' CHILLING**
COOKING
**35–40 MINUTES**

**INGREDIENTS**
- 9 OZ/250 G PREPARED UNSWEETENED PIE DOUGH
- ALL-PURPOSE FLOUR, FOR DUSTING
- 1½ CUPS CORN SYRUP
- 2¼ CUPS FRESH WHITE BREAD CRUMBS
- ½ CUP HEAVY CREAM
- FINELY GRATED ZEST OF ½ LEMON OR ORANGE
- 2 TBSP LEMON JUICE OR ORANGE JUICE
- CREAM OR CUSTARD, TO SERVE

**1** Preheat the oven to 375°F/190°C. Roll out the pie dough on a lightly floured counter and use to line an 8-inch/20-cm loose-bottom tart pan, reserving the dough trimmings. Prick the bottom of the pie dough with a fork and chill in the refrigerator.

**2** Cut out small shapes from the reserved dough trimmings, such as leaves, stars, or hearts, to decorate the top of the tart.

**3** Mix the corn syrup, bread crumbs, heavy cream, grated lemon zest, and lemon juice together in a small bowl.

**4** Pour the mixture into the pastry shell and decorate the edges of the tart with the dough cut-outs.

**5** Bake in the preheated oven for 35–40 minutes, or until the filling is just set.

**6** Remove from the oven and let the tart cool slightly in the pan before turning out and serving with custard.

## VARIATION
USE THE DOUGH TRIMMINGS TO CREATE A LATTICE PATTERN ON TOP OF THE TART, IF PREFERRED.

# NEW YORK CHEESECAKE

THIS IS AN ABSOLUTELY STUNNING EXAMPLE OF A CLASSIC AMERICAN BAKED CHEESECAKE. THE TRADITIONAL FRUITY BLUEBERRY TOPPING GIVES IT A MARVELOUSLY DRAMATIC SPLASH OF COLOR. IT IS EASY TO PREPARE AND YOU CAN KEEP IT IN THE REFRIGERATOR UNTIL YOU NEED IT.

**SERVES 8–10**

**PREPARATION**
**25 MINUTES, PLUS 10 HOURS' COOLING AND CHILLING**
COOKING
**45 MINUTES**

**INGREDIENTS**
- SUNFLOWER OIL, FOR BRUSHING
- 6 TBSP BUTTER
- 14 GRAHAM CRACKERS, CRUSHED
- 1¾ CUPS CREAM CHEESE
- 2 LARGE EGGS
- ¾ CUP SUPERFINE SUGAR
- 1½ TSP VANILLA EXTRACT
- 2 CUPS SOUR CREAM

FOR THE BLUEBERRY TOPPING
- GENEROUS ¼ CUP SUPERFINE SUGAR
- 4 TBSP WATER
- 1⅝ CUPS FRESH BLUEBERRIES
- 1 TSP ARROWROOT

**1** Preheat the oven to 375°F/190°C. Brush an 8-inch/20-cm springform pan with oil. Melt the butter in a saucepan over low heat. Stir in the crackers, then spread in the pan. Place the cream cheese, eggs, ½ cup of the sugar, and ½ teaspoon of the vanilla extract in a food processor. Process until smooth. Pour over the cracker layer and smooth the top. Place on a baking sheet and bake for 20 minutes, until set. Remove from the oven and let stand for 20 minutes. Leave the oven switched on.

**2** Mix the cream with the remaining sugar and vanilla extract in a bowl. Spoon over the cheesecake. Return it to the oven for 10 minutes, cool, then chill in the refrigerator for 8 hours, or overnight.

**3** To make the topping, place the sugar in a saucepan with 2 tablespoons of the water over low heat and stir until the sugar has dissolved. Increase the heat, add the blueberries, cover, and cook for a few minutes, or until they begin to soften. Remove from the heat. Mix the arrowroot and remaining water in a bowl, add to the fruit, and stir until smooth. Return to low heat. Cook until the juice thickens and turns translucent. Let the mixture cool.

**4** Remove the cheesecake from the pan 1 hour before serving. Spoon over the fruit topping and chill until ready to serve.

## VARIATION
YOU CAN VARY THE LOOK AND FLAVOR OF THIS CHEESECAKE BY USING OTHER BERRIES TO REPLACE SOME OR ALL OF THE BLUEBERRIES, SUCH AS RASPBERRIES OR STRAWBERRIES.

# GINGERBREAD

THIS MARVELOUSLY SPICY GINGERBREAD IS MADE MARVELLOUSLY MOIST BY THE ADDITION OF CHOPPED FRESH APPLES. IT MAKES A PERFECT AFTER-DINNER TREAT, OR A DELICIOUS SNACK AT ANY TIME OF THE DAY. IT IS VERY POPULAR WITH CHILDREN, SO GET YOUR SHARE WHILE YOU CAN.

**MAKES 12 BARS**

**PREPARATION**
**25 MINUTES, PLUS**
**50 MINUTES' COOLING**
**COOKING**
**35–40 MINUTES**

**INGREDIENTS**
- HEAPING ⅔ CUP BUTTER, PLUS EXTRA FOR GREASING
- ¾ CUP PACKED BROWN SUGAR
- 2 TBSP MOLASSES
- 1⅝ CUPS ALL-PURPOSE FLOUR
- 1 TSP BAKING POWDER
- 2 TSP BAKING SODA
- 2 TSP GROUND GINGER
- ⅔ CUP MILK
- 1 EGG, BEATEN
- 2 APPLES, PEELED, CHOPPED, AND COATED WITH 1 TBSP LEMON JUICE

**1** Preheat the oven to 325°F/160°C. Grease a 9-inch/23-cm square cake pan and line with parchment paper.

**2** Melt the butter, sugar, and molasses in a saucepan over low heat and let the mixture cool.

**3** Sift the flour, baking powder, baking soda, and ginger into a mixing bowl. Stir in the milk, beaten egg, and cooled buttery liquid, followed by the chopped apples coated with the lemon juice.

**4** Mix everything together gently, then pour into the prepared pan and smooth the surface.

**5** Bake in the preheated oven for 30–35 minutes, or until the cake has risen and a fine skewer inserted into the center comes out clean.

**6** Let the cake cool in the pan before turning out and cutting into 12 bars.

## VARIATION
IF YOU ENJOY THE FLAVOR OF GINGER, TRY ADDING 1 OZ/25 G FINELY CHOPPED PRESERVED GINGER TO THE MIXTURE IN STEP 3.

# CHOCOLATE CHIP MUFFINS

MUFFINS ARE ALWAYS POPULAR AND ARE SO VERY SIMPLE TO MAKE. THEY MAKE FABULOUS BITE-SIZE TREATS FOR CHILDREN AND ADULTS ALIKE—AND ARE PERFECT FOR PARTIES TOO. OR WHY NOT PUT THEM INTO LUNCH BOXES OR A PICNIC? THEY ARE SURE TO DELIGHT THE LUCKY RECIPIENTS.

**MAKES 12**

**PREPARATION**
**15 MINUTES, PLUS**
**30 MINUTES' COOLING**
**COOKING**
**25 MINUTES**

**INGREDIENTS**
- SCANT ½ CUP SOFT MARGARINE
- HEAPING 1 CUP SUPERFINE SUGAR
- 2 LARGE EGGS
- ⅔ CUP PLAIN YOGURT
- 5 TBSP MILK
- SCANT 2 CUPS ALL-PURPOSE FLOUR
- 1 TSP BAKING SODA
- 1 CUP SEMISWEET CHOCOLATE CHIPS

**1** Preheat the oven to 375°F/190°C. Line a 12-hole muffin pan with paper liners.

**2** Place the margarine and sugar in a mixing bowl and beat with a wooden spoon until light and fluffy. Beat in the eggs, yogurt, and milk until combined.

**3** Sift the flour and baking soda together and add to the mixture. Stir until just blended.

**4** Stir in the chocolate chips, then spoon the mixture into the paper liners and bake in the preheated oven for 25 minutes, or until a fine skewer inserted into the center comes out clean. Let them cool in the pan for 5 minutes, then turn out onto a wire rack to cool completely before serving.

**VARIATION**
THE MIXTURE CAN ALSO BE USED TO MAKE 6 LARGE OR 24 MINI MUFFINS. BAKE MINI MUFFINS FOR 10 MINUTES, OR UNTIL SPRINGY TO THE TOUCH.

# CRUNCHY PEANUT COOKIES

**MAKES 20**

**PREPARATION**
**15 MINUTES, PLUS**
**30 MINUTES' CHILLING**
**COOKING**
**15 MINUTES**

THESE RICH, CRUNCHY COOKIES WILL BE POPULAR WITH CHILDREN OF ALL AGES, SINCE THEY CONTAIN ONE OF THEIR FAVORITE FOODS—PEANUT BUTTER. THEY ARE ALSO VERY NUTRITIOUS BECAUSE THE PEANUTS ARE AN EXCELLENT SOURCE OF PROTEIN.

## INGREDIENTS
- SCANT ⅔ CUP BUTTER, SOFTENED, PLUS EXTRA FOR GREASING
- ½ CUP CHUNKY PEANUT BUTTER
- HEAPING 1 CUP GRANULATED SUGAR
- 1 EGG, LIGHTLY BEATEN
- HEAPING 1 CUP ALL-PURPOSE FLOUR
- ½ TSP BAKING POWDER
- PINCH OF SALT
- ½ CUP UNSALTED NATURAL PEANUTS, CHOPPED

**1** Lightly grease 2 baking sheets. Beat the butter and peanut butter together in a large mixing bowl.

**2** Gradually add the granulated sugar and beat together well. Add the beaten egg to the mixture, a little at a time, until it is thoroughly combined.

**3** Sift the flour, baking powder, and salt into the peanut butter mixture. Add the peanuts and bring all of the ingredients together to form a soft dough.

**4** Wrap in plastic wrap and let the dough chill for 30 minutes.

**5** Preheat the oven to 375°F/190°C. Form the dough into 20 balls and place them onto the prepared baking sheets about 2 inches/5 cm apart to allow for spreading. Flatten them slightly with your hand.

**6** Bake in the preheated oven for 15 minutes, or until golden brown. Transfer the cookies to a wire rack and let them cool.

## COOK'S TIP
FOR A CRUNCHY BITE AND SPARKLING APPEARANCE, SPRINKLE THE COOKIES WITH RAW BROWN SUGAR BEFORE BAKING.

# ALMOND BISCOTTI

BISCOTTI ARE HARD ITALIAN COOKIES THAT ARE TRADITIONALLY SERVED AT THE END OF A MEAL FOR DIPPING INTO A SWEET WHITE WINE KNOWN AS VIN SANTO. THEY ARE EQUALLY DELICIOUS SERVED WITH COFFEE OR ACCOMPANIED BY VANILLA- OR ALMOND-FLAVORED ICE CREAM.

**MAKES 20–24**

**PREPARATION**
**20 MINUTES, PLUS**
**20 MINUTES' COOLING**
**COOKING**
**25 MINUTES**

## INGREDIENTS
- 1¾ CUPS ALL-PURPOSE FLOUR, PLUS EXTRA FOR DUSTING
- 1 TSP BAKING POWDER
- PINCH OF SALT
- ¾ CUP GOLDEN SUPERFINE SUGAR
- 2 EGGS, BEATEN
- FINELY GRATED ZEST OF 1 ORANGE
- ½ CUP WHOLE BLANCHED ALMONDS, LIGHTLY TOASTED

**1** Preheat the oven to 350°F/180°C, then lightly dust a baking sheet with flour. Sift the flour, baking powder, and salt into a bowl. Add the sugar, eggs, and orange zest and mix to a dough. Knead in the toasted almonds.

**2** Roll out the dough into a ball, cut in half, and roll out each portion into a log about 1½ inches/4 cm in diameter. Place on the floured baking sheet and bake in the preheated oven for 10 minutes. Remove from the oven and let them cool for 5 minutes.

**3** Using a serrated knife, cut the logs into ½-inch/1-cm thick diagonal slices. Arrange the slices on the baking sheet and return to the oven for 15 minutes, or until slightly golden. Transfer to a wire rack to cool and go crisp.

## VARIATION
AS AN ALTERNATIVE TO ALMONDS, USE HAZELNUTS OR A MIXTURE OF ALMONDS AND PISTACHIOS.

# CHOCOLATE BROWNIES

YOU REALLY CAN HAVE A LOW-FAT CHOCOLATE TREAT. THESE MOIST BARS CONTAIN A DRIED FRUIT PUREE, WHICH ENABLES YOU TO BAKE WITHOUT ADDING FAT. SO THEY ARE THE PERFECT GUILT-FREE FOOD FOR THE AVID SLIMMER—AS LONG AS YOU HIDE THEM FROM THE REST OF YOUR HOUSEHOLD.

**MAKES 12**

**PREPARATION**
**40 MINUTES, PLUS 1 HOUR'S COOLING AND SETTING**
**COOKING**
**35–40 MINUTES**

**INGREDIENTS**
- BUTTER, FOR GREASING
- ⅓ CUP UNSWEETENED PITTED DATES, CHOPPED
- ⅓ CUP PLUMPED DRIED PRUNES, CHOPPED
- 6 TBSP UNSWEETENED APPLE JUICE
- 4 EGGS, BEATEN
- 1½ CUPS PACKED BROWN SUGAR
- 1 TSP VANILLA EXTRACT
- 4 TBSP LOW-FAT DRINKING CHOCOLATE POWDER, PLUS EXTRA FOR DUSTING
- 2 TBSP UNSWEETENED COCOA
- 1¼ CUPS ALL-PURPOSE FLOUR
- ⅓ CUP SEMISWEET CHOCOLATE CHIPS

**FOR THE FROSTING**
- 1⅛ CUPS CONFECTIONERS' SUGAR
- 1–2 TSP WATER
- 1 TSP VANILLA EXTRACT

**1** Preheat the oven to 350°F/180°C. Grease and line a 7 x 11 inch/ 18 x 28 cm cake pan with parchment paper. Place the dates and prunes in a small saucepan and add the apple juice. Bring to a boil, cover, and simmer for 10 minutes, until soft. Beat to form a smooth paste, then let it cool.

**2** Place the cooled fruit in a mixing bowl and stir in the eggs, sugar, and vanilla extract. Sift in 4 tablespoons of drinking chocolate, the cocoa, and the flour, and fold in along with the chocolate chips until well incorporated.

**3** Spoon the mixture into the prepared pan and smooth over the top. Bake in the preheated oven for 25–30 minutes, until firm to the touch, or until a skewer inserted into the center comes out clean. Cut into 12 bars and let them cool in the pan for 10 minutes. Transfer to a wire rack to cool completely.

**4** To make the frosting, sift the sugar into a bowl and mix with enough water and the vanilla extract to form a soft, but not too runny, frosting.

**5** Drizzle the frosting over the chocolate brownies and let it set. Dust with the extra chocolate powder before serving.

## COOK'S TIP

MAKE DOUBLE THE AMOUNT, CUT ONE OF THE CAKES INTO BARS AND OPEN FREEZE, THEN STORE IN FREEZER BAGS. TAKE OUT PIECES OF CAKE AS REQUIRED—THEY'LL TAKE NO TIME TO THAW.

# GLOSSARY

THIS GLOSSARY IS NOT INTENDED TO BE EXHAUSTIVE BUT TO PROVIDE A CONCISE GUIDE TO KEY TERMS WITH WHICH A BEGINNER MAY NOT BE FAMILIAR. SOME OF THE BASIC COOKING TECHNIQUES AND INGREDIENTS, INCLUDING SEVERAL OUTLINED EARLIER IN THIS BOOK, ARE LISTED HERE FOR EASE OF REFERENCE.

## A

**Agar-agar** Thickening and setting agent made from seaweed. It is a vegetarian alternative to gelatin.

**Al dente** Italian term meaning "at the teeth," indicating desired texture of cooked pasta, soft on the outside but still firm inside.

**Antipasto** Italian term, literally meaning "before pasta," denoting a hot or cold appetizer, or "hors d'oeuvre."

**Arborio rice** Medium- to long-grain type of rice, from Northern Italy, which is ideal for risotto because it absorbs liquid while retaining a firm texture.

**Arrowroot** Starch extract of maranta root used to thicken sauces.

**Aspic** Clear jelly made from clarified meat, fish, or vegetable stock mixed with gelatin. It is used to glaze or protect meat or fish and other foods, or for savory dishes set in a mold.

## B

**Bain-marie** Method of cooking ingredients where they are placed in a dish, which is in turn placed in a shallow container of water and is gently heated in an oven or on a stove. This is used to melt ingredients, such as chocolate, without burning them.

**Baking powder** Raising agent used in baking cakes, cookies, and breads. It usually contains baking soda, tartaric acid, and dried starch or flour for absorbing moisture.

**Balsamic vinegar** Dark brown vinegar from Italy, made from fermented white grape juice and aged in wooden barrels.

**Basmati rice** Small, long-grain rice grown in the Himalayan foothills. It is a creamy yellow with a nutty flavor and aroma.

**Basting** Spooning or brushing food during cooking with melted fat or stock to add flavor and color, and to prevent the food from drying out.

**Bay leaf** Aromatic herb used for flavoring meat, casseroles, and soups, often in a bouquet garni.

**Béarnaise sauce** French sauce made from reduced vinegar, white wine, tarragon, black peppercorns, and shallots, finished with egg yolks and butter.

**Béchamel sauce** French smooth white sauce made from flour stirred into milk and butter.

**Beurre manié** French term meaning "kneaded butter," a mixture of flour and softened butter, used to thicken sauces.

**Bisque** Thick, rich soup, made with cream and usually including shellfish.

**Black butter** Butter cooked over low heat until brown and usually flavored with vinegar or lemon juice, capers, and parsley.

**Black pepper** Dried whole peppercorns, which are often crushed or ground to add flavor to food.

**Blanching** Technique of plunging food into boiling water then placing it in cold water to stop the cooking process. This is used to loosen skins or preserve color and flavor.

**Blind baking** Partially cooking a pastry shell before the filling is added. This involves cooking the pie dough with a foil or paper lining and weighing it down with cooking weights (such as baking beans.) It avoids overcooking the dough or making its bottom too moist when the filling is added.

**Borscht or borsch** Eastern European soup made with beet, cabbage, and/or other vegetables, and served hot or cold with sour cream.

**Bouillabaisse** Fish stew from southern France.

**Bouquet garni** Group of herbs, usually parsley, bay leaf, and thyme, tied together to flavor soups, casseroles, and stocks, but removed before serving.

**Brochette** Cubes of meat or fish, and vegetables, cooked on a skewer.

**Buttermilk** Sour-tasting liquid remaining when milk has been churned to butter. It is often used in pancakes and soda breads.

## C

**Calvados** Northern French dry spirit made from distilled cider and used to flavor meat dishes.

**Canapés** Small appetizers, often served with drinks.

**Capers** Sun-dried flower buds of a shrub from the Mediterranean and parts of Asia. They need to be rinsed to remove excess salt or brine, and are used to provide a piquant flavor to sauces or condiments, or as a garnish.

**Caramelizing** Heating sugar until it melts and turns brown, resetting as a hard glaze, or cooking chopped fruit or vegetables in water and sugar until they brown and glaze.

**Cayenne pepper** Ground spice powder with a hot flavor, made from the flesh and seeds of chile pepper.

**Chantilly cream** Sweetened heavy whipped cream, often flavored with vanilla, used as a topping for desserts, or folded into custards or cream for fillings.

**Chiffonade** Thin strips of shredded vegetables (usually sorrel or lettuce), used raw or lightly sautéed, often as a garnish.

**Chile** Chile peppers are small, come in many varieties, and are characterized by their very hot seeds and flesh. Their potency can be reduced by removing their seeds, but this must be done carefully. It is important to avoid touching sensitive skin or eyes when handling chiles and to wash your hands thoroughly immediately afterward.

**Chinois** Conical, fine-meshed strainer used to strain soups and sauces.

**Choux pastry** Light, double-cooked dough used to make cakes and puffs. It has a hard, crisp exterior and a hollow interior.

**Clarified butter** Unsalted butter heated slowly to evaporate the water content, and then strained to separate the milk solids. The clarified butter can then be used for cooking at higher temperatures than normal butter without burning.

**Compote** Dish of fruit, slowly cooked whole or in sugar.

**Cornstarch** Fine, white, powdered starch extract of

corn, used to thicken sauces. To prevent it from forming lumps, the cornstarch should be mixed with twice its amount of cold liquid before being added to the sauce, which should be stirred constantly until it boils.

**Coulis** Thick and smooth fruit sauce or vegetable sauce. It may be served hot or cold.

**Court-bouillon** Spiced stock commonly used for cooking fish, seafood, or vegetables.

**Crêpe** French term for thin pancake. Crêpes can be made from plain or sweetened batters with different flavors and for savory and dessert dishes.

**Crème fraîche** French term for a thickened, tangy-flavored cream made from pasteurized cow's milk.

**Croûtons** Small cubes of broiled, toasted, or fried bread, which are drained and cooled. Used to garnish salads or soups.

**Crudités** Raw seasonal vegetables, sometimes sliced or grated, usually served as an appetizer with a dipping sauce.

**Custard** A smooth mixture of eggs and milk that can be used as the basis for a savory or sweet sauce or dish.

**D**
**Dariole** Small, steep-sided cylindrical mold for shaping dough, or the dough cooked in it.

**Daube** French dish of red meat, vegetables, and seasoning, slowly braised in a red wine stock. It can also refer to the method of cooking meat, some vegetables, or fish in a similar way.

**Dauphinoise (à la)** French term referring to the method of slowly baking in an oven with cream and garlic (such as potatoes).

**Descaling** Removing the scales from a fish by scraping the back of a knife along its surface, from the tail to the head.

**Dropping consistency** Required consistency of cake mixture, where it falls reluctantly from the spoon.

**E**
**Emulsifying** Combining fats (for instance, butter or oil) and vinegar or citric juices with a binding agent such as egg yolk.

**Entrecôte** French term, meaning "between the ribs," referring to a tender beef joint, cut from the short loin.

**Escalope** French term for a very thin slice of meat or fish, often flattened for quick cooking.

**Extract** Concentrated extract or oil from foods such as fish, almonds, vanilla, coffee beans, or various plants, and used to flavor foods.

**F**
**Filo dough** Very thin layers of pie dough, often used in Greek or Middle Eastern dishes, which dry out and cook very quickly.

**Fines herbes** French term referring to a mixture of chopped aromatic herbs, usually chervil, tarragon, parsley, and chives, used to flavor dishes.

**Florentine** In the style of a dish from Florence, usually referring to dishes served on a bed of cooked spinach. Also a small cookie of dried fruit and nuts, coated in chocolate on one side.

**Fond** French term for stock.

**French dressing** Cold sauce, made from olive oil and wine vinegar, seasoned with herbs, and salt and pepper, and used to dress salads.

**Fricassée** Stew made from lightly frying white meat, such as

chicken, and then cooking it in a white sauce with vegetables.

**Fritter** Piece of meat, fish, or vegetable coated in batter and deep-fried until crisp.

**Fromage frais** Fresh, soft, cream cheese that has the consistency of sour cream.

**G**
**Galangal** Spice related to ginger and used in southeast Asian cooking for flavor.

**Garam masala** Mixture of dry-roasted, ground spices, including cumin, coriander, and turmeric, mixed to form a paste, or added to a dish for flavor just before the end of cooking.

**Gelatin** Setting agent derived from the protein of animal bones, used to set sweet or savory jellies or thicken soups. Agar-agar is a vegetarian alternative, derived from red algae.

**Ghee** Type of clarified butter with a nutty, caramel-like flavor, created by simmering butter until the milk solids turn brown. It can be used for sautéing or frying at higher temperatures than normal butter without burning.

**Gluten** Flour protein, which gives dough elasticity and strength when mixed with water.

**Granita** Italian sherbet made from sweetened syrup flavored with coffee or liqueur and often served as a refreshment.

**Gratin** Any dish topped with cheese or bread crumbs mixed with pieces of butter and heated until crisp and brown.

**Gravy** Sauce made from meat juices, mixed with a stock, wine, or milk and thickened with flour. Also refers to the juices remaining in the pan after meat, fish, or poultry has been cooked.

**Grill pan** Flat, shallow, cast-iron pan, usually with ridges, for cooking food on a stove.

**H**
**Harissa** North African paste with a very hot flavor, made from chiles, garlic, cumin, coriander, mint, and oil. It is usually served with couscous, and is used to flavor soups and stews.

**Herbes de Provence** Mixture of herbs used in the Provence region of southern France, usually consisting of basil, bay, marjoram, oregano, parsley, rosemary, tarragon, and thyme.

**Hollandaise** Rich, creamy, and smooth sauce made from egg yolks, butter, and lemon juice, and usually served on vegetables, fish, or egg dishes.

**Horseradish** Herb grown for its leaves (for salads) and root. The spicy root is peeled and grated, and used to flavor sauces.

**I**
**Infusing** Imbuing a liquid (usually hot or boiling) with the flavors of herbs, spices, tea, or coffee, by letting them stand in the liquid.

**J**
**Jambalaya** Spicy Creole rice dish traditionally including ham, sausage, chilies, and tomatoes, but can also consist of any kind of meat, poultry, or shellfish.

**Julienne** Shredded or thinly cut vegetables or citrus zest, commonly used as a garnish.

**Jus** French term for "juice," referring to fruit or vegetable extract, or juice from meat.

**K**
**Kedgeree** Traditional British breakfast dish, originally deriving from India, consisting of rice, flaked fish (usually smoked haddock), and hard-cooked eggs.

**Kneading** Stretching and mixing dough by hand or mechanically, to make it smoother, softer, more elastic, and pliable. The movement helps the gluten strands in the dough to stretch and enables the dough to retain gas bubbles and rise when cooked.

**L**
**Lardons** Small chunks of fatty bacon or pork fat used to flavor dishes.

**Lemongrass** Root used in southeast Asian (especially Thai) cooking to impart a lemon flavor to sweet or savory dishes.

**Lyonnaise (à la)** French term describing dishes that include chopped onions. Lyonnaise sauce is made with sautéed onions and white wine and is then strained. It is usually served with meat or poultry dishes.

**M**
**Mace** Pungent spice made from the outer membrane of nutmeg, used to flavor various sweet and savory dishes.

**Macerating** Soaking fruit in a liquid, such as brandy, to soften and add flavor.

**Madeleine** Small, buttery sponge cake, made with sugar, flour, butter, and eggs, usually flavored with lemon or almonds.

**Marinating** Soaking food in a seasoned liquid mixture, or marinade (usually containing oil, lemon or wine, herbs, and spices), to tenderize and add flavor.

**Marinière (à la)** French term meaning "in the style of a mariner," referring to cooking shellfish, or other seafood, in white wine and herbs. It can also refer to a dish garnished with mussels.

**Mascarpone** Thick, creamy, and soft Italian cheese used in savory and sweet dishes.

**Mayonnaise** Thick, creamy dressing made from oil, egg yolks, vinegar or lemon juice, and seasoning.

**Meringue** Light, sweet dessert made by beating egg whites and sugar together and baking.

**Meunière (à la)** French term meaning "in the style of a miller's wife," referring to the method of cooking where the food (usually fish) is coated in flour, then shallow-fried in butter.

**Mille-feuille** French term for "a thousand leaves," referring to a dessert made from puff pastry, whipped cream, jelly, or fruit.

**Miso** Paste made from soybeans and used as a flavoring in Japanese cooking, including soups, sauces, and dressings.

**Molasses** By-product of refining sugar, molasses is a thick, dark brown syrup with a slightly bitter flavor.

**Mornay sauce** Béchamel sauce with grated cheese (usually Gruyère or Parmesan) added, often served with fish, egg, or vegetable dishes.

**Mustard** Plant with piquant-tasting seeds, which are used whole, ground, or in powdered form as a flavoring for seasonings, dressings, sauces, and accompaniments.

**N**
**Navarin** French stew made from lamb or mutton, potatoes, and other vegetables.

**Noodles** Thin pasta strips, made with flour and water, and egg or egg yolk.

**O**
**Olive oil** Rich oil, extracted from pressed olives, used for shallow-frying, dressings, marinades, and baking. Extra virgin olive oil is the purest form of the oil, taken from the first pressing of the olives.

**P**
**Pancetta** Italian bacon cured with salt and spices and used to flavor pasta, rice, soup, or salad dishes.

**Panna cotta** Italian term meaning "cooked cream," referring to a cold dessert made from a set custard of cream and gelatin, often flavored with vanilla or caramel.

**Papillote (en)** French term meaning "in a parcel," referring to a method of cooking food in a folded parcel of wax paper to protect it from the high heat of the oven and help it retain moisture and flavor.

**Parboiling** Boiling food until half-cooked, in preparation for adding to other ingredients with shorter cooking times or to tenderize the food before roasting (as with potatoes.)

**Parmesan** Hard, dry cheese, made from skim cow's milk, with a rich, sharp taste and used grated, usually after cooking, to flavor a dish, especially pasta and sauce.

**Pasta** Italian for "paste," referring to the dough made from durum-wheat semolina, water, and sometimes egg. Pasta comes in a wide variety of shapes and sizes and is served with sauces or soups.

**Pectin** Natural gelling agent extracted from ripe fruit and vegetables, and used in making preserves and jellies.

**Peking sauce** Thick, reddish-brown, sweet and spicy Chinese sauce, made from a mixture of soybeans, garlic, chile peppers, and spices, commonly used as a table condiment or flavoring. It is also known as "hoisin sauce."

**Pesto** Italian term meaning "pounded," referring to a green sauce made from a blend of pine nuts, fresh basil, Parmesan cheese, garlic, and olive oil. It is most commonly served with pasta or as a dressing.

**Pita** Middle Eastern flat, hollow bread made from flour or whole wheat flour and usually served with fillings or to accompany spicy dishes and dips.

**Polenta** Italian cornmeal porridge, which can be eaten hot or, when cooled and firm, fried.

**Prosciutto** Italian term for a ham that has been seasoned, salt-cured, and air dried, and served very thinly sliced, traditionally as an appetizer.

**Pureeing** Grinding or mashing fruit or vegetables to form a very smooth paste, either manually by pressing the food through a strainer, or mechanically.

**Q**
**Quenelle** Small dumpling made from seasoned ground meat, fish, or ground vegetables, bound with eggs, and usually poached in stock.

**Quiche** Open pie-dough tart, usually filled with an egg and milk custard and savory ingredients.

**Quinoa** Small, beadlike grain, very rich in protein and mild in taste, which is cooked and served like rice.

**R**
**Ragoût** Thick, well-seasoned French stew consisting of meat, poultry, fish, or vegetables, flavored with wine.

**Ratatouille** French vegetable stew consisting of eggplants, zucchini, tomatoes, onions, sweet bell peppers, and garlic simmered in olive oil.

**Reducing** Boiling a liquid, such as stock, wine, or sauce, quickly to reduce its volume by evaporation, thicken it, and concentrate the flavors.

**Relaxing** Leaving dough to "rest" after rolling in order to prevent it from shrinking.

**Ricotta** Rich, creamy, and smooth Italian cheese made from the curd of ewe's milk, used in many Italian dishes and as a stuffing for pasta.

**Rissole** Sweet or savory round pastry, filled with chopped meat or fish and bread crumbs and cooked by frying or baking.

**Risotto** Italian rice dish, made by gradually mixing hot stock and rice during cooking to ensure that the rice absorbs the liquid. Traditionally, arborio rice is used because of its capacity to absorb liquid and retain a firm texture.

**Rösti** Swiss term meaning "crisp and golden," referring to a flat, round pancake of shredded potato, shallow-fried on both sides until crisp and brown.

**Rouille** French term meaning "rust," referring to a hot, chili-flavored red sauce usually served as a garnish with fish or fish stews.

**Roulade** French term, referring to a sweet or savory rolled dish. The savory dish may be a slice of meat, poultry, or fish rolled around a filling, while the sweet dish is a filled and rolled sponge.

**Roux** Mixture of flour and fat, slowly cooked over low heat, and used as a basis for soups and sauces to thicken them.

**S**

**Saffron** Pungent and aromatic spice, yellow in color, and available whole or powdered. It is used for coloring and flavoring dishes. The spice is derived from the stigmas of the saffron crocus and is very expensive.

**Salsa** Spanish term meaning "sauce," and specifically referring to a spicy, hot-flavored, thick relish made from chiles and fruit, and served cold.

**Salt** Sodium chloride crystals, used for seasoning and preserving food. It is available in various forms, including sea salt and rock salt, from which cooking and table salt are derived.

**Samosa** Indian triangle-shaped turnover, filled with spiced meat or vegetables, and deep-fried.

**Satay** Indonesian speciality, consisting of meat, fish, or poultry cubes, broiled on a skewer, and usually served with a spicy sauce.

**Sherbet** Smooth, semifrozen water ice mixed with fruit juice or liqueur, and sometimes egg white or gelatin, and commonly served as a dessert.

**Short loin** Premium cut of tender beef, from the back, available as tenderloin steaks or joints for roasting.

**Shucking** To remove the edible part of food from its outer casing, such as removing an oyster from its shell, using a small, thick-bladed knife.

**Slaking** Mixing a thickening agent with a liquid.

**Smoothie** Thick, smooth, and cold drink made from blending fruits or vegetables, often with liquids, such as water, milk, or ice cream.

**Soy sauce** Sauce commonly used in Chinese and Japanese cooking, made from fermented and boiled soybeans. It is used to flavor sauces, soups, marinades, meat, fish, and vegetables.

**Stock** Flavored, strained liquid made by cooking meat, fish, poultry, and vegetables, with seasoning, in water. It is used for flavoring sauces, soups, stews, or braised dishes.

**Strained canned tomatoes** Smooth Italian-style tomato sauce.

**Sweating** Method of cooking ingredients, usually vegetables, in a little fat, slowly over low heat so that they cook in their own steam without browning.

**T**

**Tabasco sauce** Hot-flavored, spicy sauce made from Tabasco chile peppers, vinegar, and salt, and used to add flavor to sauces, meat, or cocktails.

**Tapenade** Thick French paste made from black olives, capers, anchovies, lemon juice, olive oil, and herbs, used to flavor sauces, marinades, stews, pasta, or meat.

**Tarte tatin** French apple tart made in a shallow dish by covering butter, sugar, and apples with a pie-dough topping and baking until the ingredients caramelize. The tart is served upside down.

**Terrine** Pâté cooked in a small, fat-lined, deep-sided dish (also called a terrine), and usually made from pieces of fish or meat.

**Timbale** Dish cooked in a mold (also called a timbale), consisting of layers, usually of rice and vegetables.

**Tisane** Infusion of herbs in boiling water, drunk hot.

**Tofu** Curd of the soybean, pressed into firm cheeselike blocks, which is bland in flavor but rich in iron and protein. Commonly used in Asian dishes, it can be cooked in soups, stir-fries, casseroles, or sauces.

**Turmeric** Spice derived from the root of a ginger-related plant, with a yellow color and bitter taste, used in Asian cooking to add color and flavor.

**U**

**Unsweetened pie dough** Crumbly pie dough used for sweet or savory pies and tarts.

**V**

**Vanilla** Sweet and fragrant flavoring extracted from the dried beans and seeds of the vanilla orchid, used to flavor sweet and savory foods.

**Vichyssoise** Rich and creamy soup, served cold, made from potatoes, leeks, and cream, and garnished with chopped chives.

**Vinaigrette** Cold sauce made from a mixture of vinegar, oil, and seasoning, normally used as a dressing for leafy salads or other cold dishes.

**W**

**White sauce** Basic smooth sauce, also known as béchamel, made from flour stirred into a mixture of milk and butter.

**Y**

**Yeast** Microscopic, live fungus that converts its food, through fermentation, into carbon dioxide and alcohol and is, therefore, used in bread-making to make dough rise, or in brewing to make alcohol.

**Z**

**Zabaglione** Italian frothy dessert made by whisking egg yolks, wine, and sugar together, while heating gently, and which is served slightly warm.

**Zest** Fragrant outer rind of a citrus fruit, grated or shredded and used to add flavor or as a garnish to a dish.

# INDEX